A Voyage Of Discovery To The North Pacific Ocean, And Round The World...

George Vancouver

VOL VI

A

VOYAGE OF DISCOVERY

TO THE

NORTH PACIFIC OCEAN,

AND

ROUND THE WORLD;

In which the Coaft of North-weft America has been carefully examined
and accurately furveyed

UNDERTAKEN

BY HIS MAJESTY's COMMAND,

Principally with a View to afcertain the exiftence of any NAVIGABLE
COMMUNICATION between the

North Pacific and North Atlantic Oceans;

AND PERFORMED IN THE YEARS

1790, 1791, 1792, 1793, 1794 AND 1795,

IN THE

DISCOVERY SLOOP OF WAR, AND ARMED TENDER CHATHAM,

UNDER THE COMMAND OF

CAPTAIN GEORGE VANCOUVER.

Dedicated, by Permiffion, to HIS MAJESTY.

A NEW EDITION, WITH CORRECTIONS,

ILLUSTRATED WITH NINETEEN VIEWS AND CHARTS.

· IN SIX VOLUMES.

VOL. VI.

London:

PRINTED FOR JOHN STOCKDALE, PICCADILLY.

1801.

T. Gillet, Printer, Salisbury-square.

VOYAGE

TO THE

NORTH PACIFIC OCEAN,

AND

ROUND THE WORLD.

⸺⊶⊙⋇⊙⊷⸺

CHAPTER X.

Procced to the Southward along the exterior Coaſt of King George the Third's Archipelago—Arrive in Port Concluſion—Tranſactions there—Two Boat Excurſions—Complete the Survey of the Continental Shores of North-Weſt America—Aſtronomical and nautical Obſervations.

OUR attention being now directed to the ſurvey of the exterior coaſt of George the Third's archipelago, at the dawn of day, on Tueſday the 29th of July, with a freſh weſterly breeze, we made ſail along the ſhore, to the ſouthward; cape Croſs bearing by compaſs N. 68 E. diſtant four or five miles. From this cape the coaſt takes a direction S. 31 E. about ſeven leagues to another promontory, that obtained the name of CAPE EDWARD;

off

off which lies a clufter of fmall iflets and rocks. The coaft between thefe capes is much broken, and has feveral openings in it that appeared likely to afford fhelter; but the vaft number of rocks and fmall iflets, fome producing trees, and others intirely barren, that extend to the diftance of three or four miles from the fhore, will render the entering of fuch harbours unpleafant and dangerous, until a more competent knowledge of their feveral fituations may hereafter be ac-quired: that which appeared to be the eafieft of accefs, lies about two leagues to the northward of cape Edward, and as it is in latitude 57° 44′, I was led to confider this opening as Portlock's harbour. We did not reach cape Edward until the afternoon, as the wefterly breeze was foon fucceeded by faint variable airs, that blew di-rectly towards the fhore, which was vifible only at intervals, owing to the thick foggy and rainy weather, and which rendered the view we had obtained of this part of the coaft, by no means fatisfactory. During the night the wind fettled in the weftern quarter, notwithftanding which, by its blowing gently, our diftance from the fhore was increafed to about three leagues, and at day-light the next morning, (Wednefday 30) cape Edward bore by compafs N. 27 W. diftant twelve miles; from whence the coaft bends more to the eaftward, and takes a direction about
S. 30 E.

S. 30 E. to a very confpicuous opening, which I
fuppofed to be that reprefented in fome late publications, as feparating the land on which mount
Edgcumbe is fituated from the adjacent fhores,
and named the Bay of Iflands by Captain Cook,
who imagined at the time he paffed it, that fuch
a feparation did exift.   We were oppofite to this
bay about eight in the morning, but the intermediate fpace between the bay of Iflands and
cape Edward was paffed in very thick foggy
weather; this difadvantage, in addition to the
diftance we had been from the land, may fubject the delineation of that fhore to fome error.
Near the land forming the fouthern fide of the
bay of Iflands are feveral fmall iflets, and from
the fouth point of the bay, which I called POINT
AMELIA, the coaft extends S. 5 E. fixteen miles,
to cape Edgcumbe, having nearly in the middle
of that fpace an opening, with two fmall iflets
lying before it, and prefenting an appearance of a
good harbour, which I called PORT MARY ; the
other parts of the coaft that were paffed at the
diftance of about a league, are indented with
fmall open bays.

As the day advanced a brifk gale from the
N. W. attended us, with fair and pleafant weather, which enabled us to afcertain the fhip's
fituation.   At noon the latitude was found to be
57° 4½′, longitude 224° 19′.   The moft nor-

thern

thern part of the coast at this time in sight bore by compass N. N. W. port Mary N. 22 E. eight miles distant; and cape Edgcumbe S. 80 E. four or five miles distant. This cape, by the same observations was found to be in latitude 57° 2′, longitude 224° 25½′, which is one mile to the south and eighteen miles and an half to the eastward of its situation, as stated by Captain Cook. We had now also a very good view of mount Edgcumbe, and notwithstanding that it must be considered as high land, yet it was intirely free from snow, and seemed to us but an inconsiderable hill, when compared with the mountains we had generally seen, extending along the shores of this continent. Cape Edgcumbe forms the north-west point of a spacious opening, that branches into several arms, and is called by Mr. Dixon Norfolk Sound; its opposite or south-east point, which I have distinguished by the name of POINT WODEHOUSE, lies from the cape S. 50 E. at the distance of seventeen miles. One of the northern branches of the found, by its communication with the bay of Islands makes, it seems, the intermediate part of the sea-coast an island. On the northern side of the found, two leagues within cape Edgcumbe, are, what appeared to us, two islands, and N. N. W. from point Wodehouse, lies an extensive group of islets and rocks that extend three or four miles

from

from the fhore, which, from that point, with
little variation, takes a courfe S. 36 E.   This
part of the coaft is much broken into fmall openings, with iflets and detached rocks lying off it.
We had advanced about fixteen miles only from
point Wodehoufe at eight in the evening, after
which, the night was paffed in ufing our endeavours to retain our ftation near this part of the
coaft; but we found ourfelves on Thurfday morning the 31ft, much further from the land than we
had expected; we had, however, a favorable breeze
from the weftward, with which we ftood towards the fhore, but the weather becoming thick
and foggy, we were under the neceffity to haul
off the coaft until ten in the forenoon, when the
land being again vifible, about four miles from
us, we refumed our examination, paffing fome
fmall openings, with feveral iflets and detached
rocks lying near to them ; but of which we were
precluded any diftinct view by the hazinefs of
the weather.

This difadvantage had attended us almoft generally fince our departure from Crofs found,
and although I have reafon to believe that we
had nearly afcertained the general line of the
coaft, yet it is poffible that there may be openings or harbours that we were unable to notice,
as circumftances would not admit of our devot-

B 3

ing

ing fufficient time to a more minute examination.

By noon we had paffed the fouth extremity of this archipelago, which was now found to ftretch a few miles further fouth than Mr. Whidbey had eftimated; our obfervations placed it in latitude 56° 10', longitude 325° 37½'. It conftitutes a very remarkable promontory, that terminates in a high bluff rocky cliff, with a round, high rocky iflet lying clofe to it, and by its fhores on its eaftern fide taking a fharp northerly direction, it becomes a very narrow point of land, which having been feen by Captain Colnett in his mercantile expedition to this coaft, was by him named Cape Ommaney, and the opening between it and cape Decifion, Chriftian Sound.

Our conjectures of foon finding a port in this neighbourhood, did not long remain unconfirmed, for after advancing feven or eight miles from cape Ommaney, we difcovered on the eaftern fhore of the archipelago an opening that took a fouth-weft direction; and as it appeared likely to anfwer all our purpofes we worked into it, with a frefh breeze directly againft us until feven in the evening; when we anchored off a cove about half a league within the entrance of the harbour. On Friday morning the 1ft of Auguft the veffels were moored head and ftern in this cove, there not being fufficient room for them

them to fwing; and whilft thofe on board were fo employed, accompanied by Mr. Whidbey and Mr. Johnftone, (who were each to undertake a diftinct expedition, and by which means we entertained the hope of being enabled to connect the furveys of the prefent, with thofe of the two preceding feafons) I rowed to the entrance of the port, in order to be better able to arrange the mode of conducting that fervice; this appeared to be no difficult tafk, as there were two given points before us, and both were nearly in view. The one was cape Decifion, where our examination of the continental fhore had finifhed the former feafon, and the other was point Gardner, from whence Mr. Whidbey had returned on his laft excurfion from Crofs found. Mr. Whidbey was directed to recommence his refearches from that point, whilft Mr. Johnftone proceeded to cape Decifion, there to begin his examination along the eaftern fhore of the found northward, until the two parties fhould meet, or be otherways informed by notes which each party was to leave in confpicuous places for the government of the other, defcribing the extent of their refpective furveys.

The fpace now to be explored occupied about a degree of latitude, and although I hoped that the examination of it with tolerable weather, would not employ the boats more than a week;

yet in order that it fhould not be left unaccom-plifhed for want of provifions, each of the par-ties was provided for a fortnight. The Difco-very's yawl and large cutter was to proceed with Mr. Whidbey and Mr. Swaine; and the Chat-ham's cutter, and the Difcovery's fmall cutter, with Mr. Johnftone and Mr. Barrie; with this arrangement both parties departed early in the morning of Saturday the 2d, in the profecution of their refpective purfuits.

The ftation we had taken, though fufficiently commodious for our purpofe, was extremely folitary; there were no inhabitants on the adja-cent fhores, nor was there the fmalleft appearance of any part of our neighbourhood being a place of their refort, fo that our time was not likely to be very intereftingly employed, or our attention diverted from fuch neceffary concerns as the ordinary fervices of the veffels now required. Thefe confifted principally in repairing our fails and rigging in the beft manner we were able. This had now become a bufinefs of conftant employment. Some of the carpenters were caulking, others cutting fuch fpars and timbers for plank us were wanted; and the brewers on fhore were making fpruce beer, which with a little famphire, and fome halibut, caught with our hooks near the entrance of the harbour, were the only refrefhments the place afforded.

The

The five following days we had light variable winds, attended by much rain; but the weather being more pleafant on Friday the 8th, I was employed in making a furvey of the harbour. Its fouthern point of entrance is fituated N. 15 E. about two leagues from cape Ommaney, its oppofite point lying N. 7 W. two miles diftant. The depth of water in mid-channel between thefe points is 75 fathoms, but decreafes to 8 or 10 clofe to the fhores, without rocks or fands, excepting near the points, which are fufficiently evident to be avoided. South fouth-weft, about half a mile from the north point of entrance, is a moft excellent and fnug bafon about a third of a mile wide, and half a mile long; but its entrance is by a very narrow channel half a mile in length, in a direction S. 70 W., with fome iflets and rocks lying off its fouth point; thefe are fteep nearly clofe to them, as are the fhores on both fides, which vary from a fixth to a twelfth of a mile afunder, with a clear navigable paffage from eight to twelve fathoms deep in the middle, and five fathoms on the fides. The foundings are tolerably regular in the bafon, from 30 in the middle, to 10 fathoms clofe to the fhores. Immediately within its north point is a fine fandy beach, and an excellent run of water, as is the cafe alfo at its head, with a third fandy beach juft within its fouth point of entrance.

In

In the vicinity of thefe beaches, efpecially the firft and third, is a fmall extent of low land; but the other parts of the fhores are compofed of fteep rugged cliffs on all fides, furrounded by a thick foreft of pine trees, which grew with more vigour than in the other parts of the harbour. From its entrance to the head, it extends about a league in a direction S. 33 W., free from any interruption, although it is inconvenient from its great depth of water. Near the fouthern fide of entrance lies a fmall iflet and fome rocks, but thefe are entirely out of the way of its navigation. The foundings cannot be confidered as very regular, yet the bottom in general is good; in fome places it is ftony, in others fand and mud; but in the cove where the veffels were at anchor the bottom is rocky. The head of this cove approaches within the fourth of a mile of the head of another cove, whofe entrance on the outfide is about two miles to the fouth of the fouth point of this harbour. In the entrance of that cove the depth is feven fathoms, weeds were feen growing acrofs it, and to the north of it is a fmall iflet with fome rocks. The furrounding fhores are generally fteep and rocky, and were covered with wood nearly to the water's edge, but on the fides of the adjacent hills were fome fpots clear of trees, and chiefly occupied by a damp moift moorifh foil, in which

were

were feveral pools of water. The furface produced fome berry bufhes, but the fruit at this
feafon of the year was not ripe. This little information I procured from fome of our gentlemen, who had made fome excurfions about the
neighbourhood. In the above cove on the weft
fide were found a few deferted Indian habitations, which were the only ones that had been
met with. Our not having been vifited here by
any of the natives, was rather a mortifying circumftance, as they generally occafioned us fome
entertainment, and frequently added fome variety to fuch refrefhments, as by our own efforts
we were enabled to procure.

From Saturday the 9th to Wednefday the
13th, the weather had been moftly boifterous,
unfettled, and rainy; this kind of weather fince
our arrival had prevented our making any lunar
obfervations, but had afforded me fufficient op-
portunities for afcertaining very fatisfactorily the
rates of the chronometers, by fuch means as were
in my power on board, not having erected the
obfervatory on fhore; for as a convenient fituation could not be found near the fhip, and as I
was in hopes we fhould not long be detained at
this ftation, I was not particularly anxious to
land the inftruments; and under the circumftances of the weather, I had not much to regret
that they had remained unremoved.

Other

Other objects began to claim our ferious attention. The plan that I had adopted for drawing our laborious examination of this coaft to a conclufion, by the furveys on which the boats were now employed, I had fully expected would have been accomplifhed in a week or ten days at the furtheft, but the whole time for which they had been provided was now expired, and Friday the 15th arrived without bringing any relief to our very anxious concern for their welfare. This unpleafant ftate of fufpence continually brought to our recollection the various untoward accidents to which our expeditions in fuch fmall open boats had been liable; and when we adverted to the very treacherous behaviour of the Indians experienced by Mr. Whidbey in his late excurfion from Crofs found, and the fimilar difpofition that had been fhewn to us the preceding feafon by thofe people who inhabit the countries not far diftant to the fouth-eaftward, our minds were filled with apprehenfion, and every hour increafed our folicitude for the return of our abfent friends. The fervice that each party had to perform, called them, if not into the immediate neighbourhood of thefe unfriendly people, at leaft into the vicinity of the places to which they frequently refort; and as they are by nature of a cunning, defigning, and avaricious difpofition, they were much to be

feared

feared; for although they could not be confidered as a courageous tribe, yet the very un-
warrantable and impolitic conduct of the feveral
traders on this coaft, in fupplying them fo amply
with fire-arms and ammunition, and in teaching
them the ufe of thofe deftructive weapons, has
not only given the natives a degree of confidence
that renders them bold and importunate, but the
dread which they before entertained of mufketry
is greatly leffened by their becoming fo familiar
to them ; and they are now fo well furnifhed,
as to confider themfelves when in their large
canoes nearly on an equality with us, and of
courfe are daily becoming formidable, efpecially
to the parties in our fmall boats. Thefe diftreffing confiderations, in addition to the pro-
tracted abfence of our friends, gave us but too
much reafon to be apprehenfive, that we had at
length hazarded our little boats, with the fmall
force they were able to take for their defence,
once too often.

Whilft we endured this irkfome anxiety, it is
a tribute that is juftly due to the meritorious exertions of thofe under my command, that I fhould
again acknowledge the great confolation I derived
on all painful occafions like this, by having the
moft implicit confidence in the difcretion and
abilities of my officers, and the exertions and ready
obedience of my people. Thefe happy reflections

left

left me no grounds for entertaining the moft diftant idea that any precaution would be wanting
to guard againft, or effort unexerted to avert, fo
far as human prudence could dictate, the threat-
ening dangers to which I was confcious they muft
neceffarily be expofed.

In the hourly hope that thefe confoling reflections would once more be proved to have been
well founded, by the fafe return of the boats, I
directed that every thing fhould be got in readinefs to proceed with all difpatch in fuch direction
as circumftances might require ; for which purpofe the veffels were moved to the oppofite fide
of the harbour, as being a more convenient fituation for our immediate departure.   Here we remained in the moft uncomfortable ftate of fufpenfe that can be imagined until Tuefday the
19th ; when, in the midft of a deluge of rain,
with the wind blowing very ftrong from the
S. E. we had the indifcribable fatisfaction of feeing the four boats enter the harbour together
from the northward.   The parties foon reached
the veffels, all well, and communicated the glad
tidings of their having effectually performed the
fervice, and attained the object that had been
expected from this expedition.

The accomplifhment of an undertaking, the
laborious nature of which will, probably, from
the perufal of the foregoing fheets, be more eafily

conceived

conceived than explained: a fervice that had demanded our conftant and unwearied attention,
and had required our utmoft abilities and exertions
to bring thus to a conclufion, could not, after the
indefatigable labours of the three preceding years,
fail of exciting in the bofoms of our little community, fenfations of a nature fo pleafing and fatisfactory, that few are likely to experience in the
fame degree, who were not participators in its
execution; and to the imagination of thofe alone,
muft I refer the happinefs we experienced on this
interefting event.

In order that the valuable crews of both veffels,
on whom great hardfhips and manual labour had
fallen, and who had uniformly encountered their
difficulties with unremitting exertion, cheerful-
nefs and obedience, might celebrate the day, that
had thus terminated their labours in thefe regions;
they were ferved with fuch an additional allowance of grog as was fully fufficient to anfwer
every purpofe of feftivity on the occafion.   This
foon prompted a defire for mutual congratulations between the two veffels, expreffed by three
exulting cheers from each; and it may be eafily
conceived that a greater degree of heart-felt fatisfaction was fcarcely ever more reciprocally experienced, or more cordially exchanged.

We had now no reafon for remaining in this
port, which, in confequence of this vifit, obtained

tained the name of PORT CONCLUSION, excepting that which a continuation of the inclement
weather produced, which detained us until the
evening of Friday the 22d.   But before I proceed
to the recital of fubfequent occurrences, it is neceffary that I fhould advert to the manner in
which the late furvey in the boats had been executed.

Agreeably to the directions Mr. Whidbey had
received, he proceeded to the ftation where his
former refearches had ended ; here he arrived
about noon on the 3d, after paffing clofe along
the weftern fhore of the ftrait, until he was oppofite to the branch leading to the eaftward.   In
his way he paffed feveral openings on the weftern fhore, fome of which he had reafon to fuppofe communicated with the ocean in a wefterly
direction, and others feemed to afford tolerably
well fheltered anchorage.   The weather at this
time was fo thick and rainy, that the party had
but a very imperfect view of the inlet before
them.   They, however, continued along its lar-
board fhore, in a direction N. 65 E. for about fix
miles and an half, paffing feveral fmall rocky
bays, and at this inlet arrived at a high fteep bluff
rocky point, named by me POINT NEPEAN,
fituated in latitude 57° 10', longitude 226° 6' ;
off which lies a ledge of rocks about half a mile,
and from this point the coaft takes a more northerly

therly direction ; but the weather became fo thick
that the party was obliged to ftop about two
miles beyond it, where the operation of the fame
caufe detained them until eight o'clock the
next morning; when, with very hazy unpleafant
weather, they refumed their inquiries, and paffed
between a coaft much indented with fmall bays,
and vaft numbers of fmall iflets and rocks, both
above and beneath the furface of the water.
The weather cleared up towards noon, and enabled Mr. Whidbey to obferve the latitude to be
57° 18′, on a fmall iflet, clofe to a point named
by me Point Pybus, lying from point Nepean
N. 38 E. ten miles and an half diftant. From
this ftation a tolerably diftinct view was obtained
of the inlet, in which the party had advanced
thus far nearly in the dark. It was now feen to
be a fpacious arm of the fea, containing, in moft
directions, many iflands, iflets, and rocks; the
country on the left hand fide, being that fhore
the party had coafted, excepting about point
Nepean, feemed in general to be but moderately
elevated, and although it is compofed of a rocky
fubftance, produced a very fine foreft, chiefly of
pine timbers; but the oppofite fide of the inlet
was too far off for us to notice any thing refpecting it. From this ftation the party proceeded
ftill along a very rocky fhore, about fix miles
further, in a direction N. 41 E. to a point called

by me POINT GAMBIER, which forms the south
point of a branch leading to the northweftward :
its oppofite point of entrance, named by me
POINT HUGH, lying from it N. 29 E. at the
diftance of five miles.   Beyond this, another extenfive branch appeared to ftretch to the northward, but the former being the object of their
firft inquiry, they proceeded along its weftern
fhore; this is low, and in many places is terminated by fandy beaches.   On one of thefe, about
ten miles from point Gambier, they refted for the
night, which was very ftormy from the fouthward, with continual rain, and dark gloomy
weather; this lafted until ten in the forenoon of
the 5th, when the wind moderating, and the
weather permitting them to fee fome little diftance before them, they proceeded, with a favorable breeze, up this branch of the ocean, called by
me SEYMOUR'S CHANNEL, which, at this place,
is from two to three miles wide, and which kept
gradually increafing to its head, where in a direction of N. E. and S. W. it is nearly two
leagues acrofs: on the weftern fide are many
fmall bays, and it terminates, at its north-weft
extremity, in a fmall brook of frefh water, in latitude 57° 51′, longitude 226°, lying from point
Hugh N. 33 W. diftant twenty-nine miles.
One mile from the fouth point of the brook is an
ifland, about three miles and an half long, and
                                          half

half a league broad; and half a mile from the
fouth point of that ifland lies another, about the
fame width, and fix miles long; both thefe
iflands lie in the above direction, and occupy the
middle of the branch, having a great number of
iflets on their north-eaft fides, and fome rocks on
their oppofite fhores. Here were feen five Indians, who were very fhy. The party caught
fome young ducks, but they were very fifhy, and
bad eating. The adjacent country is moderately
high, and was covered with timber of large
growth, excepting towards point Hugh, which
is a lofty rocky promontory, from whence extends
a ledge of rocks, where the fea broke with confiderable force. Owing to the badnefs of the
weather thefe rocks were not paffed until ten at
night on the 6th, and even then not without the
moft imminent danger, occafioned by a heavy
rain and the darknefs of the night, which prevented the party from difcovering their perilous
fituation until they were nearly amongft the
breakers, when, by timely and great exertion,
they happily paffed clear of them, and refted for
the night, about a mile on the north-eaft fide of
that point. The rain continued, with a ftrong
gale from the fouthward, until the forenoon of
the 7th, when the atmofphere becoming more
clear, their fituation was difcovered to be on the
weftern fide of the branch which was feen from

C 2

point

point Gambier, extending to the northward,
about four miles in width; but was now feen to
take a more wefterly direction, nearly parallel to
Seymour's channel, which the party had quitted;
and making the intervening fhore a long narrow
ftrip of land.   The oppofite or north-eaft fide of
this northern branch is compofed of a compact
range of ftupendous mountains, chiefly barren,
and covered with ice and fnow.   The route of
the party was along the fouth-weft fide; this is
nearly ftraight, compact, and free from rocks or
other interruptions, and favoured by a S. E.
breeze, they advanced about twelve leagues from
point Hugh; where they ftopped for the night,
oppofite to a high round ifland, lying in the
middle of the channel.

From this ftation, fituated in latitude 58° 1',
longitude 226° 3', in the morning of the 8th,
they departed with calm rainy weather, and purfued their refearches along the weftern fhore,
which now took a direction N. 10 W. eight
miles, to a point named by me POINT ARDEN,
where this branch divided into three arms; that
which appeared to be a continuation of the arm
they had been navigating took a north-eafterly
direction; the fecond, lying about a league to
the N. W. not more than half a mile wide, took
a north-wefterly direction, and, apparently, made
the land on its fouth-weft fide an ifland.   About
three

three leagues up this arm is a fmall iflet nearly in mid-channel. This afforded another inftance of the partial exiftence of the ice, which here intirely blocked up this arm, whilft the others were free from any fuch inconvenience. The third and wideft arm took a general courfe N. 81 W. and is about a league in width; this agreeably to our ufual practice was firft purfued along the fouthern fhore about five leagues to point Young, forming the eaft point of a cove, with an ifland and rock in its entrance, and another at the bottom of the cove. At this point the width of the arm decreafed to about half a league, and from it the fouthern fhore ftretched N. 42 W. At the diftance of about feven miles the eaft point of another fmall cove was reached, with an iflet lying near it. At the back of this iflet was an Indian village, and another was feen on an oppofite point lying north, about a league and a half from this cove, on the land forming the north fide of the arm, and feemed to be the north-weft point of the land before mentioned, appearing to be an ifland.

As Mr. Whidbey advanced from this cove, the fhore ftill continuing the fame line of direction, he recognized the fpot, from whence in his excurfion from Crofs found, on the night of the 18th of July he had retired, in confequence of the hoftile behaviour of the natives, and he now

became

became satisfied that he had been miſtaken in
ſuppoſing at that time the branch to be cloſed;
as it was now evident that it communicated
with that which the party had thus navigated,
making the intermediate land, which had hitherto been conſidered as a part of the continent,
one extenſive iſland, which I called ADMIRALTY
ISLAND.

In order however that no doubt ſhould in future ariſe, Mr. Whidbey proceeded to point Retreat.   After paſſing the village, which from that
point lies S. 33 E. at the diſtance of about ten
miles, the boats were followed by many large
and ſmall canoes; and as the evening was drawing near, to get rid of ſuch troubleſome viſitors a
muſket was fired over their heads, but this as before had only the effect of making them leſs ceremonious; this was proved by their exertions in
paddling to come up with our party, which they
did very faſt, until another ſhot was fired at the
largeſt canoe, and was ſuppoſed to have ſtruck
her, as the Indians all fell back in the canoe, and
were quite out of ſight; they, however, managed
to bring their canoe's ſtern in a line with the
boat's ſterns: in that ſituation they paddled back-
wards with all their ſtrength, and at the ſame
time ſcreened every part of their perſons, by the
height and ſpreading of their canoes' bows, excepting their hands, which, in the act of paddling
only

only became vifible, fo very judicioufly did they
provide for their fafety in their flight; in which,
having gained fome diftance from our party, who
had quietly purfued their courfe, the canoes ftopped for a fhort time, as if for confultation, but
foon made the beft of their way back to the village, and Mr. Whidbey proceeded without further interruption to point Retreat.   In this route
the party paffed by the fouth-weft fide of a very
narrow ifland, about half a mile broad, and about
a league and an half long; this before had been
paffed on its north-eaft fide, in the night of the
18th of July, but it was then fo dark that it was
not difcovered to be an ifland.   The channel,
about three fourths of a mile wide, which was
now purfued, is by rocks and iflets rendered
equally unfafe and intricate with that mentioned
on the former furvey, fo that the communication
between thefe two extenfive branches of the
ocean is, by thefe impediments, very dangerous
for the navigation of fhipping.   In this fouth-
weft channel, about a league from point Retreat,
on the fouthern fhore, is a deep cove, which, with
the narrow ifland lying before it, forms a very
fnug harbour, of good accefs by the paffage round
to the north of point Retreat; as the rocky part
of the channel lies to the fouth-eaft of this cove,
to which Mr. Whidbey gave the name of BAR-
LOW's COVE.   The fhores of Admiralty ifland,

C 4   which

which now had been completely circumnavigated, and found to be about fixty leagues in circuit, are, excepting at this and its fouth-eaftern part, very bold, afford many convenient bays, likely to admit of fafe anchorage, with fine ftreams of frefh water flowing into them, and prefented an afpect very different from that of the adjacent continent, as the ifland in general is moderately elevated, and produces an uninterrupted foreft of very fine timber trees, chiefly of the pine tribe; whilft the fhores of the continent, bounded by a continuation of thofe lofty frozen mountains, which extend fouth-eaftward from mount Fairweather, rofe abruptly from the water-fide, and were covered with perpetual fnow, whilft their fides were broken into deep ravines or vallies, filled with immenfe mountains of ice.

Such was the contraft exhibited at point Retreat, where Mr. Whidbey had an opportunity of feeing feveral of the points that had been fixed by his former obfervations, and which, on the prefent occafion, affifted him in correcting his furvey, for he had thus far been able to procure but one obfervation for the latitude, fince his leaving port Conclufion.

From point Retreat the party returned to Barlow's cove, where they refted for the night. The next morning a ftrong gale blew from the S. E. with a very heavy fall of rain; this greatly impeded

peded their progrefs in their way down this paffage, which dividing Admiralty ifland from the
continent, obtained the name of STEPHENS'S
PASSAGE; the point on which the northern
village is fituated, was found to be, as had before
been conjectured, the weft point of entrance into
the narrow icy arm, in which was again feen the
iflet noticed the preceding morning in an E. S. E.
direction, whence it was clearly afcertained, that
the intermediate land, forming the north fide of
Stephens's paffage was an ifland, which after
the Bifhop of Salifbury, I named DOUGLAS'S
ISLAND; it is about twenty miles long, and fix
miles broad in the middle, but becomes narrow
towards each end, particularly that to the eaftward, where it terminates in a fharp point: the
channel between this ifland and the main land,
being rendered by the ice impaffable, the boats
were fteered over to the fouthern fhore for protection againft the fouth-eaft wind, which had
now become fo violent, that it was late in the
evening before they had paffed the fouthernmoft
village; and after they had proceeded about
three miles to the eaftward of it, they refted for
the night.

Although the party had been a confiderable
time within fight of the village of thefe unfriendly people, not a fingle individual had been
feen; but they were heard making a moft hide-

ous

ous and extraordinary noife in their houfes, the
found of which reached the refting place of our
party, by whom it was fuppofed, that fome
perfon of confequence had been hurt by the fhot
fired the preceding evening at the large canoe,
and which not improbably had been the occafion
of their hafty retreat. In the morning of the
10th they were vifited by an old Indian man,
and a boy, who after receiving fome prefents
went about their bufinefs, and our party proceeded to the arm leading to the north-eaft from
Stephens's paffage, having its weftern point of
entrance, which I have called POINT SALIS-
BURY, fituated in latitude 58° 11', longitude
226° 3', in which the great quantity of floating
ice, with a ftrong northerly wind againft them,
fo retarded their progrefs, that a paffage was
with great difficulty effected; the weather here
was feverely cold, with frequent fhowers of fleet
and rain. From its entrance it extended N. 11
E., about 13 miles, where the fhores fpread to
the eaft and weft, and formed a bafon about a
league broad, and two leagues acrofs, in a N. W.
and S. E. direction, with a fmall ifland lying
nearly at its north-eaft extremity. From the
fhores of this bafon a compact body of ice extended fome diftance nearly all round; and the
adjacent region was compofed of a clofe connected continuation of the lofty range of frozen
                                        mountains,

mountains, whofe fides, almoft perpendicular, were formed entirely of rock, excepting clofe to the water fide, where a few fcattered dwarf pine trees found fufficient foil to vegetate in; about thefe the mountains were wrapped in perpetual froft and fnow. From the rugged gullies in their fides were projected immenfe bodies of ice, that reached perpendicularly to the furface of the water in the bafon, which admitted of no landing place for the boats, but exhibited as dreary and inhofpitable an afpect as the imagination can poffibly fuggeft. The rife and fall of the tide in this fituation was very confiderable, appearing to be upwards of eighteen feet. The examination of this bafon, &c. engaged the party until near noon of the 11th, when they returned along the eaftern fhore, which is a continuation of the fame range of lofty mountains rifing abruptly from the water fide; by dark they reached the ifland mentioned on the 7th, as lying in the middle of Stephens's paffage; here they took up their lodging for the night, which was very ftormy from the fouth-eaftward, and attended with a heavy rain. In the morning of the 12th the wind became more moderate, but the rain continued with an extremely unpleafant crofs fea, which the violence of the wind during the night had occafioned. This greatly retarded their progrefs down the paffage, the eaftern fhore

of

of which was found to be much indented with
fmall bays, and to take a general direction from
a fpot oppofite to the ifland they had quitted
S. 41 E., about twelve miles, to a point which
I named POINT STYLEMAN, forming the north-
weft point of a harbour, fituated in latitude 57
53', longitude 226° 22'; the oppofite point of its
entrance lying from it S. 33 E., at the diftance
of two miles.   This harbour, which obtained the
name of PORT SNETTISHAM, firft extends about
a league from its entrance in a north-eaft direction, where on each fide the fhores form an extenfive cove, terminated by a fandy beach, with
a fine ftream of frefh water.   On the north-
weft fide of entrance is a fmall cove, in which
there is alfo a run of water, with an iflet lying
before it.   The fhores are high and fteep, and
produce very few trees.   Several fmokes were
feen, but none of the inhabitants made their
appearance.   From the fouth point of this port,
which I called POINT ANMER, the fhore takes a
direction S. 29 E., nine or ten miles, to a point,
that obtained the name of POINT COKE, and
which forms the north point of a deep bay,
about four miles wide, which I called HOLK-
HAM BAY; this the party did not reach until
the morning of the 13th, when, nearly in the
middle of it, were found three fmall iflands; to
the wefternmoft of which a fhallow bank extended

tended from each fide of the bay, which is
bounded by the ftill continued lofty range of
mountains. Much floating ice was feen within
the iflands. From point Coke, in a direction
S. 43 W., two miles and an half, are two rocky
iflets, nearly in the middle of the branch, and
from the fouth point of this bay, which I called
POINT ASTLEY, the fhores are very rocky, and
contain many fmall open coves, taking a foutherly direction thirteen miles, to a point which
obtained the name of POINT WINDHAM, fituated in latitude 57° 31', longitude 230° 36'.
This point forms the eaftern point of entrance
into Stephens's paffage; here they again arrived
in the fpacious part of the inlet noticed from
point Gambier.

As the party advanced feveral iflets were feen
in various directions, and from point Windham,
on the eaftern fide, were fome bays; the fhores
took a general direction S. 25 E., twelve miles
and an half, to a point named by me POINT
HOBART, being the north point of a fmall
branch, where the party refted for the night, and
on the following morning they found its points
of entrance to lie from each other N. 1 ½ W. and
S. 11 E., about a league afunder. From its entrance it extends S. 70 E., five or fix miles,
where it terminated. Some iflets and funken
rocks lie near its fouth point, which I called

POINT

POINT WALPOLE. From point Hobart extends
a bank of fand a little diftance from the fhore,
but there is a clear paffage between it and the
iflets, within which, it forms a fnug harbour,
with foundings at a confiderable diftance from
the fhore from ten to fix fathoms water, fand
and muddy bottom. It is bounded by lofty
mountains, and from their bafe extends a fmall
border of low land forming the fhores of the
harbour, which I called PORT HOUGHTON. On
quitting this place many rocks were feen along
the fhores, which took a direction S. 12 W., fix
miles and a half, to a very confpicuous low projecting point, which obtained the name of CAPE
FANSHAW, fituated in latitude 57° 11′, longitude 226° 44½′. Here was feen an old deferted
village, and a fpacious branch of the inlet eight
miles wide, leading to the eaftward and fouth-
eaft.

From its very extenfive appearance in thefe
directions, Mr. Whidbey became apprehenfive,
left their utmoft exertions fhould not enable
them to draw their labours to a conclufion during his prefent excurfion, and for this reafon he
loft no time in proceeding along its northern
fhore, which from cape Fanfhaw takes a direction
S. 66 E., fixteen miles, to a low narrow point of
land two miles long, and half a mile broad,
ftretching fouth from the general line of the coaft

on

on each fide of it; but this diftance, owing to the
badnefs of the weather, and a ftrong gale from
the eaftward, was not reached before the 15th in
the afternoon. 'At this low point, which I
called POINT VANDEPUT, the width of the
branch decreafed to about three miles and an
half, in a fouth direction, to a fteep bluff point,
where, as alfo from this ftation, the fhores of the
branch took a more foutherly courfe.   South
from this point a fhoal extends about a mile, and
on its eaftern fide a fmall bay is formed, from
whence the eaftern fhore trends S. 34 E., feven
miles, to another point, where a fhoal ftretches
out about three fourths of a mile from the fhore;
this prevented the boats approaching the point,
although feveral attempts were made, in the
hope of gaining fhelter from the inclemency of
the weather, but it was to no effect, and the
party was obliged to remain cold, wet, and hun-
gry (having no provifions cooked) in the boats,
until the morning of the 16th; when the weather became fair and clear, and fhewed their
fituation to be before a fmall extent of low flat
land, lying immediately before the lofty mountains, which here rofe abruptly to a prodigious
height immediately behind the border.   A few
miles to the fouth of this margin the mountains
extended to the water fide, where a part of them

prefented

prefented an uncommonly awful appearance, rifing with an inclination towards the water to a vaft height, loaded with an immenfe quantity of ice and fnow, and overhanging their bafe, which feemed to be infufficient to bear the ponderous fabric it fuftained, and rendered the view of the paffage beneath it, horribly magnificent.

Soon after paffing this very remarkable promontory, the arm of the fea over which it hangs appeared to be entirely clofed by a beach, extending all round the head of it; at the foutheaft extremity was a large body of ice, formed in a gully between the mountains that approach the water-fide, from whence, much broken ice feemed to have fallen, and had entirely covered the furface of the water in that direction. From the fouth-weft corner iffued a narrow ftream of very white water, that feemed to have obtained this appearance by the melting fnow draining through the low land that was feen lying in that direction; and as it was confidered not to be navigable, Mr. Whidbey was anxious to lofe no time in the further extenfion of his refearches. Having now been abfent longer than the time for which the party had been fupplied, and being diftant upwards of an hundred miles from the veffels, towards which they had to proceed along a coaft, the principal part of which might require

quire a very minute examination; he made the beft of his way back, along the fouthern fhore of the branch.

We became afterwards informed by Mr. Brown of the Jackal, that the above narrow ftream was found, on his fubfequent vifit to this place, to afford a paffage for canoes and boats, and that it communicated with the apparently fhoal inlet that Mr. Johnftone had made feveral unfuccefs- ful attempts to enter on the 28th of Auguft, 1793. Mr. Brown alfo ftated, that the inter- vening land which had the appearance of form- ing the head of the arm between its fouth-eaft and fouth-weft extremities, is an ifland, fituated on a very fhallow bank, which, at the depth of a few feet, connects the two fhores, and at low water fpring tides becomes dry. This may ferve to account for the report of the Indians to Mr. Brown the preceding year, and which he oblig- ingly communicated to me on the 21ft of July, 1793, refpecting *Ewan Nafs*, by which means an inland navigation for canoes and boats is found from the fouthern extremity of Admiralty inlet, in latitude 47° 3′, longitude 237° 18′, to the northern extremity of Lynn canal, in lati- tude 59° 12′, longitude 224 34′. By this in- formation it likewife appeared, that our conclu- fions at the end of the laft feafon, refpecting cape

VOL. VI.   D   Decifion

Decifion being a continental promontory were not precifely correct, as, by the fhallow boat paffage difcovered by Mr. Brown, that cape is found to be feparated above the level of high water mark from the continent.

Mr. Whidbey obferves, that in no one inftance during his refearches, either in the feveral branches of Prince William's found, in thofe extending from Crofs found, or, in the courfe of his prefent excurfion, did he find any immenfe bodies of ice on the iflands; all thofe which he had feen on fhore, were in the gullies or vallies of the connected chain of lofty mountains fo frequently mentioned, and which chiefly conftituted the continental fhore from Cook's inlet to this ftation; though, in different places thefe mountains are at different diftances from the fea fide. He likewife obferves that all the iflands, or groups of iflands, were land of a moderate height, when compared with the ftupendous mountains that compofe the continental boundary, and were ftill feen to continue in a fouth-eaftern direction from this fhallow paffage, whilft the land to the weftward affumed a more moderate height, was free from fnow, and produced a foreft of lofty pine trees. Thefe obfervations more particularly applying to the former, than to the fubfequent, part of this furvey, I have, for that reafon,

thought

thought proper to introduce them in this place, and fhall now refume the fubject of Mr. Whidbey's excurfion.

The day being fair and pleafant, Mr. Whidbey wifhed to embrace this opportunity of drying their wet clothes, putting their arms in order, and giving a thorough cleaning to the boats, which, from the continual bad weather, had now become an object of real neceffity. For this purpofe the party landed on a commodious beach; but before they had finifhed their bufinefs a large canoe arrived, containing fome women and children, and fixteen ftout Indian men, well appointed with the arms of the country, but without any fire-arms. They behaved in a very friendly manner on the beach for a little time, but their conduct afterwards put on a very fufpicious appearance; the children withdrew into the woods, and the reft fixed their daggers round their wrifts, and exhibited other indications, not of the moft friendly nature. To avoid the chance of any thing unpleafant taking place, Mr. Whidbey confidered it moft humane and prudent to depart, and he continued his route down the branch along its fouth-weft fhore, paffing fome iflets that lie near it. The Indians did the fame, but kept on the oppofite fhore, and in the courfe of a little time the canoe difappeared. In the hope of being quit of thefe people the party ftopped to dine

near

near the high bluff obferved from point Vandeput, but before they had finifhed their repaft the
fame Indians, who muft have turned back un-
perceived, for the purpofe of croffing over to follow the boats, were feen coming round the point
of the cove in which was the party, and not
more than a quarter of a mile from their dinner
ftation; as the canoe approached a mufket was
fired over it, in order to deter the Indians from
advancing; but this, as on former occafions,
feemed to encourage them, and they appeared to
come forward with more eagernefs, but on a
fecond fhot being fired at the canoe they inftantly retreated with all poffible fpeed, and were foon
again behind the point: yet as Mr. Whidbey fufpected they might be inclined to attempt by fur-
prife, that which they dared not venture to do
openly, he haftened the meal of his party, and
put off from the fhore; this was fcarcely effected, when his conjectures were proved to have been
well founded, by the appearance of a number of
armed people iffuing from the woods, exactly at
the fpot where our party had dined; and nearly
at the fame inftant of time, the canoe was again
feen paddling round the point of the cove.

This conduct, on the part of the Indians, greatly attracted the obfervation of the party, and
whilft they were watching the motions of thefe
people, their attention was fuddenly and moft
agreeably

agreeably called to an object of more pleaſing concern; that of the boats under Mr. John-ſtone's direction, coming within ſight about two miles diſtant.

The ſtratagem thus practiſed by theſe Indians is alone ſufficient to ſhew, that our apprehen-ſions on board, for the ſafety of our abſent friends, had not been without reaſon; and it is one, amongſt many other circumſtances, which taught me to believe, that we were but juſt in time, for the accompliſhment of the arduous and hazar-dous ſervice in which we had been ſo long en-gaged; as the very unjuſtifiable conduct of the traders on this coaſt, has encouraged the inhabi-tants to attempt ſuch acts of hoſtility, that the means we poſſeſſed to repel their attacks, would, in all probability, have been inſufficient for our protection, had it been our lot to have tried the experiment one year later.

On the ſight of the two other boats all the Indians diſappeared, and our two parties were not long before their forces were united. It was im-mediately underſtood that Mr. Johnſtone had examined the coaſt from cape Deciſion to this ſtation. On this occaſion Mr. Whidbey re-marks, that it is not poſſible for language to de-ſcribe the joy that was manifeſted in every coun-tenance, on thus meeting their comrades and fellow-adventurers, by which happy circum-

ſtance

ſtance, a principal object of the voyage was brought to a concluſion; and the hearty congratulations that were mutually exchanged by three cheers, proclaimed not only the pleaſure that was felt in the accompliſhment of this laborious ſervice, but the zeal with which it had been carried into execution, and the laudable pride that had been entertained by both parties, in having been inſtrumental to the attainment of ſo grand an object.

The little ſquadron now proceeded to a cove about a league to the weſtward, where they took up their abode for the night. In the courſe of the evening no ſmall portion of facetious mirth paſſed amongſt the ſeamen, in conſequence of our having ſailed from old England on the *firſt of April*, for the purpoſe of diſcovering a north-weſt paſſage, by following up the diſcoveries of De Fuca, De Fonte, and a numerous train of hypothetical navigators.

Early in the morning of the 17th both parties ſat out on their return to port Concluſion, and being favored with a freſh gale from the S. E. they made great progreſs under ſail.

In the event of the two parties meeting, and conſequently a finiſhing ſtroke being put to the examination of the ſhores of North-Weſt America, within the limits of my commiſſion; Mr. Whidbey had my directions to take poſſeſſion of
the

the faid continent, from New Georgia north-
weftward to cape Spencer, as alfo, of all the adjacent iflands we had difcovered within thofe
limits ; in the name of, and for, His Britannic
Majefty, his heirs, and fucceffors : this, on the
parties ftopping to dine, was carried into execution ; the colours were difplayed, the boats'
crews drawn up under arms, and poffeffion taken
under the difcharge of three vollies of mufketry,
with all the other formalities ufual on fuch occafions, and a double allowance of grog was ferved
to the refpective crews, for the purpofe of drinking His Majefty's health. The happy meeting
of the two parties, having taken place on the
birth-day of His Royal Highnefs Frederick Duke
of York, the found in which they met I honored
with the name of PRINCE FREDERICK'S SOUND,
and the adjacent continent, north-weftward from
New Cornwall to Crofs found, with that of NEW
NORFOLK.

From hence the boats made the beft of their
way to the veffels, without any particular occurrence, until they arrived at port Conclufion, when
the wind blowing very hard from the fouthward,
brought with it a heavy confufed fea, which,
with the meeting of the tides, produced a kind
of race. Here the boats, for fome time, were in
a moft critical fituation, but by the great exertions of their crews, they were at length pre-

D 4

ferved,

ferved, and arrived fafe, as has been before related.

It now remains to recount the circumftances
attendant on Mr. Johnftone's expedition; who,
from cape Decifion, found the exterior coaft firft
take a direction N. 30 W. about three leagues,
and then N. 10 W. about the fame diftance, to
the north point of a harbour about a mile wide;
the intermediate fhore, between it and cape Decifion, has in it many fmall open bays, and at
fome diftance from it, lie many rocks. This
ftation was reached in the afternoon of the 3d,
the harbour was found free and eafy of accefs,
by keeping near the fouthern fhore; in general it
is about a mile wide. At firft it takes a north-
eaft courfe for about a league, and then terminates in a S. S. E. direction, about a league further, having fome iflets and rocks in it, notwithftanding which it affords very excellent fhelter,
with foundings from 17 to 34 and 12 fathoms
water. It is conveniently fituated towards the
ocean, has its north point in latitude 56° 17½',
longitude 225° 58', and obtained the name of
PORT MALMESBURY. Its north point, which
I have called POINT HARRIS, is rendered very
remarkable, by its being a projecting point, on
which is a fingle hill, appearing from many
points of view like an ifland, with an iflet and
fome rocks extending near a mile to the fouth-
weft

weſt of it.   North from hence, three miles and
an half, and then N. N. E. about the ſame diftance, is the ſouth point of a large bay, full of
innumerable iſlets and rocks, with a great number of very ſmall branches in various directions;
its examination occupied much time, and its
ſouthern extremity reached to the latitude of 56°
15', longitude 226° 15'; its eaſtern branch to
latitude 56° 28', longitude 226° 18'; and its
northern extremity to latitude 56° 33', longitude
226° 12'.   Between the two latter the party met
with about a dozen of the natives, who occupied
a ſingle habitation on the ſhore, and were the
firſt people Mr. Johnſtone's party had ſeen on this
expedition.   The 5th was very ſtormy, with
much rain, but the 6th was fair and pleaſant,
which enabled them to finiſh the examination
of this intricate ſound, and in the evening they
reached its north-weſt point of entrance, which
I called POINT ELLIS, where they remained
during the night.   It is ſituated in latitude 56°
31', longitude 225° 56'.   This alſo forms the
ſouth-eaſt point of another ſmall inlet, which is
equally intricate, and as much incommoded with
iſlets and rocks.   The examination of this employed the whole of the 7th.   It forms a narrow
arm, extending from point Ellis N. 56 E. for ten
miles, where it terminates.   Here they found a
ſingle houſe, ſimilar to that before mentioned,
and

and containing about as many inhabitants. From hence they returned along the northern fide of this arm, from half a mile to half a league in width, and about feven miles from its head to its north point, which forms alfo the fouth point of a bay or inlet, full of iflets and rocks, the north point of which, called by me POINT SULLIVAN, lies in latitude 56° 38', longitude 225° 51½'. From point Sullivan the fhores were lefs rocky, and became firm and compact, taking a direction N. 9 W. thirteen miles, to a confpicuous point, which after Vice Admiral Kingfmill, obtained the name of POINT KINGSMILL. From this point, which is the fouth point of the fpacious inlet, up which Mr. Whidbey had purfued his refearches to the north-eaftward; the fhores trended N. 47 E. fix miles and a half to another point, which I called POINT CORNWALLIS, and which forms the fouth-weft point of entrance into an arm leading to the fouth-eaft. The fpace between thefe two points is occupied by two bays, each taking a fouth-eafterly direction, from a mile to half a league wide, and four or five miles deep, in which as ufual along the coaft were many iflets and dangerous rocks. The examination to this extent, employed the party until the 10th in the morning, when they quitted the main inlet, and purfued the arm leading to the fouth-eaftward, which firft took a direction

tion S. 68 E. for nine miles, and then S. 26 E.
for feven miles and a half further; here a branch
was entered about half a league wide, that took
a S. S. W. direction for about eight miles, where
it terminated in latitude 56° 38½'. The fhores
of the fouthern parts of this branch, which I have
diftinguifhed by the name of Port Camden,
are pretty free from iflets and rocks, but thofe to
the north-weft of it, are lined with them, and
render the approaching of it extremely dangerous.
The termination of this branch reaches in a north
and fouth direction, within about two miles of
the north-eaft extent of the fmall inlet which the
party had examined on the 7th, and in the fame
line, within about four miles of the northern part
of that which had engaged them on the 5th and
6th. So very tedioufly and flowly were our refearches carried into effect in this very broken
and extraordinary region !

At the head of the laft mentioned branch was
a fmall Indian village confifting of three houfes,
and containing about forty or fifty perfons. On
meeting fome of the Indians here who had been
feen in the fouthern branches, it gave rife to an
opinion, that fome fmall paffage exifted which
had efcaped the notice of the party; but this
Mr. Johnftone obferves was foon explained by
the Indians who took up their canoe, and pointing to a fmall valley in a foutherly direction,

made

made figns that could not be miftaken, that they
had walked, and had brought their canoe, over
the ifthmus. The next morning, although very
wet and hazy, they returned along the eaftern
fide of this arm, and paffed its north-eaft point,
which from the head lies about N. N. E. at the
diftance of about four leagues, near which are
fome rocks. The party immediately entered
another branch, about the fame breadth, which
took firft a direction S. 68 E. for about five miles,
and then turned irregularly round to the fouthward. The weather being clear about noon, the
obferved latitude was found to be 50° 42', longitude 226° 25'. The branch in which they had
thus advanced, although two fhallow and rocky
for the paffage of any veffels larger than boats or
canoes, and even for them intricate and dangerous, would not have been further examined,
had not the tide been found running in a very
contrary direction, to that which had been obferved at its entrance, the flood tide here fetting
to the northward. This circumftance gave rife
to an opinion, that this branch would be found to
communicate with the main inlet they had left
under Mr. Whidbey's examination extending to
the north-eaft; and fhould it make the intermediate very broken land an ifland, it would
greatly facilitate their furvey of what they fuppofed to be the continental fhore.

This

This hope induced Mr. Johnſtone to perſevere, but inſtead of the channel ſtretching to the eaſtward as it was wiſhed, and expected to do, it extended to the weſtward of ſouth, and communicated with a bay in the north-weſt part of Clarence's ſtrait, which had been examined by Mr. Johnſtone on the 11th of September, 1793; but this communication was not at that time aſcertained, in conſequence of the numerous iſlets, rocks, and ſhoals, that exiſt in that bay, and render it intirely unnavigable for ſhipping. The party now diſtinctly ſaw port Protection and the adjacent ſhores, and having taken the neceſſary angles that their further ſurvey would demand, they returned by the way they had arrived; but the progreſs of the boats was rendered very ſlow by the numberleſs rocks and iſlets, and the examination of the ſeveral little bays into which the ſhores were broken. To the eaſtward were ſeen high diſtant mountains covered with ſnow, but the land in their neighbourhood was, comparatively ſpeaking, low, of a very uneven ſurface, much divided by water, and covered with wood. Mr. Johnſtone unwilling to looſe any advantage that preſented itſelf, ſtopped but a ſhort time on the night of the 12th, in order that he might take the benefit of the flood the next morning, which returning about half after one, they proceeded with it cloſe along the eaſtern ſhore round

every

every cove and corner; for they could not by any other mode have determined its boundary, as they were at this time furrounded by a very thick fog, that obfcured every diftant object until about ten in the forenoon, when a frefh wefterly breeze brought fair and clear weather, and difcovered their fituation to be near the weft point of a fmall branch, in latitude 56° 50′, longitude 226° 16′. The adjacent fhores in all directions, but particularly to the north-weft, were lined with iflets and rocks, that extended nearly two miles into the opening, which was here about two leagues acrofs.

This branch about a mile wide ftretched about five miles in an eaftwardly direction, and there it terminated; but before the party had reached this extent, Mr. Johnftone ftates, that the remains of no lefs than eight deferted villages were feen; fome of them were more decayed than the others, but they were all uniformly fituated on the fummit of fome precipice, or fteep infular rock, rendered by nature almoft inacceffible, and by art and great labour made a ftrong defence; which proved, that the inhabitants had been fubject to the incurfions of hoftile vifitors. Thefe fortified places were well conftructed with a ftrong platform of wood, laid on the moft elevated part of the rock, and projecting fo far from its fides as to overfpread the declivity. The edge of
the

the platform was furrounded by a barricade raifed
by logs of wood placed on each other. In the
vicinity of thefe ruins were many fepulchres or
tombs, in which dead bodies were depofited.
Thefe were made with a degree of neatnefs feldom exhibited in the building of their habitations. A wooden frame was raifed about ten
feet from the ground, the upper half of which
was inclofed, and in the open part below in
many, though not in all of them, was placed a
canoe ; the flooring of the upper part was about
five feet from the ground, and above that the
fides and top were intirely clofed in with boards,
within which were human bodies in boxes wrapped up in fkins or in matting. Thefe repofito-
ries of the dead, were of different fizes, and fome
of them contained more bodies than the others ;
in the largeft there were not more than four or
five, lying by the fide of each other, not one appearing to be placed above the reft ; they were
generally found near the water fide, and very
frequently on fome confpicuous point. Many of
thefe facred monuments feemed to have been
erected a great length of time, and the moft ancient of them had evidently been repaired and
ftrengthened by additional fupporters of more
modern workmanfhip. Hence it would appear,
that whatever might be the enmity that exifted
between the feveral tribes when living, their remains

mains when dead were respected and suffered to rest quietly and unmolested.

Having satisfied their curiosity in these respects, and having gained the head of the arm, they stopped to dine in a cove a little way from its termination. Hitherto the party had not seen any of the natives, but at this time they were visited by several who came chiefly from the head of the arm, where they must have been secreted, or they could not have escaped being noticed. The number of these people accumulated very fast, and in a very little time, they amounted to upwards of an hundred, amongst whom were a chief, and several of the Indians seen at the isthmus on the preceding Thursday and Sunday. Whatever might be the real intention, or the disposition of these strangers, their numbers and general appearance, induced Mr. Johnstone to desire them to keep at a greater distance; this the Indians did not seem inclined to do, although every sign to that effect was made, and our party armed in readiness for their defence. As their numbers increased, so were they encouraged to advance; on some muskets being fired they stopped for a short time, but soon again followed the boats as they returned down the arm, keeping just without the reach of musketry. Although these people had amongst them some guns, and were otherways well armed

with

with their native weapons, Mr. Johnſtone did
not impute to them any hoſtile intention, but
attributed the ardour with which they had ſtriven
to join our party, to a deſire of bartering away
their ſea otter ſkins, of which they appeared to
have many, for European commodities. The
ſituation of the party on this occaſion was in a
very confined place, and being ſurrounded by
ſuch a tribe of armed Indians, with reaſon to apprehend there might be others at no great diſ_
tance, it became prudent to avoid, if poſſible, a
nearer intercourſe, by which alone the true ſpirit
of their deſign could have been known, and in
which they muſt have been greatly intereſted, as
they continued to follow the boats, until after
they had gained a more open ſituation.   One of
the canoes now advanced before the reſt, in
which a chief ſtood in the middle of it, plucking
the white feathers from the rump of an eagle,
and blowing them into the air, accompanied by
ſongs and other expreſſions, which were received
as tokens of peace and friendſhip.   The canoe
was now permitted to come alongſide Mr. Johnſtone's boat, to whom the chief inſtantly preſented a ſea otter ſkin, for which Mr. Johnſtone
made him a ſuitable return, with every expreſſion
likely to be underſtood of his pacific diſpoſition;
the Indians ſeemed to be ſincere in their profeſ-
ſions alſo, as they now came to the boats un-

VOL. VI.   E   armed,

armed, and with the utmoft confidence in their fecurity. Expreffions of mutual friendfhip were now exchanged, and on its being fignified to the chief, that as night was approaching the canoes fhould no longer follow the boats, he returned to the reft of his countrymen; but they ftill continued to paddle after our boats until a mufket or two were difcharged, when they all dropped a-ftern and were no more feen.

However fatisfactory the latter part of the natives' conduct may appear to be, as to their friendly intentions, yet a diftruft which prudence on fuch occafions ought always to fuggeft, induced Mr. Johnftone to proceed as far as he conveniently could before he ftopped for the night; but as the fhore was quite fteep and compact they continued to row until after midnight, when they came to a grapnel, and refted in the boats. This day had proved extremely fatiguing to the people, as they had been nearly the whole of the twenty-four hours on their oars. In this route they had reached the main arm of Prince Frederick's found, and had found the fhores to form a large rounding, though not lofty promontory, in which were feveral fmall open bays, and near it feveral detached rocks. This promontory obtained the name of POINT MACARTNEY, the weftern extremity of which is fituated in latitude 57° 1$\frac{1}{4}$′, longitude 226° 12′. From hence
the

the fhore trends N. 15 E. about a league, where the width of the found is about feven miles acrofs, in a direction N. 47 W. to point Nepean. From this ftation N. 28 E., at the diftance of about a league and a half lies a fmall ifland, with patches of rocks from this point reaching nearly to its fhores. The promontory ftill took a rounding direction about N. 65 E., five miles further, from whence the fouthern fhore of the found extends N. 75 E. feventeen miles, to the weft point of a fmall cove, the only opening in the fhore from point Macartney; but off the little projecting points between this cove and that point, are detached rocks lying at no great diftance from the fhore. This extent was not reached until the afternoon of the 16th, in confequence of the wind blowing hard from the eaftward, attended with a heavy rain, againft which they contended with their utmoft exertions, left the exhaufted ftate of their provifions fhould oblige them to retire before they could join the other party. This cove extended S. 34 E. about a league, where it terminated, and according to our furvey, formed a narrow ifthmus between it and the head of Duncan's channel, about two miles acrofs in a northern direction; and is another ftriking inftance of the very extenfive, and extraordinary infular ftate of the region lying before the weftern coaft of the

E 2   American

American continent, between the 47th and 59th degrees of north latitude.

Having dined, the party refumed their furvey along the fouthern fide of the found, which took nearly an eaft direction. They had not far advanced, when about five in the evening they had the joyful fatisfaction of meeting Mr. Whidbey and his party as before recited.

Mr. Johnftone ftated, that the part of the coaft that had claimed his attention during his laft excurfion is a peninfula, connected with the more eaftern land by the laft mentioned narrow ifthmus, and that it is by no means fo high or mountainous as the land compofing the adjacent countries on the oppofite or north-eaftern fide of the found, which at no great diftance confifted of very lofty, rugged, dreary, barren mountains, covered with ice and fnow; but that the land compofing the peninfula was chiefly of moderate height, and produced a noble foreft of large and ftately pine trees of clean and ftraight growth, amongft which were a few berry bufhes and fome alders. The fhores along the bays and arms they had vifited were in general low, and prefented a probability that if the wood were cleared away, the foil of the country might be advantageoufly employed under cultivation. Thefe bays and arms abounded with a greater number of falmon and fea otters, than Mr. John-

ftone

ſtone had obſerved on any other part of the
coaſt; and as they were found in the greateſt
abundance at the heads of thoſe places, it was
inferred that ſalmon, and other ſmall fiſh, form
a large proportion of the food of the ſea otters,
which are thus induced to frequent theſe inland
channels, to which at this ſeaſon of the year ſuch
fiſhes reſort.

Mr. Whidbey in his obſervations on Admiralty iſland, remarks, that notwithſtanding this
iſland ſeemed to be compoſed of a rocky ſub-
ſtance covered with little ſoil, and that chiefly
conſiſting of vegetables in an imperfect ſtate of
diſſolution, yet like the peninſula juſt adverted
to, it produced timber, which he conſidered as
ſuperior to any he had before noticed on this ſide
of America. He alſo ſtates, that in his two laſt
excurſions ſeveral places were ſeen, where the
ocean was evidently incroaching very rapidly on
the land, and that the low borders extending
from the baſe of the mountains to the ſea ſide,
had, at no very remote period of time, produced
tall and ſtately timber; as many of their dead
trunks were found ſtanding erect, and ſtill rooted
faſt in the ground, in different ſtages of decay;
thoſe being the moſt perfect that had been the
leaſt ſubject to the influence of the ſalt water,
by which they were ſurrounded on every flood
tide: ſuch had been the incroachment of the

ocean

ocean on thefe fhores, that the fhorter ftumps
in fome inftances at low water mark, were even
with, or below the furface of the fea.

This fame appearance has been noticed before
in port Chalmers, and on this occafion Mr.
Whidbey quotes other inftances of fimilar in-
croachments not only in Prince William's found,
but alfo in Cook's inlet; where he obferved
fimilar effects on the fhores, and is of opinion
from thefe evidences, that the fhallow banks
occupying fo large a part of Gray's harbour, have
recently been produced by the operation of one
and the fame caufe: and it is not lefs reafonable
to conclude, that the waters of the North Pacific, have, poffibly for ages, had a general ten-
dency to produce the fame effect, on all the coaft
comprehended within the limits before mentioned.

A return of fair and clear weather on the 18th
enabled them to fee that large tract of broken
land lying between Crofs found and cape Ommaney, which has been defcribed as having a
range of high mountains capped with fnow extending through it; but from thefe ftill continuing to have the appearance of being difunited
in feveral places, it tended to corroborate our
former opinion; and although as before we had
not had an opportunity of afcertaining the fact,
I have been induced to confider the country as
being

being divided into many iflands, and have for
that reafon termed it an archipelago.   The ftrait
that feparates this land from the eaftern fhore,
which after Lord Chatham, I have called CHAT-
HAM STRAIT, Mr. Whidbey confiders as likely
to be one of the moft profitable places for procuring the fkins of the fea otter, on the whole
coaft; not only from the abundance obferved in
the poffeffion of the natives, but from the immenfe number of thofe animals, feen about the
fhores in all directions.   Here the fea otters were
in fuch plenty that it was eafily in the power of
the natives to procure as many as they chofe to
be at the trouble of taking.   I was alfo given to
underftand by Mr. Brown of the Jackal, who
followed us through thefe regions, that the fea
otter's fkins which he procured there were of an
extremely fine quality.

The principal object which His Majefty appears to have had in view, in directing the undertaking of this voyage having at length been
completed, I truft the precifion with which the
furvey of the coaft of North Weft America has
been carried into effect, will remove every doubt,
and fet afide every opinion of *a north-weft paffage*, or any water communication navigable for
fhipping, exifting between the North Pacific, and
the interior of the American continent, within
the limits of our refearches.   The difcovery that

E 4   no

no fuch communication does exift has been zea-
loufly purfued, and with a degree of minutenefs
far exceeding the letter of my commiffion or
inftructions; in this refpect I might poffibly
have incurred the cenfure of difobedience, had I
not been intrufted with the moft liberal, difcre-
tionary orders, as being the fitteft and moft likely
means of attaining the important end in queftion.

The very detached and broken region that lies
before fo large a portion of this coaft, rendered a
minute examination altogether unavoidable : this
had frequently the good effect of facilitating the
labours of our furvey, by its leading us through
narrow, fhallow, intricate channels, which cut
off extenfive tracts of broken land, and by thus
fhewing their feparation from the continent, their
further examination became unimportant to the
object of our inquiry.

For this reafon I have confidered it effential
to the illuftration of our furvey, to ftate very
exactly not only the track of the veffels when
navigating thefe regions, but likewife thofe of
the boats when fo employed, as well when I was
prefent myfelf, as when they were conducted by
Mr. Whidbey or Mr. Johnftone, on whom the
execution of that laborious and dangerous fervice
principally fell, and to whom I feel myfelf indebted for the zeal with which they engaged in

it

it on all occafions. The perufal of thefe parts of our voyage to perfons not particularly interefted, I am confcious will afford but little entertainment ; yet I have been induced to give a detailed account, inftead of an abftract, of our proceedings, for the purpofe of illuftrating the charts accompanying this journal; of fhewing the manner in which our time day by day had been employed ; and, for the additional purpofe, of making the hiftory of our tranfactions on the north-weft coaft of America, *as conclufive as poffible*, againft all fpeculative opinions refpecting the exiftence of a *hyperborean or mediterranean ocean* within the limits of our furvey.

I fhall now conclude the account of our tranfactions at this place by the infertion of fuch aftronomical and nautical obfervations as were made during the time we paffed at this ftation.

On the 2d of Auguft in port Conclufion the chronometers fhew the following longitudes, viz. Arnold's No. 14, 225° 37′; Arnold's No. 176, 225° 38′; and Kendall's, 225° 34′ 30″; the true longitude being 225° 37′ 30″, it appeared that Arnold's No. 14 was 30′ to the weftward, Arnold's No. 176, 30′ to the eaftward, and Kendall's 2′ 30″ to the weftward of the true longitude.

By eighteen fets of obfervations taken between the 2d and 18th of Auguft on fhore with the

artificial

artificial horizon, Arnold's No. 14 was found to be faſt of mean time at Greenwich at noon on the 18th of Auguſt   —   4^h 38$^\prime$ 13$^{\prime\prime}$ 30$^{\prime\prime\prime}$

And to be gaining on mean

    time per day at the rate of,   24 00

Arnold's No. 176, faſt of mean time

    at Greenwich on ditto   10 13 33 00

And gaining per day at the rate

    of,   —   —   49 37

Kendall's faſt of mean time at

    Greenwich on ditto   9 8 30 00

And gaining per day at the rate

    of,   —   —   26 11

The mean variation by two compaſſes and eighteen ſets of obſervations, differing from 24° 9$^\prime$ to 27° 10$^\prime$, was   —   25° 30$^\prime$

The latitude of the place of obſervation by four meridional altitudes, taken on ſhore with the artificial horizon   —   56 14 55

BOOK

BOOK THE SIXTH.

PASSAGE TO THE SOUTHWARD ALONG THE WESTERN COAST OF AMERICA; DOUBLE CAPE HORN; TOUCH AT ST. HELENA; ARRIVE IN ENGLAND.

CHAPTER I.

Depart from Port Conclusion—Arrival at Nootka— Transactions there—Visit Maquinna at Tah- sheis—Astronomical Observations for correcting the Survey between Cape Douglas and Cape Decision.

THE preparations that had been made for our departing immediately on the return of the boats, proved of little importance, as the S. E. gale which commenced on the day of their arrival, continued with little variation to blow very violently from the direction in which I pur- posed to steer, attended with very heavy rain, and thick foggy weather until Friday the 22d in the evening, when the atmosphere became somewhat clearer, and the wind more moderate. Although it continued to be contrary to our pursuit, yet being completely tired of remaining in this inactive solitary situation, I determined to put to sea, and with the Chatham departed from port Conclusion. We plied towards the ocean,

but

but made little progrefs, as we were ftill attended by adverfe winds and thick foggy weather.

It was not until the morning of Sunday the 24th that we reached the open ocean, in ac-complifhing of which, we were in imminent danger of lofing the veffels about twelve o'clock the preceding night, by being driven on cape Ommaney. The faint variable winds, and the great irregularity of the tides, fat us fo near to that promontory, and the rock that lies near it, that it required our utmoft efforts in towing to keep the veffels off from the land, and confe-quently from the inevitable deftruction that muft have followed. A very heavy weftern fwell at this time broke with great fury not half a mile from us ; and as no anchorage, or even bottom could be found, our fituation for fome time was moft ferioufly alarming ; from which however, we were moft providentially extricated, by a gentle breeze fpringing up from the N. W. when in the moft perilous and critical ftate that can be imagined.

This breeze by two in the morning, enabled us to gain a fufficient diftance from the fhore, to allow the boats, which had been employed in towing the fhip from the rocks, to be taken on board. In the execution of this bufinefs we had the misfortune of lofing Ifaac Wooden, one of the cutter's crew, who unfortunately fell overboard ;

board ; and although a boat was inftantly fent to his affiftance, yet as he was no fwimmer, and as in falling he unluckily ftruck his head againft the boat's gunwale, he funk fo immediately that no help could be afforded him.   This poor fellow had affifted in moft of the boat excurfions, was highly regarded by his comrades, and much regretted by his officers ; in fhort, he was a good man, and an active failor ; and to commemorate his unexpected and melancholy fate, I named the rock which lies off cape Ommaney, WOODEN's ROCK.

At day-light we had a frefh gale from the N. W. and having now finally accomplifhed fo much of my commiffion, as appertained to the difcovery of any navigable water communication, from the North Pacific into the interior of the American continent, my attention became directed to the adjuftment of thofe differences that had arifen in my negociation with Senr. Quadra as to the ceffion of Nootka ; under the idea that a fufficient time had now elapfed, fince the departure of Lieutenant Broughton, for the arrival of the neceffary inftructions at that place, by which I might be enabled to regulate my future conduct, with refpect to the reftitution of thofe territories to the dominion of our Moft Gracious Sovereign.

In

In this expectation our courfe was directed fouth-eaftward towards Nootka, paffing about three leagues to the weftward of the Hazy iflands; thefe form a group of fmall rocky iflets a league in extent, lying S. 7 E. at the diftance of 16 leagues from cape Ommaney; S. 62 W. from cape Decifion; and three leagues weft from Coronation ifland, which is the neareft land to them.   At noon the foothernmoft land in fight, being cape de St. Bartolom, forming the north point of entrance into Puerto del Baylio Bucareli, and difcovered by Senr Quadra in 1775, bore by compafs S. 87 E.; the neareft fhore was a con-fpicuous promontory, which I diftinguifhed by the name of CAPE ADDINGTON after the fpeaker of the Houfe of Commons, N. 73 E., diftant four or five leagues; Warren's ifland in the en-trance of Clarence's ftrait, N. 9 E.; mount Calder, N. 1 E.; Coronation ifland from N. 13 W. to N. 30 W.; and cape Ommaney, N. 44 W. In this fituation the obferved latitude was 55° 29½', and the longitude, agreeably to the pofition of feveral confpicuous ftations as fixed by former obfervations, and now very accurately correfpond-ing, was found to be 225° 58'; but by the chro-nometers, allowing their rate and error as afcer-tained at port Conclufion, the longitude was by Kendall's chronometer 226° 4', by Arnold's No. 14, 226° 3' 45", and by No. 176, 226° 15' 30";

hence

hence it would appear, that fome alteration in their rate of going had taken place fince the laft obfervations were made in port Conclufion, on the evening of the 18th ; and particularly in No. 176, which it is neceffary to remark, had been there taken on fhore for the purpofe of obfervation.

In the afternoon we paffed cape del St. Bartolom, which, according to our obfervations, is fituated in latitude 55° 12½', longitude 226° 34'. From this cape, in a direction S. 21 E. at the diftance of 14 miles, and 12 miles from the neareft part of the contiguous fhore, lies a very low flat rocky iflet, furrounded by rocks and breakers, that extend fome diftance from it; from thefe circumftances, and from its being fo far diftant from the main land, it is rendered one of the moft dangerous impediments to navigation that we had met with on the exterior coaft; and hence it obtained the name of the WOLF ROCK. S. 11 W. from this rock, at the diftance of three leagues, lies a fmall high ifland, named by Mr. Dixon, Forrefter's Ifland ; between thefe we paffed, and fo far as we became acquainted with the channel, it appeared to be clear and free from interruption.

After paffing Forrefter's ifland (Monday 25) our courfe was directed towards the north-weft point of Queen Charlotte's iflands, with an intention

tention of examining their exterior coaft, for the purpofe of correcting any error that might have occurred in our former furvey ; but this we were unable to accomplifh, on account of the thick hazy or foggy weather which for the moft part obfcured the land from our view, and when vifible, it was feen but indiftinctly. This weather was attended by calms, or light variable winds, fo adverfe to our purfuit, that it was not until Monday the 1ft of September, that we gained fight of the wefternmoft of Scot's iflands. At noon this ifland bore by compafs N. 8 E. and our obferved latitude being 50° 21′, fhewed the longitude to be 230° 35′; but by the chronometers allowing the rate as before ftated, Kendall's chronometer gave 230° 46′ 45″; Arnold's No. 14, 230° 45′ 45″; and No. 176, 231° 0′ 15″. Now, although we were not pofitively certain as to the identical part of the ifland to which thefe calculations applied, (it being but juft vifible in the horizon) yet, concluding the longitude as had been afcertained by its bearings, and the obferved latitude of the fhip to be moft correct : the former opinion, that the chronometers had varied fince our laft obfervations by them in poit Conclufion, was now very much ftrengthened, as we were thoroughly convinced that no error, either in making the prefent or any of the former obfervations, had taken place ; the moft particular

cular care and attention having ever been obferved throughout the whole voyage on all fuch
occafions.

The wind at N. W. gradually increafed to a
gentle gale, accompanied by clear and pleafant
weather, which brought us by fix in the evening
of the following day, Tuefday the 2d, to an anchor in Friendly cove, Nootka found ; here we
found His Catholic Majefty's armed veffels the
Princiffa, Aranfafu, and the St. Carlos, belonging
to the eftablifhment at St. Blas, with the Phœ-
nix bark, commanded by Mr. Hugh Moor, from
Bengal ; the floop Prince le Boo, one of Mr.
Brown's fquadron, commanded by Mr. Gordon
from China, who had been employed in collecting furs during the fummer upon this coaft,
moftly to the northward of Nootka ; befide
thefe Englifh traders, was the Wafhington, J.
Kendrick, commander, of Bofton in America ;
who had been employed in the fame purfuit, but
whofe veffel was now under repair.

The Princiffa commanded by Senʳ Fidalgo
had arrived from St. Blas only the day before,
and had brought hither Brigadier General Don
Jofe Manuel Alava, colonel of the regiment of
Puebla, and governor of Nootka.

The appointment of this gentleman as governor of Nootka had taken place in confequence
of the death of our highly valuable and much

Vᴏʟ. VI.   F   efteemed

efteemed friend Sen' Quadra, who in the month
of March had died at St. Blas, univerfally lamented.   Having endeavoured, on a former
occafion, to point out the degree of admiration
and refpect with which the conduct of Sen'
Quadra towards our little community had impreffed us during his life, I cannot refrain, now
that he is no more, from rendering that juftice
to his memory to which it is fo amply intitled,
by ftating, that the unexpected melancholy event
of his deceafe operated on the minds of us all, in
a way more eafily to be imagined than defcribed;
and whilft it excited our moft grateful acknowledgments, it produced the deepeft regret for the
lofs of a character fo amiable, and fo truly orna-
mental to civil fociety.

The Difcovery having in the courfe of the
day greatly outfailed the Chatham, the latter did
not arrive until after dark; for this reafon, our
formal vifit to the governor was deferred until
the day following.   Mr. Puget had come down
the coaft from Woody point, much nearer to the
fhore than we had done; and from him I learned
that between the entrance of the found, and the
breakers which are about feven or eight miles to
the weftward of it, he had met with much fea-
weed; growing about two miles from the fhore
in very irregular depths of water, from five to
ten fathoms, rocky bottom, until within about
two

two miles of Friendly cove, when the fea-weed
difappeared, and the depth of water greatly increafed.

On Wednefday morning the 3d, we waited
upon the governor, who ftill refided on board the
Princiffa, where we were received by him and
Senr Fidalgo with marks of the moft polite and
friendly attention.   I was foon given to underftand by Senr Alava, that his appointment to this
government had taken place as above ftated for
the particular purpofe of finifhing the pending
negociation, refpecting the ceffion of thefe territories; which, in confequence of the different
conftruction put on the firft article of the Spanifh convention, of the twenty-eighth of October
1790, by the late Senr Quadra and myfelf, had,
fince the month of September 1792, been intirely
fufpended.   The prefent governor however was
ftill unprovided with the credentials neceffary for
finifhing this bufinefs; but on his departure from
St. Blas in June, thefe documents were hourly
expected, and a veffel was waiting there in readinefs to be difpatched to this port, provided
they arrived in time for her reaching Nootka on
or before the 15th of October ; but in the event
of her not being able to effect a paffage by that
time, fhe was to repair to Monterrey.   In confequence of this arrangement Senr Alava purpofed
to remain here until that period fhould arrive;

and

and as no communication from England, either
of a public or private nature, had yet reached me,
I confidered it to be highly probable, that a duplicate of my inftructions for the like purpofe
might be tranfmitted by the fame conveyance.

Under this impreffion, and the confideration
of many other circumftances relative to the fituation of both veffels, I thought it moft advifeable
to determine on remaining till that period with
Sen' Alava; indeed it was not very likely, from
the various important duties we had now to execute, with the inadequate means we poffeffed for
doing fo, that we fhould be enabled to proceed
much before that time. Our ftore of cordage
was completely exhaufted, nor had we a fathom
of rope but what was then in ufe; the whole of it
was much worn, and had been fpliced in feveral
places, and therefore it became neceffary to contrive fome means for procuring a fupply before
we could venture to fea again. The quantity
which our Spanifh friends, or the trading veffels
in this port, were likely to afford us, was very
inadequate to our neceffities, which obliged us to
refort to the expedient of converting fome of our
cables into cordage. This would neceffarily
prove a tedious bufinefs, efpecially as we had to
conftruct a machine for that purpofe. The
Chatham was not only in a fimilar predicament
with refpect to cordage, but fhe required caulking,

ing, and immediate repair in fome of her plank, that was found to be rotten. Both veffels demanded many fpars to be cut and prepared; the fails and cafks ftood in need of great repair; and it had become effentially important, that the obfervatory fhould be erected on fhore, for the purpofe of afcertaining more pofitively the rate and error of our chronometers, in order to correct our furvey from cape Douglas to cape Decifion; for notwithftanding that I had little doubt in my own mind of the mode that had been purfued, yet I was fenfible that correfponding obfervations at this place would be very fatisfactory.

With thefe objects in contemplation, our time was not likely to be unprofitably employed; and although I would gladly have poftponed the execution of thefe feveral tafks until our arrival in a more fouthern clime, where we had reafon to believe the weather would be more favorable to our wifhes, and where the neceffary refrefhments of which we all ftood fo much in need, might have been procured in great abundance; yet it would have been highly indifcreet, and extremely dangerous, for the veffels to have put to fea again, until a fupply of cordage could be provided. In addition to this, other circumftances feemed to demand, that I fhould remain within the reach of any difpatches that might have been forwarded through New Spain; which could only be done

by

by ſtaying here, or reſorting to ſome of the ſouthern Spaniſh ſettlements, where we ſhould loſe the advantage of procuring the ſpars and plank which were now required; and as moſt of our buſineſs muſt have been ill executed on board the veſſels, I felt little encouragement, when I reflected on the treatment we had experienced the preceding year from the acting governor of California, to expect being indulged with permiſſion for performing it on ſhore, in any of the ports under his juriſdiction.

Theſe weighty conſiderations induced me to reſolve on continuing at Nootka until all our important operations were completed; and if in the mean time I ſhould receive any inſtructions for the government of my conduct, as to the reſtitution of theſe territories, by the expected Spaniſh packet, or by any other conveyance, I ſhould be upon the ſpot to act with Senʳ Alava as the nature of my orders might require.

I took an early opportunity of repreſenting to Senʳ Alava our neceſſitous condition, and requeſted his permiſſion to erect our obſervatory and tents on ſhore. To this requeſt he gave his moſt hearty concurrence, and ſeemed very earneſtly to regret, that the ſtate of their eſtabliſhment precluded him from adminiſtering to our wants in that effectual manner, to which he was prompted by his inclinations.

Senʳ

· Sen͟r Saavadra, who had remained in charge of Nootka since our former visit, joined our party on board the Princissa, where the day passed in making inquiries about the civilized world, and in deploring the turbulent and unhappy state of Europe. The melancholy circumstances that had been detailed by Mr. Brown, were now confirmed by these gentlemen to the close of the year 1793; and we became much concerned by the events that had happened, and alarmed at the fatal consequences which it was natural to suppose they must produce.

The weather was gloomy with continual rain, but it did not prevent *Maquinna* and *Clewpaneloo*, with some other chiefs, and a few of the natives, from visiting the vessels. The two former received such compliments as were suitable to their rank, with which they were highly satisfied; and the latter disposed of a scanty supply of fish at a very exorbitant price. Fish had become of great value amongst these people, as, either from the badness of the season during the preceding summer, or from their neglect and inattention in providing their usual supply for the winter, they had experienced the greatest distress for want of provisions during that period; and had not Sen͟rs Saavadra administered to their relief, many of them would probably have fallen a sacrifice to the scarcity. And although the provident care

F 4   he

he had taken was inadequate to all that was demanded of him, yet the affiftance he had been
able to afford them, was, much to the credit of
the natives, acknowledged by them with the
moft grateful expreffions.

The governor, Sen.rs Fidalgo, Saavadra, and
fome others of the Spanifh officers, honored us
with a return of our vifit on Thurfday morning
the 4th; but in confequence of our reduced ftock
of powder, I was under the neceffity of declining
the ufual ceremony of faluting, which was very
politely excufed and difpenfed with by the whole
party.

The weather continued very rainy and unpleafant until Saturday morning the 6th, when
the clouds difperfed with a breeze from the weftward, and the weather became clear and agreeable. The tents, obfervatory, and inftruments,
were now fet on fhore; the fails dried and unbent, and our various fervices were put in a train
for execution, in which we were affifted by fome
Spanifh caulkers and carpenters, who were employed on board the Chatham; and on Monday
following, the 8th, having conftructed a machine,
we began making rope from the materials of a
new bower cable.

Whilft the wind continued in the weftern
quarter, it regularly died away every evening;
and though the night light airs prevailed from
the

the land, which were fucceeded by the refrefhing
wefterly breeze from the fea in the day time,
accompanied by cheerful pleafant weather;
which, with the advantage of the fociety we here
met,. made our time pafs as agreeably as could
well be expected in thefe rude and diftant regions.

On Wednefday the 10th the wind again blew
frefh from the S. E. and exhibited another of
the very rare inftances of lightning and thunder
in this country, which with torrents of rain continued moft of the night.

The wind returned again to the weftward on
Thurfday evening the 11th, and brought with
it fair and pleafant weather; with which the
Aranfafu failed for St. Blas, and through Senr
Alava's civility, I tranfmitted by this opportunity a letter to the Admiralty, ftating our having
accomplifhed the furvey of North Weft America, and the expectation I was in of receiving
their final inftructions for the accomplifhment of
the other objects of my commiffion.

Both wind and weather, as might reafonably
be expected on the approach of the autumnal
equinox, became now very changeable; on the
13th the atmofphere was dark and gloomy, with
drifting fhowers; and the wind from the S. E.,
which in the afternoon fuddenly fhifted to the
N. E., blew in heavy fqualls, accompanied by a

very

very heavy fall of rain. Notwithſtanding that the wind came directly from the land, yet towards midnight, when the gale ſeemed to be at its height, an extremely heavy ſwell rolled in from the ocean, and broke with great fury on the ſhores of the found that were expoſed to its influence; and even thoſe of this little cove were by the ſurge greatly annoyed. This kind of weather continued until Wedneſday the 17th, and much retarded our ſeveral works, which could not yet be conſidered as in any ſtate of forwardneſs. The violence of the equinoctial gales from this time ſeemed to have abated, and a ſeries of fair weather, with regular land and ſea breezes, enabled our people to make all the progreſs that the tedious nature of their ſeveral labours would permit.

Since our arrival we had occaſionally been viſited by *Maquinna, Clewpancloo,* with ſome of the inferior chiefs, and many of the inhabitants, who ſold us a few fiſh, and brought to market ſome veniſon; but moſt of theſe people had now retired to their winter habitations up the found. Theſe Senʳ Alava expreſſed a deſire to viſit, and as we all knew that ſuch an excurſion would be highly flattering to *Maquinna,* and to the other chiefs and people, a party was formed with three of our boats, and a Spaniſh launch to carry the luggage. Notwithſtanding that we were well

perſuaded

perfuaded of the friendly difpofition of the natives, yet I confidered it neceffary that the boats
fhould be equipped for defence, as on all other
fuch occafions.   The fettled ftate of the weather had now not only favored and forwarded all
our tranfaﬅions, but was extremely inviting to
the relaxation we had in view.

Sen^{rs} Alava and Fidalgo, with Mr. Menzies,
accompanied me in the Difcovery's yawl ; Mr.
Puget, attended by fome of the officers of the
Chatham, was in the cutter ; Lieutenant Swaine,
with fome of the gentlemen of the Difcovery,
were in our large cutter ; and with thofe in the
Spanifh launch, our party confifted of fifty-fix
officers and men.   No doubt was entertained
that Maquinna, who had been informed of the
honor intended him, would be in readinefs to
receive us, and for this reafon our courfe was firft
directed towards Tahfheis, the place of his refidence.   But as we were not much affifted by
the wind, it was near fun-fet before we arrived
at a very pleafant fpot not far from *Maquinna*'s
village, where we pitched our tents ; and as the
day was too far advanced, our ceremonial vifit
was deferred until the next day, and a meffage
to that effect was fent by *Clewpaneloo*, who had
attended us from the fhips.   But *Maquinna*,
who with his people was in readinefs to receive
us, inftantly difpatched a meffenger, requefting

that

that we would repair to his refidence that evening. This however we thought proper to decline, but in order that *Maquinna* might be fatisfied of our intentions to vifit him in the morning, fome of the gentlemen walked to the village, and explained to him, that it was the late-
nefs of the hour only that prevented our then
complying with his requeft.

Matters being comfortably arranged for the
night, centinels were planted, as well to avoid
any furprize from the natives, as to prevent our
own people from ftraying to their habitations,
from whence difputes or mifunderftandings might
have arifen; ftrict orders were iffued to this
effect, and being uniformly adhered to, the night
paffed without the leaft interruption.

After breakfaft on Friday morning the 26th,
we proceeded with the four boats to Tahfheis,
and were welcomed on our approach to the fhore
by a vociferous old man, exclaiming " *Wacofh,*
Wacofh ;" by which he meant to exprefs friendfhip, and the good intentions of the natives towards us. Thefe fentiments being returned in
a fimilar manner by our party, we landed, and
were received by *Maquinna* and two of his bro-
thers, *Whaclaffe pultz,* and *Tatoochfeatticus,* with
repeated expreffions of " *Wacofh,*" until we were
almoft ftunned with their gratulations. This
ceremony being concluded, we were conducted
through

through the village to *Maquinna*'s habitation, where we were led to feats prepared and covered with clean mats at the upper end of the houfe.

Having taken our feats, about thirty men began each to beat with a ftick on a hollow board, in order to affemble the inhabitants of the village to that fpot; this fummons being readily obeyed, *Maquinna* informed the affembled crowd with great earneftnefs, and in a fpeech of fome length, that our vifit was to be confidered as a great honor done to him, and that it had taken place in confequence of the civil and orderly behaviour of all the inhabitants of the found under his authority towards the Englifh and the Spaniards. This, he obferved, was not the cafe with *Wicananifh,* or any other chief whofe people committed acts of violence and depredation on the veffels and their crews that vifited their country; but that fuch behaviour was not practifed at Nootka, and that for this reafon they had been more frequently vifited: by which means, their wealth in copper, cloth, and various other articles of great value to them, had been increafed far exceeding that of any of their neighbours. He particularly mentioned fome tribes, but by appellations we were not acquainted with, over whom he feemed to confider our vifit to him as a great triumph; and from his manner of fpeaking, there evidently appeared

peared to exift no fmall degree of jealoufy be‑
tween them. He then proceeded to enumerate
the various good qualities that marked the cha‑
racter of the Spaniards and the Englifh; that
both were ftrongly attached to himfelf and his
people, and that he hoped that we fhould be
much pleafed by being entertained according to
their manner of receiving vifitors.

The performers I believe were all in readinefs
without, and anxious to begin their part; for
the inftant *Maquinna* had ceafed fpeaking, the
hollow board mufic recommenced, and a man
entered the houfe moft fantaftically dreffed in a
war garment, which reached to the calves of his
legs, but not below them; this was varioufly
ornamented, as was alfo his face with black and
red paint, fo that his features appeared to be
moft extravagantly diftorted, or, more properly
fpeaking, they were fcarcely diftinguifhable; his
hair was powdered, or rather intirely covered
with the moft delicate white down of young
fea fowl, and in his hand he bore a mufket with
a fixed bayonet, making altogether a moft fa‑
vage, though at the fame time a whimfical
figure; this man was followed by about twenty
more, decorated with confiderable variety after
the fame fafhion, but differently armed; fome
like himfelf with mufkets, others with piftols,
fwords, daggers, fpears, bows, arrows, fifh gigs,
and

and hatchets, feemingly with intent to difplay their wealth and power, by an exhibition of the feveral implements they poffeffed, as well for the ufe of war, as for obtaining the different necef- faries of life.

This prepofterous group of figures was drawn up before us; and notwithftanding we were per- fectly fatisfied of the harmlefs and peaceable in- tentions of thefe people, yet I believe there was not one of our party intirely free from thofe fen- fations which will naturally arife from the fight of fuch unufual objects; whofe favage and bar- barous appearance, was not a little augmented by their actions and vociferous behaviour, accom- panied by an exhibition, that confifted princi- pally of jumping in a very peculiar manner. In this effort the legs did not feem to partake much of the exertion, although they fometimes raifed themfelves to a confiderable height; and we underftood that thofe were confidered to be the beft performers, who kept their feet conftantly parallel to each other, or in one certain pofition, with the leaft poffible inclination of the knees. After thefe had finifhed their part, *Maquinna* per- formed a mafk dance by himfelf, in which, with great addrefs, he frequently and almoft imper- ceptibly changed his mafk; this feemed to be a very favourite amufement of his, as he appeared to be in high fpirits, and to take great delight in

the

performance. The mafks he had made choice of, certainly did credit to his imagination in point of whimfical effect; his drefs was different from that worn by any of the other performers, confifting of a cloak and a kind of fhort apron, covered with hollow fhells, and fmall pieces of copper fo placed as to ftrike againft each other, and to produce a jingling noife; which, being accompanied by the mufic before defcribed as a fubftitute for a drum, and fome vocal exertions, produced a favage difcordant noife, as offenfive to the ear as the former exhibition had been to the eye. But as the object of our vifit was a compliment to *Maquinna*, a previous determination to be pleafed infured our plaudits, which were bountifully beftowed, and received with great pleafure and fatisfaction by the furrrounding fpectators.

A paufe now took place in the entertainments, which however was foon filled up, to the great gratification of our hoft and his friends. The prefents that had been provided for the occafion were now exhibited to public view, confifting of copper, blue cloth, blankets, ear fhells, and a variety of fmall articles of lefs value; thefe were feverally diftributed by Senr Alava and myfelf to *Maquinna* and his relations, according to the rank and confequence of each; in thefe tokens of our friendfhip we fucceeded fo well, that our

liberal

liberal donations foon refounded through the village, and the glad tidings were received with loud acclamations of applaufe. On thefe fubfiding, we had a fecond vocal and inftrumental performance, which concluded by a return from *Maquinna* for the prefents we had made. In this *Maquinna* did not perfonally appear; *Whaclaffe pultz*, acting as mafter of the ceremonies, firft addreffed Senr Alava in a fhort fpeech, refpecting the friendfhip that had fo long been eftablifhed between the Spaniards, and the tribes under the authority of *Maquinna*, who, he faid, was highly pleafed by the trouble he had taken in paying him this diftant vifit; and that, as a proof of *Maquinna*'s fincerity, he was then about to make fome return for the repeated inftances of friendfhip he had experienced, by placing a fea otter fkin at the feet of Senr Alava. I then received a fimilar compliment, as did Senr Fidalgo and Mr. Puget, after which Senr Alava and myfelf were each prefented with a fecond fea otter fkin, which concluded the ceremonies of this vifit.

The day was not yet far advanced; and being fair and pleafant, we amufed ourfelves in ftrolling through the village; and found it, although extenfive, far from being numeroufly inhabited. This was accounted for by *Maquinna*, who ftated, that many families were ftill abfent, not having

yet procured their ftock of provifions for the en-
fuing winter feafon; at which time, if all their
habitations are fully occupied, its population cannot be much lefs than eight or nine hundred
perfons. *Maquinna*'s habitation was confiderably larger than any of the others, and had a
very fuperior advantage over them all by being
lefs filthy; it was at prefent not more than half
occupied, nor was it intirely covered in, though
it did not appear to have been recently erected;
but we remained ignorant of the reafon why fo
large a proportion of the roof remained unfinifhed. The conftruction of the Nootka houfes,
efpecially with refpect to their infide, has been
fo fully treated by Captain Cook, as to preclude
any material addition from my pen; yet it is
fingularly remarkable, (although particularly reprefented in Mr. Webber's drawing of the village in friendly Cove) that Captain Cook fhould
not have taken any notice whatever in his journal,
of the immenfe pieces of timber which are raifed,
and horizontally placed on wooden pillars, about
eighteen inches above the roof of the largeft
houfes in that village; one of which pieces of
timber was of fize fufficient to have made a lower
maft for a third rate man of war. Thefe, together with the large images, were at that time
fuppofed to denote the habitation of the chief,
or principal perfon of the tribe; and the opinion
then

then formed, has been repeatedly confirmed by obfervations made during this voyage. One or more houfes in many of the deferted villages, as well as in moft of the inhabited ones we had vifited, were thus diftinguifhed. On the houfe of *Maquinna* were three of thefe immenfe fpars; the middle piece was the largeft, and meafured at the but-end nearly five feet in diameter; this extended the whole length of the habitation, which was about an hundred feet long. It was placed on pillars of wood; that which fupported it within the upper end of the houfe was about fifteen feet in circumference, and on it was carved one of their diftorted reprefentations of a gigantic human figure. We remained totally unacquainted with the intention of, or the pur-pofe that was to be anfwered by, thefe fingular roof trees; but it is natural to fuppofe that they muft be directed to fome important object, as the raifing of fuch immenfe maffes of timber twelve or fourteen feet from the ground, and placing them firmly on the pillars by which they are fupported, muft, to a people fo totally devoid of mechanical powers, be a moft tedious and labo-rious operation.

Our curiofity being fatisfied, and our pockets completely emptied by the unremitting folici-tations of the inhabitants of Tahfheis, of the ftock of trinkets with which we had been provided,

G 2   we

we proceeded to the upper end of the arm, which afforded me an opportunity of explaining to Senr Alava the manner, in which the numerous channels and branches in the continent he had feen delineated on our charts, terminated; as this ended in the fame way, by a low border of land in the front of a valley, through which fome fmall ftreams of water were difcharged; but the adjacent fhores were infinitely lefs high than we had been accuftomed to obferve; where having ftrolled a little about in the fkirts of the woods, we returned to our encampment. Here we found *Maquinna* with feveral of our Tahfheian friends, who were very folicitous that we fhould return and partake in the evening of an entertainment fimilar to that we had received in the morning; but as we had appointed to be at home on Sunday morning, and had promifed a vifit to our friend *Clewpaneloo* at his principal refidence, called Mooetchee, which was at a confiderable diftance from Tahfheis, it was not in our power to comply with the civil folicitations of *Maquinna* and his fraternity.

We were honored at dinner with the company of *Maquinna*, moft of his family, and many of the other chiefs; who, with the moft unequivocal affurances of their friendfhip, and with expreffions of the great pleafure they had derived

from

from our vifit, bad us farewell after dinner, and we departed.

As Mooetchee is fituated near the upper part of the next branch to the eaftward of Tahfheis channel, our route was directed back by the way we had come; and having reached in the evening the dividing point of thefe two arms of the fea, which is fituated about N. 6 E. fix or feven miles from Friendly cove, we pitched our tents for the night, in order to have the day before us for vifiting *Clewpaneloo*, whofe habitation was about feven or eight miles from us; towards which place, after breakfaft, on Saturday morning the 27th, we proceeded; and as our vifit was not intended to be a very long one, the Spanifh launch was left in a pleafant fituation, in order to pitch the encampment, and provide a dinner againft our return; by which means our journey to the fhip the next day would be materially fhortened. Our progrefs was not very rapid, as both wind, and the ftream which I believe in general runs down, were adverfe to our purfuit, which was through a region fo wild and inhofpitable in its appearance, as occafioned Senr Alava frequently to exprefs his aftonifhment, that it could ever have been an object of contention between our refpective fovereigns. The fhores either conftituted impenetrable forefts, produced from the fiffures of a rugged rocky

country,

country, or were formed by ftupendous barren
precipices, rifing perpendicularly from the water
to an immenfe height; fo that, excepting the ice
and cataracts to which we had been accuftomed
in many other inftances, Senr Alava was enabled
from this fhort excurfion to form a very complete idea of the general character of thofe countries to the northward of this ftation, which had
fo long occupied our time and labour.

It was nearly three in the afternoon before we
reached the village of Mooetchee, which confifted of a few houfes huddled together in a cove,
with as little regularity in the difpofal of them
as was apparent in the conduct of its inhabitants,
who crowded about us, and produced us much
inconvenience, although with the moft inoffen-
five and peaceable defign. Our friend *Clewpa-*
neloo, though their chief, feemed not to poffefs
fufficient influence to reftrain this behaviour,
even within his own habitation, to which we
were conducted by a very narrow paffage between the houfes; the filth of which, and the
combination of fo many offenfive exhalations,
rendered it highly neceffary to our feelings, that
as much difpatch as poffible fhould be ufed in
the diftribution of our prefents, which, when
effected, would leave us perfectly at liberty to
depart, without giving the leaft offence to our
hoft or to any of his friends. On this occafion,

ceremonies

ceremonies fimilar to thofe practifed at Tahfhies were here obferved; but the want of order and decorum, independently of the difference in point of numbers between Tahfheis and Mooetchee, evinced the fuperiority of *Maquinna*'s authority, when compared with that of the neighbouring chiefs; amongft whom *Clewpaneloo* was reputed to be one of the firft in wealth and power; and I certainly noticed as many of their large fquare boxes, in which they generally keep their valuables, in his habitation, as I had done in almoft all the other houfes collectively taken, but what they contained we did not entirely learn; yet, if credit were to be given to our landlord, they were all well appropriated, being, according to his account, filled with the fkins of the fea otter, bear, deer, martin, and other animals of the country, or with copper, iron, cloth, and other European commodities.

Our part being performed, and our ftore of prefents exhaufted, we returned to our boats, accompanied by *Clewpaneloo*, who made us in return prefents fimilar to thofe we had received from *Maquinna*; to which he added one infinitely more valuable than all the reft. This was a very fine buck, juft killed; which being depofited in our boat, we took leave of Mooetchee, amidft reiterated acclamations of " *Wacofh, Wacofh,*" with repeated intreaties of the moft friendly

G 4   nature

nature to prolong our ftay; but as the day was now far advanced, no time was loft in making the beft of our way towards the ftation where the Spanifh launch had been left; this we reached in the evening, and found every thing comfortably prepared for our reception.

As we bent our way homewards the next morning, we ftopped at an anchoring place called by the natives Mowenna, in great repute with the traders on this coaft, and particularly fo with the Americans. It is fituated on the weftern fide of the found, between four and five miles to the northward of Friendly cove, over which it poffeffes (though further from the fea) feveral advantages in point of fecurity and accommodation. The land in its neighbourhood continues to be low to a greater diftance than about Friendly cove, and feems to be compofed of lefs rocky materials. The extent of this harbour is but fmall, but being well protected againft all winds, and its diftance from the ocean preventing its being much affected by the fwell, feveral veffels might ride here in perfect fafety; and as it has a fair navigable channel out of it in a foutherly direction, veffels can fail out of this harbour whenever the land wind prevails to pufh them clear of the found, with infinitely more eafe than from Friendly cove; out of which, they are firft obliged to warp a confiderable diftance,

tance, and to anchor not only in an inconvenient
depth of water, but on an uneven rocky bottom;
in addition to which, in the event of the wind
fuddenly fetting in ftrong from the fea, their
fituation becomes by no means pleafant. The
departure from Friendly cove, although not difficult in the fummer feafon, yet (as I have been
given to underftand) is fubject in the winter to
great, and indeed dangerous, inconvenience, from
the heavy fea which rolls in ftormy weather into
the found; efpecially during the S. E. gales,
againft which, from its vicinity to the ocean, it is
not fufficiently protected. As a military eftablifhment however, it is greatly to be preferred to
Mowenna, as nothing can pafs or repafs into the
found unobferved at Friendly cove.

About noon we arrived on board. Nothing
of any moment had occurred during our abfence; the weather, which had been favorable
to our excurfion, had been fo likewife to the feveral employments of re-equipment, though we
had yet much remaining to perform.

On Monday afternoon the 29th, arrived a very
fmall fhip called the Jenny, belonging to Briftol;
the fame veffel that had vifited Nootka in October, 1792, then rigged as a three-mafted fchooner, and commanded by Mr. Baker, who had
proceeded in her to England, with the cargo of
furs he had then collected. She was now commanded

manded by a Mr. John Adamſon, who had returned with her from England, and had in the
courſe of the preceding ſummer in the neighbourhood of Queen Charlotte's iſlands, collected upwards of two thouſand ſea otter ſkins, with which
he was bound to the Chineſe market, and from
Canton was to be employed as packet in the ſervice of the Eaſt India Company.   He brought
us the agreeable intelligence of having met Mr.
Brown in the Jackal on the coaſt, in the latitude
of 54°, for whoſe ſafety we had entertained ſome
apprehenſion; for when we left Mr. Brown in
port Althorp, it was his intention to proceed to
the ſouthward through the inland navigation,
and as the inhabitants of thoſe ſhores had acted
a very ſuſpicious part towards Mr. Whidbey, we
were fearful leſt Mr. Brown's ſmall force might
not have been equal to his protection.

The ſerenity of the weather continued to favor
our operations with little interruption.   The
wind blew for a few hours on the afternoon of
Tueſday the 30th, from the S. E. attended with
rain; but the N. W. wind again prevailed, and
the weather became fair and pleaſant the next
morning, Wedneſday the 1ſt of October.

On the day following, Thurſday the 2nd, I was
honored with the company of the Governor,
Senrs Fidalgo, Saavadra, and moſt of the Spaniſh
officers to dine on board the Diſcovery.   The
very

very exhausted state of my stores, and stock of articles necessary on such occasions, had precluded my receiving this pleasure so frequently as I could have wished.

I was very agreeably surprized by receiving a message from the governor on Saturday the 4th, in the afternoon, purporting that the expected Spanish packet from St. Blas was in the offing; these however were but short-lived hopes, for we no sooner had recourse to our glasses, than we became of opinion that the vessel in question was the Jackal.   But as the wind at this time blew strong from the S. E. attended with dark, rainy, hazy weather, and as she could not reach the port before dark, she stood to sea again; during the night the S. E. gale increased with incessant rain, and a very heavy swell rolled into the sound; the next day, Sunday the 5th, the weather was more moderate, and in the evening the Jackal arrived. It was now that I received the information of Mr. Brown's having passed through the shallow passage mentioned in Mr. Whidbey's last survey in the boats, which appertaining immediately to the region then under consideration, I thought it most properly introduced in the narrative of that expedition.   Since our separation with the Jackal, Mr. Brown had collected upwards of a thousand prime sea otter skins, and several of inferior quality.   Most of these had been procured

cured

cured from thofe people, whofe conduct had put
on fuch a fufpicious appearance in the opinion
of Mr. Whidbey and his party, in his way from
Crofs found: they had behaved very properly to
Mr. Brown, whofe readinefs to enter into a traf-
fic with them might probably operate in gaining
their good opinion; for it had been evident, on
many occafions, that our difinclination to a commercial intercourfe had excited the difpleafure of
feveral tribes we had met with; this opinion
was confirmed, by their ufual formalities on firft
vifiting the veffels, which generally concluded
with a defire to open a negociation for the difpofal of their merchandize.

As the month of October advanced, we knew
perfectly well, both from our former and prefent
experience, that the fummer feafon of this country
was faft drawing to a conclufion, and as moft of
our material bufinefs with the fhore was now
nearly finifhed, I took the advantage of Monday,
being a fair day, to receive on board the obfervatory inftruments and tents. Our fuel and
water was yet, however, to complete, which
would unavoidably detain us three or four days
longer, fo that waiting the ftipulated time, after
which the Spanifh packet was not to be expected, could now be of little moment, when
compared to the importance her arrival might
poffibly be of, in expediting our return to England.

land. This, however did not happen, nor did any circumſtance worthy of notice take place during this anxious interval. At midnight on the 16th we put to ſea, in company with the Chatham. The Princiſſa, Captain Fidalgo, with Governor Alava on board, was to follow us the next day. Monterrey was appointed as the next rendezvous, where theſe officers entertained little doubt of our meeting a reception, and every re-ſpect ſuitable to our ſituation and wiſhes. In this opinion I was induced to concur, from a con-verſation that had lately paſſed between Senʳ Alava and myſelf, when I became acquainted that the repreſentation I had made to Senʳ Quadra of the treatment we had received on our former viſit to New Albion, had in conſequence of his deceaſe been tranſmitted to the viceroy at Mexi-co, whoſe very humane and liberal intentions towards us, had no doubt, been materially miſ-underſtood by Senʳ Arrillago.

Having bad farewell to Nootka, and made ſuch remarks on our ordinary tranſactions there. as appeared to me deſerving attention, I ſhall now proceed to ſtate the reſult of our labours at the obſervatory, and ſhew from what authority I deduced the longitude of the various ſtations in our late ſurvey, which in many inſtances differs materially from the longitude aſſigned to them by Captain Cook. I have already ſtated my

reaſons

reafons for fubfcribing to our own calculations in preference to thofe made by Captain Cook ; and muft again repeat, that I have prefumed fo to do, under the conviction of our having had the means of being accurate, more fully in our power than fell to the lot of that renowned and illuftrious navigator.

On September 6th, in Nootka found the chronometers fhew the following longitudes; viz. Arnold's No. 14, 232° 32′ 50″; Arnold's No. 176, 232° 32′ 53″. The true longitude being 232° 31′ 30″, it appeared that Arnold's No. 14, and Kendall's, were each of them 1° 0′ 40″, and Arnold's No. 176, 44′ 25″ to the weftward of the true longitude.

On the 6th of October at noon, Arnold's No. 176 was found by the mean of twenty-nine days equal altitudes, to be faft of mean time at Greenwich   -   -   -   10ʰ 49′ 45″ 56‴

And to be gaining on mean
time per day at the rate of,   41 57

Arnold's No. 14, faft of
mean time on the fame day, 4 57 10 56

And gaining on mean time
per day at the rate of,   -   23   4

Kendall's, faft of mean time
on ditto,   -   -   -   9 30 52 56

And gaining on mean time
per day,   -   -   28 30

By

By obfervations taken on fhore with the artificial horizon, between the 6th of September and
11th of October, 1794, the chronometers were
found to be gaining on mean time, viz. Arnold's
No. 176, 41ʺ 57ʹʹʹ; Arnold's No. 14, 23ʺ 6ʹʹʹ;
and Kendall's, 28ʺ 29ʹʹʹ per day; by which it
appeared, that when opportunities did not offer
of obtaining equal altitudes for afcertaining the
rates of the chronometers, common altitudes if
taken with care, would anfwer the fame purpofe; this is exemplified by the above obfervations, as the difference of the rate between two
of the chronometers was only one fourth, and
that of the other, viz. Arnold's No. 176, rather
more than half a fecond, which is accounted for
by the very unequal rate in general of that chronometer.

The latitude, longitude, variation, and inclination of the magnetic needle, were found to be
the fame as on our firft vifit to this place in the
year 1792.

CHAPTER

CHAPTER II.

Depart from Nootka Sound—Violent Storm—Arrive at Monterrey—Receive on board the Deserters from the Chatham and Dædalus—Excursion into the Country—Examine a very remarkable Mountain—Astronomical and Nautical Observations.

A LIGHT breeze from the land favored our progress out of Nootka found, and by daylight on Friday the 17th, we were about three leagues from the land, when the wind suddenly died away, and was succeeded by a calm with thick hazy weather continuing the whole of the day, and giving the vessels an appearance of being stationary; the depth of water continued to be the same from noon until midnight, 75 fathoms, muddy bottom. At this time the haze was succeeded by a very thick fog, without the least breeze of wind; and although by the depth increasing we imagined that we were proceeding from the coast, yet our motion was so slow, that by six in the evening of Saturday the 18th, we were still in soundings at the depth of 100 fathoms, muddy bottom, and by the lead when on the ground, the vessel seemed to lie as if at anchor.

This

This obfcurity in the atmofphere had prevented
our feeing the Chatham fince the preceding
evening, but the ferenity of the weather, and the
apparent ftationary fituation of the Difcovery,
made me conclude that fhe could not be far off.
Our powder being much exhaufted, the fog fignal
had not been made; but in order to afcertain
the fact, a gun was now fired, and to our great
aftonifhment it was not anfwered. The fog and
calm ftill continued, and the depth of water
gradually increafed, at eight o'clock we had 105
fathoms, with fandy bottom. The fog now difperfed, and the calm was fuceeded by a light
breeze from the E. N. E.; another gun was now
fired, and a falfe fire burnt as a fignal to our
confort, but neither was anfwered. After re-
peating thefe fignals in the fame manner, at three
o'clock on Sunday morning the 19th to no
effect, we made all fail, fteering to the S. S. E.
At day-light the high land over Nootka and
Clayoquot, was ftill in fight, bearing by compafs
from N. 6 W. to E. N. E.; our diftance from
the coaft was 10 or 12 leagues. The foundings
we had gained at midnight at the depth of 135
fathoms, proved to be at the diftance of about
feven leagues from point Breakers, and fomething more from the general line of the coaft to
the eaftward of that point. This I confidered to
be the edge of a bank of foundings that appeared

to lie along the coaft, which commenced a-breaft of cape Lookout, and terminated a little to the northward of Nootka. Near the entrance of De Fuca's ftraits it feemed to ftretch further into the ocean, as at the diftance of eight leagues from thofe fhores we had only 58 fathoms water, with muddy bottom.

In looking round for the Chatham a veffel was difcovered a-ftern, for which we immediately fhortened fail, but foon finding it to be the Spanifh fhip Princiffa, we again directed our courfe as before with all fail fpread to a pleafant eafterly breeze and fair weather; with this however we were not long indulged, for in the evening the wind veered to the S. S. E., and by Monday the 20th in the afternoon, increafed to fo ftrong a gale as to oblige us to clofe-reef our topfails. The wind fixed in the fouth-eaftern quarter, and became variable, with fometimes clear, and at others cloudy weather: this gale did not reduce us below our topfails, although we plied not only againft it, but againft a very heavy fouth-wefterly fwell to fo little purpofe, that by noon on Friday the 24th we had by our reckoning (for we were unable to gain any obfervation) only reached the latitude of 47° 12', longitude 232° 12'. In the evening the wind veered to the S. S. W., with which we made a tolerably good progrefs to the fouth-eaftward

until

until Sunday morning the 26th, when it became light and variable, with alternate calms, and a very heavy fwell from the W. S. W.

This uncomfortable weather was fuccceded by a frefh breeze from the N. E., which as ufual veered to the S. E. on Monday morning, and in the afternoon increafed to a gale fo violent, as to make it neceffary that we fhould ftrike the topgallant-mafts, and bring to, under the ftorm ftayfails; this gale was attended with an ex-tremely heavy rain until midnight, when the ftorm fuddenly moderated, and the wind veer-ing to the S. W. we ftood to the S. E. under our courfes and clofe-reefed topfails.

The obferved latitude on Tuefday the 28th was 44° 14′, longitude by account 233° 27′; in the afternoon all our canvafs was again fpread, but by Wednefday morning the 29th the wind had refumed its fouth-eaftern direction, with hard fqualls and heavy rain, which again reduced us to the forefail and ftorm ftayfails.

Since our departure from Nootka we had con-ftantly been incommoded by a very heavy weft-erly and fouth-weft fwell, which at this time was greatly increafed, notwithftanding the fea, raifed by the violence of the wind from the fouth-eaft; thefe together caufed a very confufed agi-tation of the ocean, and although the fhip was made as fnug as poffible by the top-gallant mafts

H 2   being

being ftruck, and by every thing, that conveniently could be taken from aloft, yet fhe was
extremely uncomfortable, and fhipped great quantities of water. About noon the gale moderated,
and on the wind returning to the S. W., we again
made fail to the fouth-eaftward. The afternoon
was tolerably fair; vaft flocks of wild geefe and
ducks were obferved, flying to the fouthward,
which indicated that in a more northern climate
the winter had fet in with much feverity.

The wind, although variable between S. E. and
S. W. was moderate, with frequent calms, and
the weather, comparatively fpeaking with that
we had fo recently experienced, might be confidered as tolerably fair, notwithftanding which,
we made little progrefs until Monday morning
the 3d of November, when the wind feemed
fixed in the north-weft quarter, with very pleafant
weather. To this favorable gale we fpread all
our fails, fteering for cape Mendocino; the fouthern promontory of which, at noon, bore by compafs S. 51 E., and with the coaft to the north of
it, in fight to the N. E., was about 9 or 10 leagues
diftant. The obferved latitude 40° 42′, longitude according to our former calculations of the
fituation of cape Mendocino, 235° 30′, the variation 14° eaftwardly.

At this time the longitude by the chronometers agreeably to the Nootka rate, was by Kendall's,

dall's, 235° 27'; Arnold's No. 14, 235° 22'; and
No. 176, 235° 55'.

As we drew in with the ſhores of the northern
part of the cape, having ſince noon ſteered S. E.
by compaſs about three leagues, we ſuddenly
came into diſcoloured water, with a very irregular ſea ; but ſoundings could not be gained
with the hand line, nor at the rate we were then
going, could bottom have been reached at a
greater depth than from 7 to 10 fathoms.

As I intended before we proceeded to Monterrey to viſit the bay of Sir Francis Drake, and
from thence in our boats to acquire a better
knowledge than we had hitherto gained of port
Bodega, our courſe after paſſing this promontory
was directed along the coaſt to the ſouth-eaſt for
that purpoſe.

In the evening about ſun-ſet a very ſingular
appearance was obſerved over the interior mountains, immediately behind the high land of this
lofty projecting promontory. An immenſe body
of very denſe clouds enveloped the ſummits of
thoſe mountains, riſing in a confuſed agitated
ſtate like volumes of ſteam from a boiling caul-
dron of great magnitude ; theſe expanded to the
northward, and obſcured all that part of the horizon, whilſt to the ſouthward, it was perfectly
clear and unclouded. From our own experience,
as well as from the information we had derived

H 3   from

from the Spaniards, we had long been led to confider cape Mendocino as fituated on the divi-
fionary line between the moderate and boifterous
climates of this coaft.   For this reafon, however
unfcientific it may appear, we could not avoid
entertaining an idea, that from the immenfe ac-
cumulation of exhalations, which the ftupendous
mountains in this immediate neighbourhood
arreft, arofe thofe violent fouth-eaft ftorms, with
which, further to the northward, we fo frequently contended, and by which, the coaft of New
Albion to the fouthward of this ftation, is certainly but feldom, and never in fo violent a degree affected.   This extraordinary appearance inclined us to believe that fome turbulent weather
was not far remote, but from what quarter we
could not guefs, as the fteady favorable north-
weft gale, and the appearance of clear and fettled
weather, in the direction we were fteering, did
not give us reafon to apprehend any inconvenience from the wind fhifting to the fouth-eaftward; and its blowing from the oppofite point
had always been confidered as the harbinger of
moderate and pleafant weather.   This general
rule was on Tuefday morning the 4th partly
confirmed, and partly contradicted, as the vapours
we had obferved collecting on the preceding
evening, were now found to have been deftined
to difcharge their fury from a quarter we had
                                           leaft

leaft expected.   During the night we had made fuch progrefs along the coaft, that by four in the morning it became neceffary to haul to the wind, in order that we might not overfhoot our intended port before day-light.   At this time the wind at N. N. W. attended with a moft tremendous fea from the fame quarter, had increafed to fuch a degree of violence, as allowed us to haul off the fhore under our forefail and ftorm ftayfails only; but the forefail, though a very good one, not being able to refift the violence of the ftorm, was about fun-rife on Wednefday the 5th, blown nearly to pieces; this was immediately replaced with the beft we had, the topgallant-mafts were ftruck, and the fhip made as fnug as poffible; but unable to fcud with fafety before the ftorm, we lay to, with the fhip's head to the weftward, under the ftorm ftayfails, it being impoffible to fhow more canvafs, and of courfe too hazardous to fteer for that part of the coaft I wifhed to make, or to attempt running under our bare poles into a port, of which we had fo little knowledge as that of the bay of Sir Francis Drake; to keep the fea, was therefore our only prudent alternative.

During this ftorm I felt a high degree of fatisfaction, that we had not made a more fpeedy paffage from Nootka to Monterrey, as from the direction in which it had blown, I confidered, that had we been arrived in that port, we fhould have been expofed to the whole of its fury, and the violence of the fea that had attended it. As Monterrey was now lying S. 50 E. of us, I could not fuppofe from the diftance of that port, that the gale had not reached fo far, for excepting the ftorms we experienced at and off New Zealand, this was certainly the moft violent of any we had met with during this voyage ; the fhip however was by no means fo uncomfortable as we had found her on many other occafions. The waves, although extremely high, were long and regular, the fky was hard and clear, and intirely free from clouds. About the horizon and a few degrees above it, was feen a bright glaring haze ; and as this at intervals became more perceptible, the violence of the wind was conftantly obferved to be increafed.

In this fituation we remained until the ftorm moderated, though it ftill blew extremely hard: we now wore and ftood for the land under the forefail and ftorm ftayfails, in the hope, that by the time we fhould arrive near the fhore, now at the diftance of 45 leagues, the violence of the ftorm would in a great meafure have abated. It was not however before ten at night that it had fufficiently moderated to allow of our fetting the clofe-reefed topfails ; at midnight we had the topgallant-fails fet for about an hour, but the

wind

wind foon again increafed, and feeing the land
at no great diftance about two o'clock in the
morning of Tuefday the 6th, we hauled off fhore,
and plied under an eafy fail to wait the return
of day, when finding ourfelves about three or
four leagues from point Anno Nuevo, point Pinos
in fight bearing by compafs S. E. ½ E. and having a moderate breeze with fine pleafant weather,
we fteered for Monterrey, where about two in
the afternoon we anchored, and moored nearly
in our former fituation.

Here we found the Chatham, fhe having arrived in the evening of the 2d. By Mr. Puget
I was informed, that whilft we were becalmed
and ftationary off Nootka, the Chatham on the
evening of the 17th of October was favored with
a light breeze from the eaftward, which gradually increafed; with this Mr. Puget fteered to
the fouth-eaft, concluding we were doing the
fame, and he was not undeceived until noon of
the 18th, when the fog with them had fufficiently difperfed, to fhew that the Difcovery was
not within their vifible horizon. Mr. Puget was
equally at a lofs with ourfelves, to account for
the feparation that had then taken place; but as
he confidered that we had preceded the Chatham, and fhe having at that time a pleafant
breeze from the eaftward, he thought it moft
advifeable to make the beft of his way to the
fouthward,

southward, and on the 19th in the morning whilst he continued to be within sight of Nootka, the Chatham had increased her distance near 40 leagues from the shore.   This circumstance, in consequence of the succeeding winds, afforded the Chatham a superior advantage in getting to the southward, and which in all probability was considerably augmented, by her having stood further from the coast to the south-westward, than we had done during the prevalence of the south-easterly winds.   On reference to the journals it appeared Mr. Puget had been enabled so to do, by the wind having been much further to the southward with the Chatham than with the Discovery; by which means on the wind's shifting to the S. W. as is most frequently the case after the south-easterly gales, our consort made much better slants along the coast to the southward, than we were able to do, because we were so much nearer to it.   The Chatham had to contend with nearly the like boisterous weather we had experienced until she had passed cape Mendocino on the 30th of the preceding month; when, at the distance of 40 leagues from the cape the weather was pleasant, with westerly and north-west winds.   The greatest distance she had on this passage been from the coast, was stated by Mr. Puget at 93 leagues from cape Disappointment, and from thence, southward to cape

Mendocino

Mendocino from 60 to 70 leagues; the greateft diftance we had been from the coaft did not exceed 78 leagues off Deftruction ifland, but to the fouthward of cape Lookout we were not more than from 16 to 40 leagues from the land.

The north-weft ftorm we had fo lately contended with, and to which I had confidered this anchorage as dangeroufly expofed, Mr. Puget informed me had been here felt, at the fame time; but that the gale had been principally from the weftward; and although it certainly blew ftrong, yet it neither prevented the ufual communication with the fhore, nor would have caufed any apprehenfion for the fecurity of veffels riding in the bay, if tolerably well provided with anchors and cables. Indeed the Chatham rode it out, with cables that had been long in ufe, and were in the laft ftage of being ferviceable. This was by no means an unpleafant fact to afcertain, as it tended to prove, that although the weather may be extremely boifterous out at fea, and in the offing, yet this bay may be approached with the greateft facility, and will afford extremely good fhelter againft thofe winds, to which, apparently, it is moft expofed.

Our profeffional inquiries being mutually fatisfied, I had the pleafure to underftand from Mr. Puget, that he had met the moft cordial reception from our former friend Senʳ Arguello, the

lieutenant

lieutenant of the Prefidio, who then, as on our firft vifit to this place, in the abfence of the governor of the province, officiated in that capacity. From this gentleman we were likely to meet very different treatment to that which we had received from Senr Arrillago, whofe reftrictive arrangements on our laft vifit to Monterrey, had obliged us to feek that hofpitality and protection from the untutored inhabitants of the Sandwich iflands, which we defpaired of obtaining in any of the ports under his jurifdiction. Senr Arrillago having been ordered to fome inferior eftablifhment, had refigned his authority at this place, and had departed about two months previoufly to our arrival, and a lieutenant in the Spanifh army, Don Diego de Borica, had been appointed fome time fince, to the government of this province, and was now daily expected at Monterrey.

As foon as the fhip was fecured, an officer was fent to the Prefidio with the ufual ceremonious compliments, and with an apology for our not having faluted. On landing I was received by Senr Arguello, to whofe kind and benevolent offices we had before been greatly indebted, with marks of the greateft friendfhip and refpect. He expreffed the fatisfaction he fhould receive by having it now in his power to fupply us with the various neceffary refrefhments the country afforded;

afforded: and being without the leaft reftraint,
he fhould endeavour to adminifter to our amufement and recreation.   Whatever means he poffeffed that were likely in any way to contribute
to the happinefs or comfort of the prefent time,
or to our future welfare, he was now impower-
ed, by the orders that had been tranfmitted to
this government from the viceroy of New Spain,
feduloufly to afford, and prompted by the intereft
he felt in our accommodation, he fhould with
great pleafure carry thofe orders into effect.

The people who, on our firft vifit to this
Prefidio, had deferted from the Dædalus and
Chatham, we found here, with directions for
their being delivered up to me ; but as the governor of the province was fo foon expected, I deferred taking any fteps in this bufinefs until he
fhould arrive ; nor did I erect our tents or obfervatory on fhore for the fame reafon, as I confidered it would be more refpectful to fubmit
thefe matters to the approbation of Governor
Borica himfelf than to Sen[r] Arguello, from whom
I only folicited permiffion to recruit our wood
and water, and to obtain fome neceffary refrefhments.

On Friday morning the 7th I received from
Sen[r] Arguello the only letter that had arrived at
this place for me ; this letter was from the Conde
Revilla Gigedo, the late viceroy of New Spain,

in reply to one I had written to his excellency
on the 22d of May, 1793. In the moſt polite
and friendly terms the count informed me of Mr.
Broughton's ſafe arrival at Madrid, and expreſſed
the higheſt approbation of the conduct of Senʳ
Fidalgo, whoſe ſervices I had repreſented to him
we had been greatly indebted to, on heaving the
Chatham down at Nootka. Thoſe very obliging offers he had before made, in wiſhing to contribute to our health and welfare, by whatever
means of affiſtance this country could beſtow,
were in this letter repeated. It was dated on
the 20th of October, 1793, about the time when
we firſt felt the influence of Senʳ Arrillago's diſ-
inclination towards our little ſquadron. It was
addreſſed to me at Monterrey, with directions
there to remain for my reception, until it ſhould
be underſtood I had taken my leave of theſe regions, and in the event of my ſo doing, without
repairing to this place again, the letter was then
to be tranſmitted to me in England. From theſe
circumſtances it would appear, that the correſpondence I had been thus honored with, was not
intirely of that complimentary nature that Senʳ
Arrillago had thought proper to conſider it ; and
that the viceroy *did expect* that I ſhould make,
at leaſt, a ſecond viſit to Monterrey, was evidently
proved by the deſerters having been ſent hither,
inſtead of being forwarded to Nootka, as he had
formerly

formerly intended to do, but which determination, Sen' Arguello informed me, he had been induced to alter, under the perfuafion of this being the moft likely place of our meeting with them.

Not having received official intelligence at this port from England, and there being here no difpatches waiting the arrival of Sen' Alava, through which channel I might poffibly have obtained fome fort of information, by which my future proceedings might, in fome degree, have been regulated, I could not help feeling very great difappointment, anxiety, and concern. I was not, however, totally deftitute of hope, that fome letters might have arrived at St. Diego. To afcertain this fact, notwithftanding that it was from hence to St. Diego more than four hundred Englifh miles, Sen' Arguello very obligingly ordered an extraordinary courier to be ready the next day, whofe return from St. Diego might be expected in ten or twelve days, and before the expiration of that time, I had no idea of quitting this ftation. Under the circumftances of the mortifying difappointment I now felt, I was unable to form any plan for our future operations, excepting that which I had before meditated, of remaining here a fufficient time to recruit the health and ftrength of our little community. For, notwithftanding that we were not materially af-

feted

fected with indifpofition, yet the health of moft
of us demanded care and attention.   The fatiguing fervice in which we had now been fo long
employed, and the very few frefh meals we had
been enabled to obtain fince the middle of the
preceding month of March, muft be fufficient
to convince the judgment, without the appearance of actual difeafe, that three weeks or a month
would be well dedicated in availing ourfelves of
the refrefhments and recreation, in which we had
now fo favourable an opportunity to indulge.

Frefh beef, which was extremely good, was
daily and unlimitedly ferved to the crew of each
veffel ; but vegetables were a fcarce commodity,
owing to the drynefs of the feafon, which gave
the country an appearance of being parched up ;
and the few articles which had been produced
on the fmall portion of land allotted here to the
purpofe of garden ground were nearly exhaufted.
We, however, were not apprehenfive of wanting
fufficient variety to cover our tables, as in the
immediate neighbourhood of the bay there were
an immenfe number of wild geefe, ducks, plovers,
curlews, and other wild fowl; to which, by
little excurfions into the country, our fportfmen
added an abundance of very fine quails and fome
hares, which afforded us excellent repafts in addition to their amufement. It was fomething
fingular that none of thefe fpecies of wild fowl,
had

had been found in any degree fo numerous on either of our former vifits to Monterrey.

The weather was fair and pleafant, with a moderate breeze from the fea, which in the evening brought in the Princiffa. We had confidered this veffel to have been to the northward of cape Mendocino, whilft we contended with the north-weft ftorm to the fouth of it, and an idea had arifen, from the appearance of the evening that preceded the gale, that the Princiffa muft, in that fituation, have experienced much blowing weather from the fouth-eaftward; but on inquiry this was not found to be altogether the cafe; fhe was, however, to the north of the promontory in queftion at that time, and her progrefs, like ours, had been greatly retarded by contrary winds; but on the 1ft of November, in the latitude of 45° 30', fhe having generally kept about 30 leagues from the coaft; thefe adverfe winds were fucceeded by a pleafant gale from the north weft, which continued during the remainder of the paffage.

This fact, though not proving cape Mendocino to be fo fingularly fituated as we had fuppofed it to be, with refpect to moderate or boifterous weather, yet ferves to fhew that it has an influence on the winds that prevail during the winter feafon, as the fouth-eafterly ftorms are fcarcely ever known to the fouthward of cape Mendo-

Vol. VI.   I   cino;

cino; where, whilft the north-weft gale reduced us to our ftorm ftayfails for twenty-four hours, the Princiffa to the north of it, felt nothing of its fury; but, on the contrary, had only a moderate north-weft gale, to which the whole of her canvafs was fpread.

We had the pleafure to meet our friends in the Princiffa very well, though much difappointed, like ourfelves, in not receiving any official communications from Mexico; but as the courier was in readinefs to depart the next morning, Senr Alava embraced this opportunity to make the neceffary inquiries at St. Diego.

In the night the wind blew ftrong from the northward; and on the return of the day it confiderably increafed from the north-weft. Notwithftanding the veffels rode without the leaft inconvenience or apparent danger, yet, as our cables had been a long time on board, and had endured great trials, the topgallant mafts were got down, the yards and top-mafts ftruck, and the veffels made perfectly fnug; by noon, however, the wind moderated, and we had a return of fair and pleafant weather; all hands were now employed in different fervices, amongft which, recruiting our ftock of fuel and water, was no inconfiderable labour; no difficulty was experienced in procuring the former, but the drynefs of the feafon had rendered the latter very fcarce.

The

The wells that we had dug, on our firſt viſit to Monterrey, though not perfectly dry, afforded too ſmall a quantity to anſwer our demand, and we had no means of obtaining a ſufficiency of water nearer than up a valley about half a mile to the eaſtward of the Preſidio, and full that diſtance from the ſea-ſide, where a ſluggiſh ſtream ooſed through the bed of a water-courſe, compoſed of a looſe ſandy ſoil; and here, by ſinking ſeveral caſks, temporary wells were formed, which afforded only a ſcanty ſupply, though the water was extremely good. This mode of procuring it was very tedious, and the diſtance which the caſks, when filled, had to be rolled, through a looſe ſandy gully, to the boats, was very great, and proved to be a very laborious taſk, yet the water was infinitely preferable to any that could have been collected from the ſtagnated brackiſh pools, in the vicinity of the Preſidio.

On Sunday part of the ſhip's company were indulged with a run on ſhore, and the day following, Monday the 10th, we were buſily employed in facilitating, as much as poſſible, the procuring of our water, by the beſt arrangement in our power, notwithſtanding which we could not prevent its being a very laborious buſineſs.

The weather continued to be remarkably pleaſant, and on Tueſday evening, the 11th, Senʳ Don Diego Borica arrived at the Preſidio,

where,

where, the next morning, accompanied by Mr. Puget and moft of the officers of both veffels, I waited upon him, to congratulate him on his fafe arrival, and to acquaint him with my reafons for vifiting the countries under his jurifdiction; thefe attentions, I had the pleafure to find were perfectly fatisfactory, and were received in a manner that was highly compatible with the refpective ftations that each of us had the honour to fill.

The indulgence I had folicited, and which had been granted by Senr Arguello, was now very politely extended by the governor, with further permiffion to erect our tents and obfervatory on fhore, under the direction of our officers, and protection of our own guard, to which he very obligingly added the affurance of doing every thing in his power that could in any way contribute to make our ftay as pleafant and agreeable as their limited fociety and the lonelinefs of the country would afford.

After this introductory difcourfe, we underftood from Senr Borica, that accompanied by his wife and daughter, a young lady about eleven years of age, and a fuitable number of attendants, he had come from Mexico to this place on horfeback; as no other mode of conveyance was to be procured, They were provided with a fmall camp equipage, which was occafionally pitched, either as a retreat from the heat of the

sun,

fun, or for reft during the night. Upwards of
eight months had been employed in performing
this journey, through a country very thinly inhabited, and which afforded but little comfortable accommodation for travellers.

In the evening an exprefs arrived from Mexico, which brought difpatches from the viceroy
of New Spain to the governor, together with the
long expected inftructions to Senr Alava, refpecting the ceffion of Nootka to the crown of Great
Britain, but nothing addreffed to me accompanied thefe credentials; and, from a converfation
with Sen.^t Borica, I was not flattered with the
leaft probability of receiving any intelligence
from St. Diego, becaufe it was not likely, had
any difpatches for me arrived there, that he
fhould have remained ignorant of the circumftance; and as the deftination of Senr Alava was
well known to the officers commanding the
fouthern pofts of this province, letters for either
of us would moft likely, immediately on their
arrival, have been tranfmitted hither.

The embarraffment I had been long under was
now very materially increafed, and I was greatly
at a lofs as to what meafures were beft to be purfued. From this dilemma, however, I was very
unexpectedly relieved the next day, Wednefday
the 12th, by Senr Alava very obligingly confiding to me that part of his inftructions which

ftated, that no further altercation would take place with refpect to the precife meaning of the firft article of the convention of the 20th of October, 1790, as the documents tranfmitted by the late Sen' Quadra and myfelf, had enabled our refpective courts to adjuft that matter in an amicable way, and nearly on the terms which I had fo repeatedly offered to Sen' Quadra in September 1792. In addition to which the Spanifh minifter's letter fet forth, that this bufinefs was not to be carried into execution by me, as a frefh commiffion had been iffued for this purpofe by the Court of London.* The fame was announced to governor Borica by the new viceroy of Mexico, the Marquis de Branciforte, with inftructions to receive the perfon acting under this commiffion into their Prefidios.

Having maturely confidered the feveral parts of this intelligence, I concluded that from the length of our voyage, and the various accidents to which the fervice in which we were employed would neceffarily render us liable, Government did not expect we fhould remain longer in thefe feas, than the furvey of the American coaft might require; and in truth we were not now in a fit condition to protract our ftay in thefe regions.

---

* This however was not the fact, as the frefh inftructions were addreffed in the firft inftance to me.

The

The very exhaufted ftate of our ftores and provifions not only demanded fuch fupplies as were not eafily within our reach, but as the Difcovery had been frequently aground, it was highly probable that her bottom might ftand in need of fome very material repair, of which we had remained intirely ignorant, not having been fo fortunate as to meet with a proper fituation for the purpofe of her undergoing this neceffary examination.

One of the great objects of our voyage, the furvey of the coaft of North Weft America, being now accomplifhed, and relying on the authenticity of the intelligence I had derived from Senr Alava, I did not long hefitate, but determined on making the beft of my way towards England, by the way of cape Horn, agreeably to my inftructions; and as I had no intention of vifiting any part of the American coaft to the northward of the 44th degree of fouth latitude, I purpofed that our courfe from hence fhould be directed towards that latitude without ftopping, unlefs we fhould be fo fortunate as to fall in with the Gallapagos iflands, whofe undefined fituation I much wifhed correctly to afcertain; and of courfe it would neceffarily be fome time before we reached our next refting place. On this account it became highly expedient that we fhould fail from hence with as great a quantity

I 4

of water as we might be enabled to procure, for
the reception of which the coopers were directed
to repair, and put into order every cafk on board
capable of holding water; in many cafes this
was attended with great trouble, from the length
of time they had been in ufe, and the hard fervice that many of them had endured.

Although the very great diftance, and the badnefs of the road we had to pafs in getting the
water down to the fea-fide, made the obtaining
of this indifpenfable article a very tedious and
fatiguing bufinefs, yet as we were in the mean
time benefitting from the air, the exercife of the
fhore, and the excellent refrefhments of the country, I could not confider our detention here as a
lofs of time, becaufe I was affured that it would
be attended with the ineftimable advantage of
fecuring to us all, that ftate of health which the
remainder of our voyage we had yet to perform
homewards, would neceffarily require.

Some doubts having arifen in my mind, as to
the fafe arrival in England of the copies (which
I had forwarded thither) of our furvey of the
American coaft to the northward, from Fitz-
hugh's found to cape Decifion, and fouthward
from this port to the 30th degree of north latitude, I deemed it expedient that a duplicate of
the former papers, together with a copy of our
furvey during the preceding fummer, as alfo that

of

of the Sandwich iflands, fhould from hence be
tranfmitted to the Admiralty ; that in the event
of any mifchance having befallen the others, or
any unfortunate accident happening hereafter to
us, our labours might not be intirely loft to our
country.   The like information, in conformity
to my original promife to my much lamented
friend the late Senr Quadra, had been folicited
by Senr Alava, for the ufe and information of
the Spanifh court, and with which of courfe I
complied.   The preparation of thefe documents
would neceffarily occupy fome time, but I had
little doubt of their being finifhed by the time
we fhould in other refpects be ready to depart.

The deferters from the Chatham and Dædalus had, at my requeft, been delivered up to me,
at leaft fuch of them as were the fubjects of
Great Britain. An account of expences, amount-
ing to three hundred and twenty-five dollars and
an half, was exhibited againft them ; but as I
did not confider myfelf authorized to difcharge
this debt, (though of its having been incurred
by the deferters. I could entertain no doubt) of
which I acquainted Governor Borica, by letter,
on Sunday morning the 10th, and at the fame
time added, that I fhould reprefent the bufinefs
fully to the Board of Admiralty, and that I had
no doubt that the ftricteft juftice would be done.
With this the governor feemed to be completely
                                    fatisfied,

fatisfied, and in his letter to this effect, after expreffing the greateft approbation, he, in virtue of
the harmony and good underftanding that continued to exift between us, folicited my good offices in behalf of the deferters before mentioned.

The weather, fince the 8th, had been delightfully pleafant; in the day time the wind blew a
gentle gale from the fea, and during the night a
calm, or gentle breeze, prevailed from the land,
fo that the precaution we had taken of ftriking
our yards and topmafts, fince the moment of
our having done fo, ceafed to be neceffary. This
agreeable weather caufed the water in the bay to
be fo very tranquil, that landing was eafily effected
on any of its fhores, and rendered our intercourfe
with the country extremely pleafant.

The fame caufe operated to invite the excurfions of feveral parties into the country on foot
and on horfeback. Thefe were rendered further
agreeable and pleafant, by the friendly and at-
tentive behaviour of our Spanifh friends, of which
I was feldom able to avail myfelf, not only from
the various matters of bufinefs in which I was
deeply engaged, but from the very debilitated
ftate of my health, under which I had feverely
laboured during the eight preceding months; I
was, however, on Wednefday the 19th able to
join in a party to the valley through which the
Monterrey river flows, and was there gratified

with

with the fight of the moft extraordinary mountain I had ever beheld.   On one fide it prefented
the appearance of a fumptuous edifice fallen into
decay ; the columns which looked as if they had
been raifed with much labour and induftry, were
of great magnitude, feemed to be of an elegant
form, and to be compofed of the fame cream-
coloured ftone, of which I have before made
mention.   Between thefe magnificent columns
were deep excavations, refembling different paf-
fages into the interior parts of the fuppofed building, whofe roof being the fummit of the mountain appeared to be wholly fupported by thefe
columns rifing perpendicularly with the moft
minute mathematical exactnefs.   The whole had
a moft beautiful appearance of human ingenuity
and labour ; but fince it is not poffible, from the
rude and very humble race of beings that are
found to be the native inhabitants of this country, to fuppofe they could have been capable of
raifing fuch a ftructure, its being the production
of nature, cannot be queftioned, and it may not
be prepofterous to infer, that it has been from
fimilar phænomena that man has received that
architectural knowledge, by which he has been
enabled to raife thofe maffy fabricks, which have
ftood for ages in all civilized countries.

In this excurfion I had an opportunity of feeing what before I had been frequently given to
underftand ;

underftand ; that the foil improved in richnefs and fertility, as we advanced from the ocean into the interior country.

The fituation we had now reached was an extenfive valley between two ranges of lofty mountains, whofe more elevated parts wore a fteril and dreary afpect, whilft the fides and the intervening bofom feemed to be compofed of a luxuriant foil. On the former fome pine trees were produced of different forts, though of no great fize, and the latter generally fpeaking was a natural pafture, but the long continuance of the dry weather had robbed it of its verdure, and had rendered it not very interefting to the eye ; yet the healthy growth of the oak, both of the Englifh and holly-leaved kind, the maple, poplar, willow, and ftone pine, diftributed over its furface as well in clumps as in fingle trees, with a number of different fhrubs, plainly fhewed the fuperior excellence of the foil and fubftratum in thefe fituations, to that which was found bordering on the fea fhore.

The fame uninterrupted ferenity of the weather continued, and on Friday evening the courier from St. Diego returned, but he brought no kind of intelligence whatever ; and the 24th being the day fixed for the return of the exprefs to Mexico, I embraced that opportunity for tranfmitting to the Admiralty a brief account of

our

our tranfactions during the preceding fummer, and a copy of our furveys made in that and the former year, which had been prepared for that purpofe. Thefe documents, agreeably to the advice of the governor and our other Spanifh friends, I took the liberty of addreffing to the marquis of Branciforte, viceroy of New Spain, and requefted that he would do me the favor of forwarding them to England by the moft early and fafe conveyance.

All expectation of Mr. Broughton's return and of his refuming the command of the Chatham being now at an end, I appointed Lieutenant Puget to that office, Mr. Baker, and Mr. Swaine I removed to be the firft and fecond lieutenants of the Difcovery; Mr. Thomas Manby I appointed to the vacant lieutenantcy, and Mr. H. Humphreys, to be the mafter of the Chatham in his room.

Our bufinefs with the fhore now began to draw nigh to a conclufion; the yards, topmafts, and topgallant-mafts were got up, and the rigging put into condition for fea fervice, but a fufficient ftock of water was however not yet obtained; whilft this was completing, I difpatched Lieutenant Swaine on Thurfday morning the 27th with three boats over to the miffion of Sta Cruz, in order to procure a fupply of garden ftuff, as the continuation of the dry weather, here, had

made

made every fpecies of efculent vegetables extremely fcarce. Mr. Swaine returned on Saturday evening the 29th, having been tolerably
fuccefsful, fo that with our live ftock and the
other refrefhments that Monterrey had afforded,
we were likely to take our leave of it, with as
good a ftore for the prefervation of health, and to
be as well provided for the long and diftant paffage we had to perform, as from any port in the
known world. The two following days were
employed in receiving on board the tents, obfervatory, inftruments, and all other matters from
the fhore, and in getting the fhip in readinefs to
proceed.

The variety of objects that had occupied my
time whilft at Monterrey, had, as at Nootka, precluded my attending to little more of our aftronomical bufinefs, than that of afcertaining the
rate and error of the chronometers, according to
the meridian of thefe places as fixed by our former obfervations: yet I had confidered thefe to
be of fufficient authority to anfwer all the purpofes of correcting our furvey of the coaft in the
refpective vicinity of thofe ftations. By com-
parative obfervations made by Mr. Whidbey
with Mr. Ramfden's circular inftrument, and
thofe made with the artificial horizon by myfelf,
I was in hopes of adducing further reafons in fupport of the means I had adopted for fixing of the
longitude,

longitude, and for correcting our general survey of this coast during the preceding summer, between Trinity islands and cape Decision; and I had the satisfaction to find the same corresponding accuracy at Monterrey as had appeared at Nootka.

On the 13th of November in the bay of Monterrey the chronometers shewed the following longitudes:

Arnold's No. 14, - - - 238° 0′ 50″

Ditto, 176, - - 238 33 5

Kendall's - - - 237 59 15

The true longitude being 238° 25′ 45″, Arnold's No. 14 appeared to be 24′ 55″, Kendall's, 26′ 30″ to the westward, and Arnold's No. 176, 7′ 20″ to the eastward of the true longitude. And by altitudes taken on shore with the artificial horizon on the 28th of November, Arnold's No. 14 was found to be fast of mean time at Greenwich, at noon on that day, - - - 5ʰ 19′ 23″ 0‴

And to be gaining on mean time per day at the rate of - 24 1

Arnold's No. 176 was fast of mean time at Greenwich, - 11 28 21 30

And gaining on mean time per day at the rate of - - 50 25

Kendall's faft of mean time at
Greenwich,   -   - 9^h 58' 23"

And gaining on mean time per
day at the rate of   -   -   30 53

By equal altitudes taken on
fhore with the circular inftrument between the 13th and 29th
of November, the following are
the rates at which the chronometers were found to be gaining
per day ; (viz.)

Arnold's No. 14,   -   -   23 55
Ditto   176,   -   -   50 19
Kendall's,   -   -   -   30 52

The very inconfiderable difference between the
rates thus found, and thofe afcertained by the
artificial horizon, muft be received as a proof of
the correctnefs of that method, which fhould be
reforted to, whenever better authority cannot be
had.

The above true longitude, latitude, variation,
and inclination of the marine dipping needle,
were found to correfpond with our obfervations
made on our former vifit to this place in December, 1792.

CHAP.

CHAPTER III.

*Leave Monterrey—Some Account of the three Marias
Iſlands—Proceed to the Southward—Aſtronomical and nautical Obſervations.*

THE method that had been purſued to pre-
ſerve as great a regularity as was poſſible
in the rate of the chronómeters, had ſo far ſuc-
ceeded with No. 14, that its rate as aſcertained
at Nootka and at Monterrey, differed only 54‴;
this made me very anxious to fall in with ſome
place whoſe longitude had been ſettled by pro-
feſſed aſtronomers, by which means the accuracy
of our calculations would be confirmed, or the
error they might have been liable to, would by
ſuch compariſon become apparent; leaving it at
the diſcretion of geographers, or of thoſe who
might hereafter follow us, to adopt or reject ſuch
correction as their own judgment might direct.
For this purpoſe, no ſtation appeared to me to be
ſo eligible as cape St. Lucas, at the ſouth extremity of the peninſula of California, (on a moderate computation not more than eight or ten days
ſail from Monterrey,) as at St. Joſeph's, in the
immediate neighbourhood of that promontory,

VOL. VI.   K   the

the tranfit of Venus had been obferved, and other aftronomical obfervations had been made by pro-feffors in that fcience, whence its pofitive fitua-tion had been correctly determined. But as our obfervations during the preceding autumn for fixing the longitude of the coaft of New Albion, fouthward from hence to the 30th degree of north latitude, had been all reduced to port St. Diego as a central ftation, and the rate of the chrono-meters for correcting that furvey had been there afcertained; I deemed it expedient to fteer firft for the ifland of Guadaloupe, for the purpofe of examining whether the fituation we had before affigned to that ifland from the refult of thofe obfervations, would agree with the longitude in which we had now placed Monterrey.

With a frefh breeze from the N. E. attended with fair and pleafant weather, on Tuefday the 2d of December we quitted Monterrey, and bad adieu to governor Alava, and the reft of our Spa-nifh friends, from whofe great kindnefs and hof-pitality we had not only derived much relaxation and happinefs, but by their attention to our future wants, we had every profpect of a continuation of that health, which now feemed to be eftab-lifhed, by the refrefhments we had there pro-cured.

From Monterrey bay our courfe was directed to the S. E. but in the evening the gale died

away,

away, and after about twelve hours calm, it was
fucceeded by light variable adverfe winds, which
continued until near noon on Thurfday the 4th,
when it fixed in the weftern quarter, blowing a
pleafant gentle breeze. The obferved latitude
was 35° 29′, longitude 238° 16′. The coaft of
New Albion was ftill in fight, bearing by compafs from N. E. to N. W. by N. This was the
laft we faw of it; the wind between W. N. W.
and N. N. W. gradually increafed to a pleafant
gale, which by the evening of Monday the 8th
brought us in fight of the ifland of Guadaloupe;
this we paffed in the night, and from the obfervations made on the preceding and following
day, which exactly agreed with the fhips run by
the log, I had the fatisfaction of finding its fituation exactly to correfpond with that which we
had before affigned to it ; hence it is fair to pre-
fume, that the whole of this coaft which has
fallen under our examination, has been laid
down relatively correctly, however our longitude
may be found to vary from other navigators or
obfervers.

Having afcertained this fact, and being unwilling to lofe any opportunity by which the advancement of geography might in the flighteft
degree be furthered, I fteered over to the coaft of
California, for the purpofe of fixing in our way
towards cape St. Lucas, the pofition of fome of

K 2   the

the moſt projecting points between that promontory, and the part where we had quitted its ſhores
the foregoing autumn; but in ſo doing I had no
intention of approaching ſufficiently near to attempt a minute delineation of the coaſt.

At day-light in the morning of Tueſday the
9th we had ſight of the iſland of Cerros, bearing
by compaſs from E. N. E. to N. E. about ten
leagues diſtant.   This is repreſented in the Spaniſh charts to be about ten leagues long, and to be
lying before an extenſive bay, on the ſhores of the
peninſula.   The ſouth-weſtern point of this bay
is a very projecting promontory named Morro
Hermoſo : weſt from thence is laid down a ſmaller
iſland called Natividad.   To theſe as the day
advanced we drew ſomewhat nearer, but the
land was ſtill too far off to admit of our forming
any correct judgment as to the productions of the
country, or the ſhape of its ſhores.   Thoſe of the
iſland of Cerros wore an uneven broken appearance, though on a nearer view they ſeemed to be
all connected.   The ſouthern part, which is the
higheſt, is occupied by the baſe of a very remarkable and lofty peaked mountain, that deſcends in
a very peculiar rugged manner, and by projecting
into the ſea, forms the ſouth-weſt end of the
iſland into a low craggy rocky point ; this as we
paſſed at the diſtance of five or ſix leagues, ſeemed, like the other part of the iſland, to be deſtitute

tute of trees, and nearly fo of all other vegetable productions. Natividad appeared to be more moderately elevated, and at noon bore by compafs N. 70 E.; the fouth-eaft point of the ifland of Cerros, N. 46 E.; the peaked mountain, N. 37 E.; its fouth-weft point, N. 27 E.; its north-wefternmoft part in fight, N. 20 E.; and ifle de St. Benito, which is a fmall ifland, feemingly with fome rocks and iflets about it, N. 11 W. diftant eight or nine leagues. In this fituation the obferved latitude was 27° 51', longitude by Arnold's No. 14, 244° 38½', by Kendall's 244° 38¼' and by Arnold's No. 176, 244° 54'. The variation, by the furveying compafs, was at this time 8° eaftwardly.

The weather continued to be fair and pleafant, and, with a gentle breeze from the north-weft, we proceeded along the fhore. In the afternoon we had fight of what we fuppofed was Morro Hermofo, which at that diftance appeared to be infular, and, like Natividad, feemed to be moderately elevated. Although we were too far diftant to attempt an accurate delineation of thefe fhores, yet we were enabled pretty clearly to af-certain the pofition of their moft prominent points, and, from the refult of our calculations, the ifland of Cerros appeared to form on its weft-ern fide a deep bay, between its north-weft and fouth-weft points, which are about five leagues

K 3   apart,

apart, in a direction N. 20 E. and S. 20 W.; the peaked mountain being the part whofe fituation we were beft able to fix, is in latitude 28° 8′, longitude 244° 58′. From this mountain the ifland St. Benito lies N. 65 W. at the diftance of twenty miles, and the ifland of Natividad S. 4 E. diftant fourteen miles. The latter appeared to be about four miles long, in a S. E. and N. W. direction, and, like the ifland of Cerros, prefented a barren and dreary afpect. Behind it was the point which we had taken for Morro Hermofo, in latitude 27° 52′, longitude 245° 7′. The channels round thefe iflands, and between them and the main land, are, in the Spanifh charts, reprefented as clear and navigable; we were not, however, fufficiently nigh to them to fatisfy ourfelves in this particular. During the night our courfe was directed more foutherly, which, although it kept us within fight of the land, yet by the morning of Wednefday the 10th, it had increafed our diftance further from the coaft than I had reafon to expect, from the way in which it has been laid down. We were now at the diftance of 12 to 14 leagues, and whether the parts in fight were or were not immediately on the fea fhore, it was not poffible for us to determine, but the fhore was fufficiently marked to admit of our making the neceffary obfervations, as we failed along it, for the object I had in view,

view. The northernmoft point in fight at noon, being the fame land that had formed the northern extremity ever fince the morning, bore by compafs N. 3 W. diftant feventeen leagues, a particular high part, appearing to form the north point of a bay or opening on the coaft, N. 17 E. at the fame diftance ; and what appeared to form a very confpicuous point, from whence the coaft feemed to take a very eaftwardly turn, N. 25 E. diftant thirteen leagues. In this fituation the obferved latitude was 26° 48′, longitude 245° 26¼′; and, if the above eftimations be correct, the latter point will be found to lie in latitude 27° 20′, longitude 245° 49′. Several turtles were feen at this time on the furface of the fea, one of which was taken by our fmall boat. Towards fun-fet the weather became cloudy, the wind veered to the fouthward, and threatened us with a heavy rain, but by midnight the wind refumed its north-weft direction, and the weather became fair and pleafant. Not being in fight of the coaft, on Thurfday morning the 11th, I fteered more to the eaftward, and by day-light on Friday the 12th we were within fight of a high round mountain, which we fuppofed was on the main land of the peninfula, bearing by compafs N. E. ½ E.

The part of the ocean in which we had now arrived abounded with bonitos, albicores, and

K 4   various

other fifhes of the tropical regions, with a great
many turtles. Thefe feemed fo perfectly indifferent to any interruption that we occafioned
them, either by paffing near to, or even over
them, that I was induced to fend the fmall boat
to take fome of them up, and in about half an
hour fhe returned loaded with thirteen very fine
green ones, each weighing from feventy to two
hundred pounds. They all proved to be extremely good eating. Some of them were ftuck
with the turtle peg, but moft of them were taken
into the boat unhurt. The obferved latitude
at noon was 25° 11′, longitude 247° 48¼′, and
the variation of the compafs 9° eaftwardly. The
above high round mountain at this time bore
N. 30. E. diftant 25 leagues, and land fuppofed
by us to be an ifland, S. 35 E.; to the eaftward
of which our courfe was directed until two in the
afternoon, when our conjectures were difcovered
to have been ill founded; for, inftead of this
land proving to be an ifland, it formed the weft
point of a fpacious open bay, the contiguous
fhores to which were very low, and bounded by
breakers, whilft the more interior country rofe
in fmall detached hillocks, giving the whole from
the deck the appearance of a group of iflands, but
from the maft-head it was feen to be all connected, for which reafon we hauled our wind,
and paffed to the weftward of this land, which,

in

in every point of view, even at a very little diftance, feemed to be infular, owing to the lownefs
of the land to the eaftward of the elevated part
that forms the point, and which, in a fouth-eaft
and north-weft direction, appeared to occupy an
extent of about five miles. It is higheft in the
centre, from whence its north-weftern extremity
fhoots out and defcends gradually to a low point
of land, with an even furface, but in every other
part the acclivity was fteep and irregular; and
the furface, broken into deep chafms, terminates
at the water-fide in abrupt rocky cliffs. On its
northern fide lies an iflet with fome rocks at a
little diftance from the fhore, on which there was
an appearance of fome verdure and fertility, but
where its furface was rocky and broken it had a
fteril and barren afpect. In the evening we paffed within about five miles of this point, which
I fuppofed was the fouth point of the bay de la
Magdalina, and which, according to our obfervations, is fituated in latitude 24° 53ʹ, longitude
247° 56ʹ, from whence, in a fouth-eaft direction,
at the diftance of about three or four leagues, is
another elevated part of the coaft, which, like the
former, at a little diftance, has the appearance of
being infular. As the coaft, for fome extent to
the fouth-eaftward of this ftation, is in the Spanifh
charts reprefented as low, and dangerous to approach, we ftretched to the fouth-eaftward during
the

the night, and on Saturday morning the 13th, there being no land in fight, we ftood to the eaftward, and foon regained a diftant view of the coaft, which was high and mountainous.

Being favored with a fine gale from the north-weft, and delightfully pleafant weather, we made great progrefs towards the land, for which we continued to fteer until nine in the evening; when, being in 80 fathoms water, and conceiving the land to be not far off, we hauled to the wind and plied under an eafy fail, with foundings from 80 to 90 fathoms, until five on Sunday morning the 14th, when we again ftood towards the land, and to our great furprize, at day-light, found it to be eight leagues diftant, and bearing by compafs from N. 54 E. to S. 68 E. By ten in the forenoon we were within about three leagues of the fhore, at which time we bore away, and fteered for cape St. Lucas. The parts of the coaft to which we were now oppofite were in a great meafure compofed of fteep white rocky cliffs, from whence the country rofe with a very broken and uneven furface to a ridge of ftupendous mountains, which were vifible at a great diftance into the ocean. The fhores jut out into fmall projecting points that terminate in abrupt cliffs, and having lefs elevated land behind them, gave them at firft the appearance of being detached iflands along the coaft, but, on

a nearer

a nearer approach, this did not feem to be the cafe. The general face of the country was not very inviting, being deftitute of trees and other vegetable productions.

The obferved latitude at noon was 25° 12', longitude 250°, and the variation of the compafs 7° eaftwardly. At this time the northernmoft part of the exterior coaft of California in fight bore by compafs N. 15 E. the neareft fhore N. 63 E. diftant three leagues, and a point to the northward of, and intercepting our view of cape St. Lucas S. 39 E. diftant fix leagues, beyond which the cape foon appeared, and was found to lie from that point S. 47 E. diftant two leagues. In the afternoon we paffed this point, or promontory, which gradually, though not very regularly, defcends from the range of mountains before mentioned, and terminates at its fouth extremity in a hummock of low, or very moderately elevated land, that had the fame rocky fteril appearance as that we had been oppofite to in the morning.

The weather had been very favorable to the object I had had in view in thus directing our courfe to the fouthward. According to our obfervations cape St. Lucas is fituated in latitude 22° 52' longitude 250° 16' 18". The very fharp turn which the coaft takes from that point towards the gulph of California, enabled us in a

very

very precife manner to afcertain the moft projecting part of the cape, which according to the
Spanifh charts, and the information I had procured from the Spaniards themfelves, is fituated
under the fame meridian as their eftablifhment
of St. Jofeph, and which agreeably to the Spanifh
printed chart compiled by Miguel Coftanfo in
1770, is ftated to be in latitude 23° 3' 42″, longitude 250° 17' 30″.   On the confirmation of
our calculations by this authority I derived much
gratification, as I had now great reafon to pre-
fume, that the pofition of the weftern coaft of
America between cape St. Lucas in California,
and cape Douglas in Cook's inlet, as heretofore
ftated by me, would be found tolerably correct.
The very trivial variation that had occurred in
the rate of Arnold's No. 14 for the preceding
two or three months, induced me to place my
principal reliance upon it, and by which the longitude of cape St. Lucas differed from the above,
only 1' 12″.   By Arnold's No. 82 on board the
Chatham, the longitude of the cape was 250° 9';
Arnold's No. 176, gave 250° 37'; and Kendall's, 250° 21' 30″.   From thefe feveral refults
it fhould feem, that Arnold's No. 176 varied
moft from the truth; and as I have had occafion
before to obferve, this deviation may poffibly
have arifen by the motion it received on its
being

being taken on fhore, for the purpofe of difcovering its rate of going.

As the fituation of the Marias iflands lying between cape St. Lucas and cape Corientes before the port of St. Blas, had been varioufly defined by different perfons, and as thefe iflands were nearly in our route, an opportunity was likely to be afforded me for determining their pofition; and on confidering the length of the paffage we had yet to perform, I was induced to hope we might at thofe iflands be able to recruit our ftock of water; for thefe reafons our courfe was directed towards the Marias, with a frefh gale from the northward, and delightful weather. The fea ftill abounded with fifh, and feveral turtle were feen; but as our former fupply was not yet exhaufted, and as the gale was too favorably tempting to admit of a moment's delay, they remained unmolefted.

According to Dampier, the iflands for which we were then fteering are fituated E. S. E. at the diftance of 40 leagues from cape St. Lucas; according to the Spanifh chart 47 leagues; and by the Spanifh MS. chart they are ftated to be 60 leagues from that promontory. This irreconcilable difference rendered it no eafy tafk to determine on which to rely; the difference in the Spanifh charts rendered the accuracy of each equally queftionable, and our own experience

had

had proved both of them to be very erroneous in
feveral inftances.   Under this uncertainty, about
nine o'clock on Monday the 15th, at night, being
then 42 leagues from cape St. Lucas, and in the
direction in which the Marias were faid to lie,
we plied under an eafy fail until the next morning,
Tuefday the 16th, when we made all fail, fteering
to the E. S. E. which courfe, by nine in the
forenoon, brought us in fight of thofe iflands,
bearing by compafs E. ½ N.; in this direction we
inftantly fteered, but as we were not fufficiently
up with the land to gain anchorage before dark,
the night was paffed in preferving our fituation
with the land, and in the morning of Wednefday the 17th, we fteered for the paffage between
the northernmoft and the middle, or Prince
George's ifland, fo diftinguifhed by Dampier.
The moft northern and largeft ifland of this
group, is about thirteen miles long, in a S. E.
by E. and N. W. by W. direction, which is
alfo nearly the line in which thefe iflands feemed to lie from each other.   As we paffed along
the northernmoft ifland it appeared to be but
moderately elevated, notwithftanding that we
had defcried it at the diftance of near 18 leagues;
its higheft part is towards the fouth, from whence
it gradually defcends and terminates in a long
low point at its north-weft extremity, which
according to our obfervations is fituated S. 68 E.

and

and at the diftance of 64 leagues from cape St.
Lucas.   A low detached iflet, and a remarkably
fteep white cliffy rock, lie off this point of the
ifland, whofe fhores are alfo compofed, but particularly fo on its fouth-weft fide, of fteep white
rocky cliffs ; the fame fort of fubftance feemed
to be its principal component part, and although
in fome places it was tolerably well covered with
low fhrubs, yet upon the whole it prefented but
a dreary and unproductive fcene.   Its fouth-eaftern extremity, which likewife defcends gradually
from the fummit of the ifland, terminates alfo
in a low projecting point with fome rocks lying
off from it.   On either fide is a fmall bay ; that
on the eaftern fide is bounded by a beach, alternately compofed of rocks and fand, and as we
gained foundings of 35 fathoms at fome diftance
as we paffed by it, little doubt was entertained
of its affording good anchorage, provided the
bottom fhould be good ; as it is protected againft
the general prevailing winds.   The furf however
broke with fome violence on its fhores, and as
it did not feem from the fcanty portion of its
vegetable productions, and the apparent drynefs
of the foil, to poffefs what we principally, and
indeed only wanted, water; we proceeded towards that ftation which Woods Rogers defcribes
to have occupied, and where about the fame
feafon of the year, he procured a great fupply of
excellent

excellent water.   This was on the north-eaſt
ſide of Prince George's iſland.   In our way thither we paſſed between Prince George's and the
north weſternmoſt iſland, in a paſſage about ſix
miles wide, with ſoundings from 20 to 40 fathoms, ſandy bottom, and ſo far as we became
acquainted with its navigation, it is free from
danger or interruption.   The ſouth-weſt ſide of
Prince George's iſland is bounded by detached
rocks lying at a ſmall diſtance from its ſhores ;
theſe in general, but more ſo on its northern and
eaſtern ſide, deſcend gradually from the center
of the iſland (whoſe ſummit is nearly as high as
that of the northernmoſt iſlands) and terminate
at the water-ſide in a fine ſandy beach.   This was
infinitely more verdant than the other iſland, as
its vegetable productions extended from the more
elevated parts to the waſh of the ſea, and grew
with ſome luxuriance though we did not perceive any trees of great ſize on the iſland, nor
did it ſeem to afford any ſtreams or runs of freſh
water.   Some gullies were ſeen as we paſſed
along, which in addition to the cheerful appearance of the country, flattered us with the hope,
that on further examination they would be found
to afford us the ſupply of water we needed.
Having ſhortly after noon, reached the ſpot
pointed out by former viſitors as moſt likely to
furniſh this eſſential article, we anchored on a
                                                    clear

clear fandy bottom, in 10 fathoms water, about three quarters of a mile from the fhore, on the north-eaftern fide of Prince George's ifland; its eaft point bearing by compafs S. 16 E. about two miles and a half diftant; its north-eaft point, N. 68 W. diftant two miles; the north point of the northernmoft ifland, N. 46 W. about fix leagues diftant; and the moft fouthern ifland, which is the fmalleft, from S. 21 E. to S. 45 E. about four leagues diftant.

Two boats were immediately difpatched with Mr. Whidbey and Mr. Manby in different directions in queft of water, which however, if found, could not be got on board without fome difficulty, on account of the furf which broke on every part of the fhore, but not fo violently as to prevent the parties from landing. In the evening both returned; Mr. Whidbey had extended his excurfion to the north-weftward from our anchorage, without finding any water, and Mr. Manby had been equally unfuccefsful to the fouth-eaftward round the fouth point of the ifland. On its fouth-eaft fide the beds of many fpacious water courfes were feen, which in the rainy feafon appeared to give vent to copious ftreams, as fome of them were twenty feet in width. In fome a moiftnefs was obferved, and Mr. Manby was of opinion, that by digging wells, water might have been procured. A fupply by

VOL. VI. L this

this means was however precarious, and as we could not devote any time to uncertainties, I determined to depart without further delay, and at eight o'clock we were again under fail.

Our vifit to thefe iflands not having afforded us an opportunity of making a very accurate delineation of their fhores, or of acquiring fuch information as might render them objects worthy the particular attention of future vifitors to thefe feas, I have not fubjoined any fketch of them, and fhall content myfelf by noticing, that the anchorage we quitted, is fituated according to our obfervations made on the preceding day, and the day after we failed (not having obtained any obfervations on the day of our arrival and departure) in latitude 21° 28′, longitude 253° 54′; and that in a direction N. 50 W. and S. 50 E.; thefe iflands occupy a fpace of about 14 leagues; the length of the northernmoft has been already ftated, its breadth is about nine miles; the next in fize and direction is Prince George's ifland, this is about eight leagues in circuit; and the third, or fouth-eafternmoft, is about nine miles round. In navigating near them we obferved no danger; fome detached iflets and rocks are about the fhores, but all are fufficiently confpicuous to be avoided; and the regularity of the foundings, fo far as our examination extended, gave us reafon to believe, that

fecure

fecure anchorage might be obtained againſt the prevailing winds, at a commodious diſtance from the ſhore.

From the gentlemen who had landed (being myſelf from the the ill ſtate of my health unable to go on ſhore) I became acquainted, that the ſoil of Prince George's iſland ſeemed to be prin-cipally of a ſandy nature, on which the chief valuable production was *lignum vitæ*, beſides which, was an almoſt impenetrable thicket of ſmall trees and buſhes of a thorny nature, toge-ther with the prickly pear, and ſome plants of the orange and lemon tribe ; the whole growing as cloſe to the water ſide as the waſh of the ſurf would permit. Some of the *lignum vitæ* which was cut cloſe to the beach and brought on board, worked up full eight inches in diameter at heart; this wood was very ponderous, of a cloſe black grain, and extremely hard. Before this time I did not recollect to have met with this ſpecies of wood growing on any of the iſlands in theſe ſeas, and it is not improbable, that in the more inte-rior parts of this iſland the trees may be of a much larger ſize. About the outſkirts of the woods, for excepting where in the rainy ſeaſon the deſcending waters had formed a path, the thicket was impenetrable ; many birds were ſeen, thoſe of the larger kind were hawks of ſeveral ſorts, green parrots with yellow heads, paroquets,

L 2 pigeons,

pigeons, doves, and a variety of fmall birds, many
of which were of beautiful plumage. Pelicans,
gulls, curlews, terns, and fandpipers were obferved, but no quadrupeds were feen, although
in the fand on the bottom of fome of the water-
courfes Mr: Manby noticed the footing of an
animal, which he confidered to be about the fize
of a fox; many turtle tracks were on the beach,
and nearly a hundred of dead *manatee*, or fea-
cows, were lodged at fome diftance beyond the
prefent range of the furf. The carcaffes of thefe
animals, from their then ftate of putrefaction,
were confidered by Mr. Manby to have been fo
left about ten or twelve days before, and as they
all feemed to be nearly in the fame ftate of decay, the only conjecture that could be reafonably
formed, was, that they had been fo depofited in a
violent foutherly ftorm. They were eagerly devoured by the vultures, hawks, and other birds of
prey that had affembled about them in great
numbers, and it appeared to be not improbable
that the carnivorous animals of the Marias are
frequently regaled with fuch fumptuous repafts,
for, befides the fea-cows that remained intire,
the fkeletons of many hundreds of the fame or
fimilar animals had been in like manner caft on
fhore, at more remote and different periods. A
variety of fifh common to the tropical regions
were feen in great numbers about the fhores;
amongft

amongft thefe the fharks were very bold and daring, they followed the boats, and made repeated attempts to catch the oars, in which one of them at length fucceeded, but with the lofs of five of its teeth, which were left in the blade of the oar.   A few fnakes and guannas were alfo feen, and fome of the latter were very good eating.   No traces of human vifitors were perceived, though on fhore fome drift wood was found, with evident marks of its having been worked or hewn with European tools.

This appeared to me to be the fubftance of the information we acquired by calling at thefe iflands, which are not more than 160 leagues from Acapulco, and in the immediate vicinity of St. Blas.   In the Spanifh M. S. chart they are placed weft from that port, at the diftance of about 20 leagues, which appeared to correfpond exactly with our obfervations, in refpect to the bearings from cape St. Lucas, and to differ only three leagues in the diftance from that promontory ; this was further proved (fo far as eftimated diftances could be relied upon) by the diftant view we had had of the continent in that direction at our laft place of anchorage ; notwithftanding which, thefe iflands do not feem to have engaged or attracted the attention of the Spanifh government.

As on leaving the Marias it was my intention

to

to make cape Corientes, in order to afcertain its latitude and longitude, our courfe was directed between the iflands and the main land; fteering well to the eaftward at firft, in order that we might avoid a fhoal faid to extend fome diftance from the fhores of the fouthernmoft of the Marias; at midnight we purfued a more foutherly courfe, but the wind, though attended with fine pleafant weather, was fo moderate, that at day-light on Thurfday the 18th, the iflands we had left were ftill in fight, bearing by compafs the fouthernmoft from N. 82 W. to N. 72 W.; Prince George's ifland, from N. 70 W. to N. 64 W.; the eaft point of the northernmoft, N. 58 W.; and a diftant view of the continental fhore from N. E. by N. to E. by S. This was too remote to form any judgment refpecting the country, further than its appearing to have a very lofty and uneven furface, fwelling into various eminences of different forms and magnitude.

The obferved latitude at noon was 21°, longitude 254° 27′, and the variation of the compafs 7° 30′ eaftwardly. In this fituation the high land over cape Corientes bore by compafs S. 25 E., land appearing like a fmall ifland, lying at fome diftance from the continent S. 66 E.; the northernmoft part of the main land in fight N. N. E., and the fouthernmoft of the Marias flands N. 58 W., diftant nine leagues. Much

to

to our furprize, in the afternoon we approached
a fmall black rugged rock, or, more properly
fpeaking, a clofely connected clufter of fmall
rocks, which though deferving of attention, from
their fituation, and the fafety of the navigation
between cape Corientes, St. Blas, and the Marias,
yet they are not inferted in either of the Spanifh
charts, nor do they appear to have been noticed
by any former vifitor with whofe obfervations I
have become acquainted. The fpace they occupy does not appear to exceed the dimenfions
of a large fhip's hull, nor are they much higher.
They are at a great diftance from any land, and,
fo far as we could perceive on paffing by them
at the diftance of about half a league, the water
near them appeared to be deep in every direction.
We could not gain foundings clofe round them
with the hand-line, nor did this fmall rocky
group feem to be fupported by any bed of rock
or fhallow bank. The fhores of the main land,
to the eaftward of them, at the diftance of about
eight leagues, appeared to be broken, and about
ten miles within them are two fmall iflands.
Thefe rocks, according to our obfervations, are
fituated in latitude 20° 45', longitude 254° 27',
lying from the land mentioned at noon as appearing like an inlet S. 76 W. fix leagues diftant, and from the fouthernmoft of the Marias
S. 36 E. at the diftance of 12 or 13 leagues.

L 4

In

In the evening the breeze that had been very moderate all day, freshened, and towards midnight we passed cape Corientes, at the distance of about five leagues; this time was rather unfavourable for the fixing of its position; but as it was still in sight at day-light the next morning, Friday the 19th, bearing by compass N. 8 E. and having been constantly within our view during the night, I should suppose that it's situation as resulting from our observations will be liable to no very material error. These placed cape Corientes in latitude 20° 22', longitude 254° 40'; from whence if this statement be correct, the above rocky group will be found to lie N. 26 W. at the distance of nine leagues.

The American coast to the southward of cape Corientes not continuing to take a direction favorable to our route, we were no longer desirous of keeping near its shores, and I therefore made the best of our way towards the island of Cocos and the Gallipagos, with an intention of stopping at one or both of those places. At noon the observed latitude was 19° 15', longitude 254° 48'; the coast at this time was still in sight, bearing by compass north, from N. 85 E. and its nearest part N. E. about ten leagues from us. We were now accompanied by many of the tropical fishes, and oceanic birds, and notwithstanding that we had a fresh breeze from the north-westward, the

weather

weather was very fultry and unpleafant. The thermometer within thefe two days had rifen from 70 to 81, and the heat that we now experienced was attended with a degree of oppreffive inconvenience, that exceeded any thing of the fort I had ever before felt, under fimilar circumftances of fuch an alteration in the height of the mercury. The unpleafantnefs of the atmofphere on Saturday morning became greatly increafed by the north-wefterly wind dying away, and by its being fucceeded by calms of light variable airs. The atmofphere was perfectly clear, ferene, and unincumbered either with fogs or clouds, which made it very difficult to account for the extraordinary change in the climate between our then ftation and the three Marias iflands, as the diftance did not exceed 70 leagues. This may poffibly be acounted for by the projecting promontory of cape Corientes, and other parts of this mountainous country intercepting thofe cool refrefhing gales from the north that are fo grateful and acceptable to the human conftitution.

That part of the globe we had now to pafs over having been little frequented by perfons poffeffing the means of making due obfervations on the vertical inclination of the magnetic needle, I purpofed to procure fome obfervations at different intervals when the fhip was fufficiently fteady

for

for this purpofe. This day in latitude 18° 20',
longitude 255° 40', the marked end, north face
eaft, fhewed   -   -   38° 17'
    Ditto   Ditto   Weft,   38   3
    Ditto   South face Eaft,   34   3
    Ditto   Ditto   Weft,   36   20
Mean vertical inclination of the
north point of the marine dipping
needle   -   -   -   36   41
The horizontal inclination or variation was
about 60° eaftwardly.

A continuation of very light winds made our
progrefs very flow, through an ocean on whofe
furface great numbers of turtles, in every direction, were lying afleep, and we had only to lower
down the boat, and without interrupting the progrefs of the fhip, make choice of as many as we
required; though under our prefent circumftances we would readily have waved the acqui-
fition of thefe luxuries for a little more wind, as
with that which now prevailed, the fhip's motion through the water was fcarcely perceptible.

We had again fight of the American coaft on
Sunday morning the 21ft; it bore by compafs
from N. 5 E. to eaft, to N. 72 E.; but at fo remote a diftance that we loft every appearance of
it by noon, when the obferved latitude was 17°
56', longitude 255° 52'. During the two preceding

ceding days we had very light variable winds
from the eaftward and S. E. with alternate calms,
and very oppreffive fultry weather ; but by
Thurfday the 25th we had fome little alleviation,
as the wind then blew a moderate fteady breeze
from the north-weftward. Whilft the light
winds continued we were greatly incommoded
by a very heavy fwell from the fouth-eaftward,
which made the fhip extremely uneafy ; this had
now in a great meafure fubfided ; but the weather though perfectly clear was ftill very hot and
fultry, the thermometer night and day varying
from 81 to 83.   Had it not been for our anxious
folicitude to get forward, and the exceffive heat
of the weather, our fituation would have been by
no means unpleafant ; the ocean was tranquil,
and abounded with a great variety of fifh ; its
furface as it were was covered with turtles, and
the numerous fea fowls hovering over, and diving
for their prey, prefented fuch an animated fcene,
as the ocean, unaffifted by intervening land, or
other objects, is feldom, I believe, found to exhibit.   We were here at no lofs to provide a repaft for this our fourth Chriftmas day fince we
had quitted the civilized world ; and with the
addition of the frefh beef, mutton, and poultry
we had brought from Monterrey, the officers
tables prefented fuch an appearance of luxury as

is

is not frequently feen in fuch diftant regions of
the ocean. In addition to our frefh provifions,
and what the fea afforded, the people were ferved
fuch an extra allowance of grog as was fufficient
for the celebration of the day, and to call to their
recollection their friends and favorites at home;
on which occafion, though perhaps the circumftance may appear too trivial here to be noticed,
yet as the fentiment arofe fpontaneoufly from the
gratitude of the crew, I am induced to mention
it; the memory of Senr Quadra, and the health
of *Tamaahmaah* were not forgotten.

The fame light baffling winds continued to
impede our progrefs, which was tardy and irkfome beyond all defcription; in addition to
which, fome of our water cafks were found to
have leaked out; this, very contrary to my
wifhes, obliged me to reftrain the allowance of
water to three quarts a man per day. So very
flowly did we proceed, that by Wednefday the
31ft at noon we had only reached the latitude of
13° 50', longitude 259° 5' 30"; the latter was
deduced from 116 fets of lunar diftances, as follow, with the fun and aldebaran on different fides
of the moon between the 27th and 31ft of December. Thofe taken on the 27th, and brought
forward by Arnold's No. 14, gave the following
refults.

The

The mean of

6 fets ☽ a ☉ weft of her, by Mr. Whidbey, 259° 38 50″

4	ditto	Mr. Baker,	259 32 45
6	ditto	Mr. Manby,	259 52 45
6	ditto	Mr. Orchard,	259 50 27
6	ditto, taken on 29th, by Mr. Whidbey,		259 45 40
6	ditto	Mr. Baker,	259 37 35
6	ditto	Mr. Manby,	259 55 22
6	ditto	Mr. Orchard,	259 56 35
6	☽ ab aldebaran eaft of her,	Mr. Whidbey,	259 52 2
6	ditto	Mr. Baker,	260 14 17
4	ditto	Mr. Manby,	260 8 10
6	ditto	Mr. Orchard,	259 55 38
6	☽ a ☉ weft of her, taken 31ft	Mr. Whidbey,	259 46 50
6	ditto	Mr. Baker,	259 41 47
6	ditto	Mr. Manby,	259 47 43
6	ditto	Mr. Orchard,	259 47 2
4	☽ ab aldebaran eaft of her,	Mr. Whidbey,	259 52 4
6	ditto	Mr. Baker,	259 58 10
6	☽ ab aldebaran eaft of her,	Mr. Manby,	259 55 7
6	ditto	Mr. Orchard,	260 1 52
3	ditto	Myfelf,	259 58 25
3 days' obfervations, in 28 fets,		Mr. Whidbey,	259 47 5
	ditto 28	Mr. Baker,	259 48 55
	ditto 28	Mr. Manby,	259 55 51
	ditto 29	Mr. Orchard,	259 54 19

The mean of the whole, collectively taken,
being the refult of 116 fets of lunar diftances,
fhewed the longitude, at noon on the 31ft of
December, 1794, to be　　-　　-　　259 51 45

At which time Arnold's No. 14 fhewed　　260 6 30

　　　　　　　　No. 176　　-　　260 53 36

　　　　　　Kendall's　　-　　-　　260 46 45

　　And by the dead reckoning　-　260

Hence,

Hence, as I confidered the longitude deduced from the lunar obfervations to be correct, or nearly fo, it will appear evident that the chronometers, fince the commencement of the very hot weather, had been gaining confiderably lefs than the rate we were allowing as afcertained at Monterrey; for which reafon a new rate was, from thefe and fubfequent obfervations, found and adopted for pointing out our longitude, by the chronometers, from this ftation fouthward to the ifland of Cocos.

By this mode No. 14, at noon, on the 31ft of December, appeared to be faft of mean time
at Greenwich, - - 5^h 31' 36'' 45'''

And to be gaining on mean time per day at the rate of, -   20

No. 176, faft of mean time at Greenwich on the fame day,   11 51 59 45

And to be gaining on mean time per day at the rate of, -   41 5

Kendall's faft of mean time on the fame day, - -   10 11 43 45

And to be gaining on mean time per day at the rate of, -   21 35

CHAP.

CHAPTER IV.

Viſit the Iſland of Cocos—Some Deſcription of that
Iſland—Aſtronomical and nautical Obſervations
there—Proceed to the Southward—Paſs between
Wenman's and Culpepper's Iſlands—See the Gal-
lipagos Iſlands, and aſcertain their Situation.

DURING our paſſage thus far from Monterrey, it did not appear that we had been
much affected by currents, the log and the obſervations having in general correſponded very
nearly, and the difference between the longitude,
by the dead reckoning, and that which I conſidered to be the true longitude, had not exceeded
half a degree, the dead reckoning having been in
general to the eaſtward of the truth.

The wind in the north-weſtern quarter continued to blow a ſteady breeze, and as we advanced to the ſouth-eaſtward it increaſed in its
force; the heat was leſs oppreſſive, and the mercury in the thermometer fell to a general temperature of about 78; the atmoſphere was commonly clear, and the ſea, which was remarkably
ſmooth, abounded with immenſe numbers of
flying fiſh, dolphins, bonitos, albicores, and a

great

great variety of fmaller fifh; of turtles we eafily procured as many as we could difpenfe with.

By noon on Monday the 5th we had reached the latitude of 9° 27′, and the longitude, brought forward from the preceding lunar obfervations, with the new rates of the chronometers, was fhewn by Arnold's No. 14 to be 263° 36′ 15″, No. 176, 263° 34′ 15″, and by Kendall's 263° 40′; the dead reckoning at this time fhewed 265° 33′; whence it became evident that we were now materially affected by a current fetting to the weftward, as this deviation had been gradually increafing fince the 31ft of December, and by our daily obfervations for the latitude, the direction of this current feemed to be irregularly between the north, fometimes correfponding, and at others to the fouth of the obfervations.

In this fituation the vertical inclination of the magnetic needle was as under :

Marked end North face Eaft	-	24° 50′
Ditto ditto Weft	-	25 30
Ditto South face Eaft,	-	24 45
Ditto ditto Weft,	-	24 30
Mean inclination of the marine dipping needle	- - -	24 54

The variation being about 7½ degrees eaftwardly.

The two fucceeding days we were fet to the fouthward, at the rate of about half a mile per hour,

hour, and on Wednefday the 7th the wind from
the north-eaftward again became very light, and
I found it neceffary to begin diftilling frefh water
from the fea ; by this procefs, without any great
additional expenditure of fuel, a fupply of from
twelve to eighteen gallons of frefh water was procured in the courfe of each day ; and although it
could not be confidered of the firft quality, yet it
was perfectly frefh, and applicable to all the purpofes of cooking. In this refpect it was highly
acceptable, as by the affiftance of the diftilled
water, we were enabled to appropriate to greater
advantage the abundant refrefhments which the
fea ftill continued to afford, and which were fome
compenfation for the very tedious and tardy progrefs that the faint baffling winds permitted us
to make.

Since Wednefday we had frequently noticed
very ftrong riplings on the furface of the water,
but felt fcarcely any effect from currents. The
obferved latitude on Sunday the 11th was 7° 47′,
longitude, by Arnold's No. 14, 266° 27′ ; No.
176, 260° 20′ ; Kendall's, 266° 33′ ; and by the
dead reckoning 268° 32′ ; fo that admitting No.
14, as I conceived it to be, neareft the truth, the
error in the reckoning, fince the 5th, had only increafed 19′. The variation of the compafs was
now about 8° eaftwardly. During the laft week
the clouds, particularly in the northern quarter,

had fometimes hung about the horizon very dark and heavily, but they had now difperfed without any rain, excepting about noon on the preceding day, when we had a fmart fhower that lafted nearly two hours, and was the firft rain that had fallen with us fince our arrival at Monterrey in the beginning of November laft.

As we thus gently advanced to the fouth-eaft-ward, the riplings on the furface of the water became more frequent, and were attended with a greater degree of agitation, making a ruftling hiffing noife, like a tide in fhoal water; and though we felt fomething of their influence, they feemed infinitely more to affect the Chatham in her fteerage; yet, from the refult of our obfer-vations, they did not appear to be the confequence of any current, which gave rife to an idea, that probably the fpace we were then paffing over was of very uneven bottom. To afcertain this fact foundings were tried, but no bottom was found in thefe riplings with 140 to 170 fathoms of line. During the night of Monday the 12th, and until noon the following day, we had a frefh breeze from the N. N. E., which afterwards veered round to the eaftward and E. S. E, nearly in the direction in which I wifhed to fteer. On Wednefday noon we had reached the latitude of 5° 37′, longitude 268° 31′, approaching nearly to the parallel of the ifland of Cocos, and about two

or

or three degrees of longitude to the weftward of
its meridian, according to the different accounts
of its fituation in the ocean; and as we had no
indication whatever of our having left it to the
weftward of us, our courfe was directed eaftwardly, as the moft probable means of finding
the ifland.

We were ftill attended by vaft numbers of
fifh, varying both in fize and fpecies; few birds
were now about us, and the abundance of turtles
was fo much decreafed, that, on Thurfday the
15th, notwithftanding the day was for the moft
part calm, our boat's crew caught only two.
The weather ftill continued clear, and gave us fo
good a view all around us, that had any land
been within the limits of our horizon, it could
not have efcaped our notice. After having paffed
to the fouth of the 6th degree of north latitude,
we again found ourfelves under the influence of
the current, that, during the 14th, had fet us 18',
in a direction S. 47. E., and, during the laft
twenty-four hours, at the fame rate, in a direction N. 62 E. A light breeze fpringing up foon
after noon from the north, we purfued our eaftwardly courfe, intending to incline a little to the
fouthward. This however we were prevented
doing, from the current continuing to fet to the
E. N. E. at the rate of a mile per hour; fo that at
noon the following day, Friday the 16th, our obferved

ferved latitude was 5° 51', and the longitude
269° 32'.

The tranquil ftate of the wind and fea, which
with fo little interruption had for fuch a length
of time attended us, now feemed likely to un-
dergo a very material change. A very heavy
fwell rolled from the weftward, and the atmofphere became loaded with denfe, heavy clouds,
particularly between the S. E. and S. W.; in
this direction our view was limited to a very few
miles. The wind now blowing a gentle breeze
from the N. W. a more foutherly courfe was purfued, in the hope of regaining what we had loft
by the current having driven us to the northward. Towards midnight, after about three
hours calm, the wind came from the fouthward,
and obliged us to fteer again to the eaftward;
this I much regretted, as we had not, with all
our efforts, yet been able to get fo far fouth, as
the latitude affigned to the ifland we were in
queft of, which according to Lord Anfon's voyage is ftated to be in 5° 20', and by the Bucca-
neers in 5° 15'. I could not help being apprehenfive, that a continuation of thefe adverfe
winds and currents would oblige us to pafs to the
northward of the ifland without feeing it; for,
by our obfervations on Saturday the 17th, after
making every allowance, inftead of our being in
latitude 5° 22', which was fhewn by the reckon-

ing,

ing, the refults of our meridional and d ı ble altitudes (which agreed extremely well t gether)
proved our latitude to be 5° 46', and that we
were alfo feveral miles to the eaftward of our account, the longitude being 270° 37'. The variation at this time was $8\frac{1}{4}$° eaftwardly.

Between this and the preceding noon, we had
paffed over upwards of a degree of longitude,
without being able to fee far to the fouth of the
latitude of 5° 30', owing to very thick hazy
gloomy weather; hence it was very poffible, that
we might have paffed to the northward of the
ifland of Cocos. This was confidered by fome
on board to have been highly probable, from the
circumftance of our being now attended by vaft
numbers of the different fpecies of birds that are
generally found frequenting the fhores of the uninhabited tropical iflands; but this did not
amount to proof, as thofe birds might have been
attracted to the neighbourhood of our then fituation by the great numbers of bonitos, albicores,
and other fifhes, with which the fea at that time
abounded: and as we were fuccefsful in taking
as many of them as we could make ufe of, they
made us ample amends for the deficiency of turtle,
which did not appear to be an object of much
regard, as I believe moft of us began to be tired
of that food, which was only ufed to diverfify our
other provifions.

The

The currents with which we had met, fhewed that little reliance was to be placed on the longitude, affigned to any land in this part of the ocean, from the teftimony of thofe who had fo long fince vifited thefe regions, but who had not been provided with the means we poffeffed for afcertaining the ftrength and direction of thefe ftreams.

For fome days paft we had been fet confiderably to the eaftward, and as, from the feveral authorities I had confulted, it did not appear that we had yet reached the moft eaftern fituation affigned to the ifland in queftion, the prefumption was that it was ftill to the eaftward of our prefent track; and although I fhould have been greatly mortified to have been obliged to abandon an object that had fo much attracted my attention, yet, from the reduced ftate of our water in confequence of this unexpectedly tedious paffage, and the worn-out and defective ftate of our water-cafks, the reaching of the ifland of Cocos became a matter more of neceffity than choice; as I was very unwilling to enter any port in the continent. There feemed, however, no profpect of effecting this, unlefs we fhould be able to fhape fuch a courfe as would counteract the ftrength of the adverfe north-eafterly current. For this purpofe, with the wind at S. S. W. we fteered to the S. E. and in the evening had a to-

lerably

lerably diftinct view a-head, but the fouth-weft
horizon was ftill obfcured in dark denfe clouds,
and haze; the night was moftly calm, but in the
following morning, Sunday the 18th, the weather
was ferene and clear, attended with a gentle
breeze from the N. W, with which we fteered
to the fouth and at noon were in latitude 5° 33',
longitude 271° 7'; having been fet during the
laft twenty-four hours 13' to the north, and 11'
to the eaft of our reckoning.

The clear weather was not of long continuance
in the fouthern quarter, although the oppofite
fide of the horizon retained its former appearance;
for by fun-fet we could not fee a mile from the
fhip in the eaftern, fouthern, or fouth-weftern
quarters.   The various kinds of birds became
more numerous, and having at length reached
the ftated parallel of the ifland, we plied during
the night, which was attended by variable winds,
fome rain, and dark gloomy weather.   This continued until noon the next day, Monday the 19th,
when the obferved latitude was 5° 14', longitude
271° 9'; being 10' to the north, and 4' to the
eaft of what the log fhewed.   The weather now
admitted of an extenfive view all round, but no
land was in fight; and as the number of birds
was confiderably leffened, fome additional reafons
were offered in fupport of the former opinion,
that we had left the ifland to the fouth-weftward

M 4   of

of us. Of this however I was by no means convinced, as in my feveral traverfes over the Pacific
Ocean, I had feldom found that fuch indications
amounted to a proof of the very near vicinity of
land.

With the wind between the fouth and S. W.
although I had continued during the night to
the fouth-eaftward, we were not able to keep
our fouthing; for the obferved latitude at noon
the following day, Tuefday the 20th, was 5° 16',
the longitude 271° 52', which was 24' further
north, and 10' further eaft than was given by our
reckoning.

In the courfe of the laft three or four days we
had, in different inftances, been deceived for a
fhort time both by night and day, by very heavy
dark clouds which affumed the appearance of
land. Shortly after noon a fimilar refemblance
was feen from the maft-head at a great diftance,
bearing E. N. E. which was not given credit to
as being land, until aided by a gentle breeze and
the current, we had approached nearer to it by
three leagues, when it was decided beyond all
queftion to be land. Concluding it to be the
long-looked for ifland of Cocos, at the diftance
of 14 or 16 leagues, the glad tidings were communicated by fignal to our little confort. All
the turtles had now left us, but we had ftill many
fifhes and fea fowl attending us, though thefe

were

were not quite fo numerous as on the preceding evening. The night was calm or accompanied with light variable winds, which continued with rain and dark gloomy weather until noon the next day, fo that no obfervations could be obtained for afcertaining the fhip's fituation : we had however made fome progrefs, as the ifland now bore by compafs N. 73 E. to N. 81 E. not more than 6 or 7 leagues from us. In this we had been much affifted by the current fetting us directly towards the land, the fouth-weft extremity of which appeared in this point of view, to rife abruptly from the fea in fteep rugged cliffs to a confiderable height; and then in a moderate afcent to its moft elevated part; this was a hill of no very great fize; from whence it defcended with a more uniform declivity to its northern extremity, which appeared like a detached iflet.

The wind, which had been variable in the evening, became very light, and I was not without my apprehenfions that the current might force us paft the ifland, before we might have an opportunity of making choice of a fituation for anchoring. That no time might be loft, about two in the following morning, being then fufficiently near the land for one of our boats to be in with the fhores by day-light, Mr. Whidbey was difpatched in the cutter to make the neceffary examination. During this and the three or four

preceding

preceding nights the fea had prefented a very lu-
minous appearance, but I was not able to afcertain
with fatisfaction the caufe of it. After the boat
had left the fhip, we ufed our utmoft endeavours
to preferve our ftation to the fouth-weft of the
ifland, but to no effect; the current foon after
day-light drove us beyond its weftern end, and
although our head was to the fouth-weft, we
were driven at a great rate paft its northern fide,
within a few miles of its fhores. Thefe appeared
to be indented into fmall bays, with rocks and
iflets lying near them; but they by no means
exhibited that inviting appearance which has
been reported of them by Lionel Wafer* and
others. The fhores were chiefly compofed of
broken perpendicular cliffy precipices, beyond
which the furface rofe unevenly to the fummit
of the ifland; the whole compofing one rude
connected thicket of fmall trees near the fhore,
but on the more elevated and interior parts many
large fpreading trees were feen; fome cocoa nut
trees were alfo obferved in the chafms of the
rocky precipices, but they did not feem now to
flourifh in fuch abundance, as was moft likely the
cafe when their fruit gave a name to the ifland.

Being intirely without wind, the current fat
us faft to the north-eaftward from the land,

* Vide Collection of Voyages to the Southern Hemifphere, in
2 vols. 8vo. publifhed in 1788.

which

which at noon bore by compaſs from S. 17 W·
to S. 35 W. diſtant ſeven or eight miles.   The
weather at this time afforded us a good opportunity for aſcertaining the ſhip's place, which by
ſeveral correct obſervations was found to be in latitude 5° 40′, longitude 273° 8′.   By theſe and other
obſervations that had been made on the 20th, the
ſhip appeared to have been ſet by the current
during the two days 60 miles, in a direction N.
50 E.; this ſhewed that the iſland, which we did
not conſider to be more than moderately high
when firſt ſeen, was upwards of 20 leagues diſtant.

   In the morning, as we were driving near to
the ſhores of the iſland, ſome falls of water were
obſerved deſcending from the cliffs into the ſea,
and as we ſtood much in need of this neceſſary
article, as more of our caſks were found to have
leaked out, no ſmall degree of impatience was experienced for the return of the boat, as her long
abſence had been attributed to want of ſucceſs in
finding a ſafe place for anchorage.   This however
did not prove to be caſe, for her ſuppoſed detention was wholly occaſioned by the great diſtance
to which the current had ſet the ſhip from the
iſland.   About four o'clock I had the ſatisfaction
of being informed by Mr. Whidbey, that the
ſhores abounded with ſtreams and falls of moſt
excellent water, together with ſome cocoa nuts,
and plenty of wood for fuel, eaſily to be procured;

cured; especially in two small bays, both of
which afforded anchorage sufficiently sheltered
from the prevailing winds at this season of the
year; the one on the north-east, the other on the
north-west part of the island. Mr. Whidbey
gave the preference to the most eastern, for
which, therefore, with a light breeze from the
north, we immediately steered, but were unable
to stem the current till about nine at night, when
the wind freshened from the N. E.; and with
this, about four on Friday morning, the 23d, we
reached the situation Mr. Whidbey had chosen,
and moored in 33 fathoms water, sandy and
gravelly bottom, and (so far as we became acquainted,) good holding ground, and free from
rocks. The east point of the bay, which is a
small conical islet lying close to the north-east
extremity of the island, bore by compass S. 51 E.
distant half a mile; the west point of the bay
S. 75 W.; a steep rocky islet lying off it bore
from S. 87 W. to N. 66 W.; and the watering
place at the mouth of a very fine stream empty-
ing itself over a sandy beach, S. 13 W. about
three quarters of a mile distant; the Chatham
moored within us in 26 fathoms water, on the
same kind of bottom.

As soon as the ship was secured I went on
shore, and found that all our wants could be
easily supplied; that although there was some
surf

furf on the beach it was inconfiderable, and that
not only water and fire-wood, but that cocoa
nuts were alfo to be procured in great abundance. No time was now loft in fetting about
obtaining a due fupply of thefe effential articles,
and in the performing fuch other bufinefs as had
become requifite on board; where, at noon, by
the mean of four obfervations, with different
perfons and inftruments, the latitude was fhewn
to be 5° 35' 15". This differing fo materially
from the latitude as ftated in Lord Anfon's and
other voyages, and the general appearance of this
ifland fo little correfponding with the defcription
given of the ifland of Cocos, efpecially by Dampier, and Wafer, gave rife to fome doubts in my
mind as to its being the identical ifland fo defcribed by thofe gentlemen. Be that as it may,
the advantages it afforded us, not only in the
articles already mentioned, but in an abundance
of very fine fifh, were very important; and as the
foil was apparently capable of affording a variety
of ufeful vegetables, this ifland did not fail to attract our particular attention; and being anxious
to acquire every information refpecting it that
the fhort ftay I purpofed to make would allow
of, I difpatched Mr. Whidbey on Saturday morning, the 24th, in the large cutter, to take a fketch
of its fhores. This fervice he performed, and
returned about four in the afternoon, having
found

found them to be compofed of fteep perpendicular rocky cliffs, with fome iflets and rocks lying near them; on which the fea broke with fo much violence as to preclude any attempt to land in any part, excepting in the bay to the weftward of the anchorage we had taken, where Mr. Whidbey had been before, and in that in which the veffels were moored; which were the only two fituations on the ifland to which veffels could refort. On Sunday morning I made a fhort excurfion to the weftern bay, and although a more copious ftream of frefh water was found to flow into it, yet it is certainly not fo eligible a fituation for procuring the good things which the ifland afforded as that which we occupied. It was about half ebb when we reached its fhores, where we landed with tolerable convenience. After we had breakfafted, we fatisfied our curiofity in taking a view of the adjacent country; this was confined by an impenetrable thicket nearly to the limits of the fandy beach, which compofes the bottom of the bay, where, on our return to the boats, we found fome difficulty in re-embarking, owing to an increafe of the furf which at that time broke upon the beach.

At the place on fhore, where our operations were going on, I had obferved evident marks of European vifitors, from the trees having been felled with axes and faws, whilft the decayed

ftate

ftate of the remaining ftumps proved that they had not been very recently cut down. In this weftern bay, near to the frefh-water brook, a bottle was fufpended on a tree, containing a note directed to the commander of any veffel that might vifit the ifland, and figned " James Colnett;" ftating, that the fhip Ratler, South-fea whaler, of London, had arrived on the 26th of July, 1793, and, after procuring wood, water, and other refrefhments, had proceeded on her voyage, all in good health: that, previoufly to her departure, a breed of hogs and goats had been left on the ifland, and a variety of garden feeds had been fown, but the fpot where thefe valuable articles had been depofited did not happen to fall within the limits of our obfervation.

By the time we reached the veffels the rain fell very heavily, and I became acquainted, on my arrival on board, that the furf had fo much increafed, as very materially to retard our bufinefs with the fhore. The rain was accompanied by a frefh gale from the S. W. at the commencement of which the current, which, though by no means regular in its force, (fometimes being barely perceptible, at others running at leaft at the rate of two miles per hour,) yet had hitherto fet uniformly to the E. N. E. now changed its direction and fet to the weftward, but at a very gentle rate.

This

This uncomfortable weather continued, though with some intermiffion, during the 26th; we, however, made great progrefs in completing our water and fuel, and having nearly exhaufted the neighbouring fhores of their cocoa nuts, I difpatched two boats with Mr. Manby, the next morning, to the weftern bay, where they were produced in great plenty, to procure a full fupply of them. The boats returned about noon, not having been very fuccefsful, as the heavy furf prevented their landing in that part of the bay where the fruit was moft abundantly produced.

By the afternoon we had taken on board about thirty-five tons of water, with as much wood as we could ftow; and having thus finifhed all our bufinefs with the fhore, we quitted this ifland in the evening, and made the beft of our way to the fouthward.

Having adverted to the fituation and advantages which this fmall fpot of land poffeffes, I fhall now more particularly notice fuch matters as occurred to our obfervation whilft we remained there.

It does not appear from any account with which I am acquainted, to whom we are indebted for the difcovery of this valuable little ifland; nor, indeed, do the feveral defcriptions of the ifland of Cocos much accord with each other,

or

or agree with what we found to be its fituation or appearance. The ifland feen by Lord Anfon, of which he was within fight for five days, and confidered by him to be the ifland of Cocos, is ftated in his voyage to be fituated 13′ to the fouth of what was found by our calculations to be the latitude of this ifland; and fhould this error in the latitude be confidered as reconcilable, it is likely we may both intend the fame ifland. I have not the leaft doubt that the ifland we laft quitted is the fame which Chipperton vifited, and called it the ifland of Cocos. He, I fhould fuppofe, anchored in the weftern bay, but his defcription is too confined to draw from thence any fatisfactory conclufion; but the greateft difference is in the accounts given of the ifland of Cocos by Dampier and Lionel Wafer; thefe differ fo very materially from our obfervations, in point of extent of fituation and appearance, that their reprefentations muft either be exceffively erroneous, or they muft belong to fome other ifland. After taking all thefe circumftances into confideration, it appeared to me by no means unlikely, that fome other ifland might exift not very far remote from this, to which thefe apparently contradictory reports might more properly apply.

Two opinions were formed refpecting an infcription that was found cut on a rock near to our watering place; the letters, which had been originally but ill executed, were much defaced.

Look ⛎ as' you goe for ye I Coco.

This I confidered as purporting, " Look to " fouth as you go, for the ifland of Coco," but the more prevailing opinion amongft us was, that it meant, " Look as you go for the ifland of " Coco," meaning this identical ifland. The defaced character after the word " look" might poffibly have originally been intended to fignify the north, yet as we met with no other in its vicinity, it is probable that this latter opinion was moft correct; for which reafon I have adopted the name of Cocos for the ifland in queftion.

According to the fketch made by Mr. Whidbey, the ifland of Cocos is about four leagues in circuit, lying in a N. E. and S. W. direction; it is about four miles long, and two miles broad, with feveral detached rocks and iflets fcattered about its fhores; thofe lying off its fouth-weft part extend to the greateft diftance, which is nearly two miles, but they cannot be confidered as dangerous becaufe they are fufficiently high to be feen and avoided. The fmall bay in which we had anchored at the north-eaft end of the ifland is greatly to be preferred to the other weftward of it; for the fmall iflet that lies off its north-weft point adds greatly to its protection from

the

the wind and fea. The width of the bay from point to point of the two iflets that form each of its extremities is about a mile, in a direction S. 52 E. and N. 52 W. and from this line its extent to the bottom of the bay is alfo about a mile; the foundings are regular from 12 to 50 fathoms, and veffels may ride very fnugly within lefs than half a mile of the beach, in about 20 fathoms water, but in a lefs depth the bottom did not appear to be fo free from rocks. The weftern bay is more extenfive and more expofed, and its foundings are neither fo regular, nor is the bottom fo good; but from the abundance and great variety of vegetable productions that grow clofe to the verge of high water mark in both bays, it fhould feem that neither of them are fubject to very violent ftorms, or heavy feas. The climate was confidered by us as temperate and falubrious, for although the thermometer was ufually between 78 and 80, we did not feel that oppreffive heat which we had experienced further to the northward; and notwithftanding that our people were greatly expofed to the heavy rains that fell while tranfacting our bufinefs on fhore, yet not the leaft interruption from want of health took place, which in various other tropical iflands frequently attends the execution of fimilar fervices.

N 2

This

This ifland cannot be confidered as having a pleafant appearance in any one point of view, for although its inland furface is much diverfified by hills and vallies; yet the only low land of any extent that we were certain it poffeffes is in the bottom of the two bays, each of which form the extremity of one of thefe valleys bounded by craggy precipices, from the foot of which extends a narrow ftrip of low flat land that terminates in a beach at the water fide, refembling more the dreary profpect exhibited at the heads of the feveral branches of fea we had fo recently ex-plored on the coaft of North Weft America, than any thing elfe I could compare them to. Every other part of the fhore feemed to be com-pofed of fteep, broken precipices of rock, of which fubftance the interior of the ifland was apparently compofed, as the naked cliffs were fre-quently feen protruding their barren fides through the thicket, which otherwife covered the furface of the ifland. This thicket, fo far as we were enabled to afcertain, was chiefly compofed of a great variety of trees of a moderate fize, with an impenetrable underwood of the vine or fupple-jack kind, which oppofed any excurfion into the country ; fome attempts were, I believe, made to penetrate thither by the water courfe, but this, from rocky precipices and other obftructions, was found to be equally impracticable ; our know-ledge

ledge of its productions muſt conſequently be
confined to our obſervations on the ſmall margin
between the woods and the ſea ſhore, the only
part that was acceſſible to us. In reſpect of its
future utility, the firſt object of conſideration to
maritime people is the abundant ſupply of water
that it affords. This abounds in every part of
the iſland, and is to be eaſily procured at the
ſtations to which veſſels can reſort. From its
purity and limpid appearance, and from its being
deſtitute of any colour or unpleaſant taſte, either
from dead leaves or other putrid or rotten matter, though very heavy rains had fallen during
the time we had been at anchor there, it may
reaſonably be inferred that the larger ſtreams of
water have a more remote and permanent ſource
than the accidental ſhowers that at this ſeaſon
of the year may deſcend upon the iſland. The
ſoil in the immediate neighbourhood of the
ſtreams that fall into each of the bays is of a poor,
looſe, ſandy nature; but at a little diſtance behind the beach, and in the fiſſures of the rocks,
a rich black mould was obſerved, apparently capable of affording much vegetable nouriſhment;
and this may alſo be the caſe in other parts of
the iſland, although we had no power of aſcertaining the fact. All its vegetable productions
appeared to grow luxuriantly, and covered the
iſland in one entire wilderneſs. On the rocky

N 3   cliffs

cliffs near the fea fide, whofe uneven furface admitted the growth of vegetables, a coarfe kind of grafs is produced, that afforded an excellent retreat for the different kinds of fea fowl which reforted thither to rooft and build their nefts, or more properly fpeaking to lay their eggs, as they are at little pains to form a neft of any defcription. About thefe cliffs grew a very particular kind of tree, fomething like the cloth plant of the South Sea iflands, but much larger; fome of thefe grow to the height of about thirty feet, are of a lightifh coloured bark, free from branches to the top, which is fomewhat bufhy, and for that reafon was called by us the umbrella tree. There were fome few other trees whofe foliage ftrongly refembled that of the bread fruit, but as no one of them was in bearing near the beach, I was not able pofitively to determine their fpecies. Many of the trees that compofed the foreft, efpecially in the interior and elevated parts of the ifland, feemed to be of confiderable fize, fpreading out into large branches towards their tops, which in point of height greatly furpaffed the others. I was inclined to believe that thefe trees were of the fame fort with thofe from which we principally obtained our fuel, although near to the fea-fide they did not grow fo large as on the hills; Mr. Manby, who moft commonly fuperintended that fervice, gave me the following

ing account of them. This tree is very generally produced all over the ifland, its trunk grows
very ftraight to the height of twenty or thirty
feet before it throws out its branches, which are
fo clofe, large, and fpreading, as to afford extremely good fhelter againft both fun and rain ;
the ftems of feveral were capable of fquaring to
twelve or fourteen inches ; the grain is clofe,
fomewhat variegated, and reddifh towards the
heart ; it yielded to the axe with tolerable eafe, to
the faw it was equally fitted, and being free from
knots, it fplit without much labour ; its leaves
are of a dark green colour, fmooth at the edge,
and not much unlike the laurel, though rather
longer ; the feed refembling a fmall acorn is
borne in clufters. The wood is well calculated
for burning. Mr. Manby defcribes another fort,
(which we cut for fuel alfo,) as having a whitifh
fmooth bark, growing tall and ftraight, and producing but few branches. Its leaf is large, and
in fhape refembling that of the horfe-chefnut,
of a light green colour, with a velvet furface ; it
appeared to be fit for little elfe than fire-wood,
and not the moft proper even for that purpofe,
as it has a thick pith in the center of it that
occupies a large portion of the ftem or branches.
The wood is of a white clofe grain, fplits readily,
but does not burn remarkably well. The cocoa-
nut trees, which grow not only on the fea-fhore

N 4   but

but high up on the fides of the hills, were the
only trees we faw that bore any fruit, although,
in one of the rivulets, an unripe guava was
picked up, which, moft probably, had come from
the interior country: in addition to thefe, we
noticed an abundance of different forts of fern,
fome of which produced a ftem nearly fix inches
in diameter, and grew to the height of nearly
twenty feet; thefe, as well as I recollect, were
exactly of the fame defcription as thofe commonly found in New Zealand. Such were the
moft general vegetable productions of this ifland
that fell under our obfervation, to which we further added the feeds of apples, peaches, melons,
pumkins, with beans, peas, &c. Thefe were
fown by Mr. Swaine, in a fpot cleared for that
purpofe, where he was of opinion they were
likely to thrive.

With refpect to the animal kingdom, fifh and
fowl feemed to be in great abundance, and we
entertained hopes that future vifitors may benefit
by Captain Colnett's liberality; as juft before
Mr. Swaine left the ifland a young hog, in very
excellent condition, was feen by him and fome
of his party, but on his difcovering our people
he haftily retreated into the thicket. Although
at no very great diftance from the ifland we had
feen fuch numbers of turtle, it was fingularly remarkable that there was not the moft diftant
                                        fign

fign of their reforting to thefe fhores.   The land
abounded with white and brown rats, and vaft
numbers of land crabs.   All the birds of the
oceanic tribe, common to the tropical regions,
repaired hither in great flocks, and were by no
means bad eating. Befides thefe were feen hawks,
a fpecies of brown and white herons, rails, a kind
of blackbird, and a few others, that chiefly inhabited the woods; which, with fome ducks
and teals, were what was obferved principally to
compofe the feathered race. A great variety and
abundance of excellently good fifh frequented
the fhores; fharks alfo were very numerous, and
the moft bold and voracious I had ever before
feen. Thefe affembled in the bay in large fhoals,
conftantly attended on our boats in all their motions, darting at the oars, and every thing that by
accident fell, or was thrown overboard. They frequently took the fifh from the hooks before they
could be got clear of the water, and what was ftill
more fingular, when one of their own fpecies was
fo taken, and they perceived he could no longer
defend himfelf, he was inftantly attacked, torn to
pieces, and devoured by his companions, whilft yet
alive; and, notwithftanding that thefe monfters
fubjected themfelves to be greatly annoyed by the
harpoons, knives, &c. of our people, by which
they received many deep wounds, yet even that
did not deter them from renewing the attack upon
the

the one which was caught, until every part of the
victim's flesh was thus torn from its bones.   On
this occasion we had an opportunity of observing,
that it is erroneous to suppose the shark is under
the neceffity of turning on his back for the purpose of taking his prey, as these sharks most commonly attained their object without first turning
themselves, as has been generally believed.

The general warfare that exists between sea-
faring perfons and these voracious animals, afforded at first a species of amusement to our
people, by hooking, or otherways taking one for
the others to feast upon, but as this was attended
with the ill consequence of drawing immense
numbers round the ship, and as the boatswain
and one of the young gentlemen had nearly fallen
a sacrifice to this diversion, by narrowly escaping
from being drawn out of the boat by an im-
mensely large shark, which they had hooked,
into the midst of at least a score of these voracious animals, I thought proper to prohibit all
further indulgence in this species of entertainment ; which, independently of its being likely
to be attended with serious confequences, was in
itself of too cruel a nature to be witnessed without pain.   These sharks appeared to be of three
distinct forts ; the most numerous were of the
tyger kind, these were beautifully streaked down
their sides ; the other forts were the brown and
the

the blue fharks ; and it was fingularly remarkable, that although they all voracioufly devoured
the two former fpecies, yet when one of the
latter was caught, it remained unmolefted by
the reft, and even when killed, and cut up, its
flefh was not eaten by its companions.

The other kinds of fifh that fell under my notice, befide thofe common to the tropical feas,
were two forts of bream, the large fnapper of
the Weft Indies, a fort of rock fifh, and another
kind commonly called yellow tail ; thefe were
all very excellent, and took the hook readily;
and to thofe who may follow us, and ftand in
need of refrefhments, they may prove a moft defirable refource ; and there can be little doubt
but that perfons under fuch circumftances would
foon fall upon fome expedient, to evade the inconvenience to which they might be liable from
the extreme vigilance of the fharks.   Nor is it
improbable, that on a more minute examination,
the furface of this little ifland may be found to
produce many articles of refrefhment; but as we
did not ftand much in need of any, excepting
the neceffary article of water, our attention was
not directed to fuch inquiries, being wholly en-
groffed in ufing every poffible means of difpatch
in providing ourfelves with thofe few particulars
with which we could not difpenfe.

We

We happily ſtood in no great need of ſearch-
ing for refreſhments at any great diſtance from
the ſhores of the iſland; for, excepting that I
continued to be in a very feeble and debilitated
ſtate, there was not on board either of the veſſels
a ſingle individual who was not in the higheſt
health imaginable.   In conſequence of the in-
diſpoſition under which I had ſo long laboured,
I was only able to go once on ſhore in each of
the bays, or I might poſſibly have acquired more
knowledge reſpecting this ſmall though valuable
ſpot of land.   The comfort we derived from the
water, and the few other ſupplies there obtained
juſtly entitled it to our conſideration; and as
from its ſituation it is not unlikely that it may
become a place of importance to thoſe whoſe
purſuits may direct them to this part of the Pacific Ocean, I truſt I ſhall be excuſed for having
dwelt ſo long on a ſubject which I could not but
regard as deſerving attention; not only as far as
it reſpects the productions of the iſland, but alſo
to ſhew, that the deſcription of the iſland of
Cocos given by Dampier from the obſervations
of others, and that ſtated by Lionel Wafer from
his own, are either extremely inapplicable to its
preſent circumſtances and appearance, or have
reference to ſome other iſland in its neighbourhood.   It is much to be regretted that Dampier
                                        had

had not himſelf viſited this iſland, as from the
great accuracy of moſt of the obſervations made
by that judicious traveller, few doubts could have
ariſen concerning the identity of the iſland he
meant to deſcribe.   I am more inclined to at-
tribute this deviation from the truth to miſre-
preſentation, than to any other cauſe, from our
having acquired a tolerably competent knowledge of that part of the ocean between the 5th
and 6th degrees of north latitude, for at leaſt
four degrees of longitude to the weſtward of the
iſland in queſtion, in which ſpace there is not
much likelihood of there being any other iſland.

For the purpoſe of commemorating our viſit
to the iſland of Cocos, I directed that the date
of our arrival, with the names of the veſſels and
the commanders, ſhould be cut on the ſame
rock where the other inſcription was found : the
two former I underſtood was executed, but it
ſeems that ſome obſtacle aroſe to prevent the
inſertion of the latter.   The reaſons before ſtated
for ſuppoſing that this iſland may hereafter prove
uſeful to thoſe who may traverſe theſe ſeas, demanded that the utmoſt attention ſhould be paid
to the fixing with accuracy its true poſition.   By
the reſult of all our obſervations, comprehending
152 ſets, taken between the 29th of December
1794, and the 16th of January 1795 ; and 155
ſets taken afterwards between the 28th of January,

nuary, and the 16th of February following, the longitude of the anchorage deduced thus from 306 fets of lunar diftances from the fun and ftars, each fet as ufual containing fix obfervations, appeared to be as follow:

The mean of
37 fets on both fides ☽ before our arrrival by

			Mr. Whidbey,	272° 54' 46''
37	ditto	ditto	Mr. Baker,	273 1 43
37	ditto	ditto	Mr. Manby,	273 3 3
38	ditto	ditto	Mr. Orchard,	273 4 58
3	ditto	ditto	Myfelf, ·	273 2 55
32	ditto after our departure		Myfelf,	273 8 42
34	ditto	ditto	Mr. Whidbey,	273 10 38
36	ditto	ditto	Mr. Baker,	273 14 55
25	ditto	ditto	Mr. Manby,	272 53 15
27	ditto	ditto	Mr. Orchard,	273 21 53

The mean of the whole 306 fets collectively taken, and reduced to the anchorage by Arnold's No. 14, according to its new rate, fhewed the true longitude to be · — 273 5 34

From this authority, and from feveral fets of altitudes of the fun carefully taken whilft in the bay, the errors and rates of the chronometers were found to be as follow:

Arnold's No. 14, faft of mean time at Greenwich at noon on the 27th of January 1795, 5ʰ 41' 3'' 20'''

And to be gaining per day on mean time
at the rate of — · — 20 2

Arnold's No. 176, faft of mean time at
Greenwich at fame time, — 12 11 18 20

And to be gaining per day on mean time, 41 5

Kendall's

Kendall's faft of mean time at Greenwich
at fame time,   —   — $10^h \ 21' \ 19'' \ 20'''$

And to be gaining per day on mean time   21   35

The latitude by twenty meridional altitudes of the fun and fea horizon, by the back obfervation taken by five different obfervers with different inftruments, and varying from $5° 33'$ to $5° 37' \ 20''$, fhewed the mean refult to be   —   —   — $5° 35' \ 12''$

The longitude according to the Monterrey rate was,

By Arnold's chronometer, No. 14, $273° 36' \ 40''$
   Ditto   ditto   176,   274   47   55
And by Kendall's,   —   274   55   10

By which it appeared that No. 14 was $31' \ 5''$, No. 176, $42' \ 20''$, and Kendall's chronometer, $1° 49' \ 35''$ to the eaftward of the true longitude.

The variation of the compafs by four fets of azimuths differing from $8° 14'$ to $7° 21'$, fhewed the mean refult to be   — $7° 45'$ eaftwardly.

The vertical inclination of the magnetic needle,

Marked End, North Face Eaft, $19° 47'$
   Ditto   ditto   Weft,   20   17
   Ditto   South Face Eaft,   19   17
   Ditto   ditto   Weft,   19   40

Mean inclination of the north point of the magnetic dipping needle,   19   45

The rife and fall of the tides were, by the fhore, found to be very confiderable and regular

twice

twice in the twenty-four hours without any apparent ftream, and were not in the leaft influenced by the currents. The night tides appeared
to be the higheft, and were eftimated to rife
nearly ten feet perpendicularly, though the furf
was too high to admit of any correct meafure-
ment. The time of high water was pretty clearly
afcertained to be about 2^h $10'$ after the moon
paffes the meridian.

Having, as before ftated, put to fea from the
ifland of Cocos, on the evening of the 27th of
January, and having no intention of ftopping
fhort of the ifland of Juan Fernandez, or fome
port on the coaft of Patagonia, for the purpofe
of again recruiting our water and ftore of fire-
wood, the fhip's courfe was directed fouthwardly,
but with fo gentle a breeze during the night,
that although we had all fail fet, yet, in the
morning of Wednefday the 28th, the ifland continued in fight until about nine in the forenoon,
when it bore by compafs N. 30 W., diftant forty-
fix miles; fhortly after this time we loft fight of
it, not from its being beneath the horizon, but
from its being obfcured by clouds and an hazinefs in the atmofphere. At noon the obferved
latitude was 4° 43', the longitude 273° 17'; by
which it appeared that, fince quitting our anchorage, a current had fet us in a direction
S. 12 E., eighteen miles. In the afternoon fuch
immenfe

immenfe fhoals of fifh were playing about on the
furface of the water as to be miftaken at firft for
breakers.   During the night the wind was very
light from the weftward, and on the following
morning, Thurfday the 29th, the weather was
calm, with very heavy rain; but in the forenoon,
although the atmofphere continued very gloomy,
we procured the neceffary obfervations to fhew
the latitude to be 3° 29', the longitude 273° 25',
whence we appeared to have been fet by a current 46 miles, in a direction S. 5 E.; a few turtles were this day about the fhip, fome of which
were taken.   In the afternoon we had a light
breeze variable between the eaft and S. S. E.,
with which we ftood to the fouth-weftward;
the night was nearly calm with very heavy rain,
but the next morning, Friday the 30th, we had
again a fouth-eafterly breeze with fome rain,
which in the forenoon ceafed, and permitted us
to obferve the latitude at noon to be 2° 35', which
was 30' to the fouth of what was fhewn by the
log.   With a moderate breeze, varying between
S. by W. and S. E. we ftood on fuch tacks, as
would enable us to make the beft of our way
to the fouthward, and at noon on Saturday the
31ft the obferved latitude was 2° 11', the longitude 272° 12', from which it appeared that the
current during the laft twenty-four hours had
fet us 12 miles to the fouth, and from the 29th

at noon 41 miles to the weftward. Since leaving the ifland of Cocos we had obferved many
riplings on the water, and had experienced an
uncomfortable irregular fwell from the fouthward. On Sunday the 1ft of February the weather became more pleafant, and the wind at
S. S. E. blew fo fteady a breeze, that I concluded
we had at length reached the regular trade wind.
In the forenoon we paffed by fome fea weed and
drift wood, a cocoa-nut, and a ftick of fugar
cane about nine feet long; all of which, excepting the former, appeared to have been no great
length of time in the water. The obferved latitude at noon was 1° 31′, longitude 270° 26′;
the former agreed exactly with the log, but by
the latter we appeared to have been fet fince the
preceding noon 10 miles in a weft direction.
The vaft numbers of fifh that ftill attended us
afforded us a very profitable amufement, and
many birds were ftill about us. The wind
which now hung far to the fouth, obliged us to
make a much more wefterly courfe than I could
have wifhed, as I had entertained hopes of being
able to pafs near enough to the Gallipagos iflands
to have had an opportunity of afcertaining their
true fituation; but as the wefternmoft of them
are faid to be under the meridian of the ifland of
Cocos, which was now nearly three degrees to
the eaftward of us, the chance of fucceeding in
                                              this

this expectation was now fo little, that I gave up every idea of accomplifhing that object.

Land was difcovered on Monday forenoon to the W. S. W.; it then appeared to be a very fmall ifland, which at noon bore by compafs S. 72 W., eight or nine leagues diftant. As our obferved latitude was 1° 26', longitude 268° 43', and the variation of the compafs 8° eaftwardly, we appeared to have been fet in the courfe of the laft twenty-four hours 10 miles to the north, and 28 miles to the weftward. The influence of this current fetting to the W. N. W. was very perceptible, for although with a light air of wind during the afternoon our courfe was directed to the fouth-weftward, yet fo rapidly were we driven in the above direction of the current, that, at fun-fet, this ifland bore by compafs S. 46 W., and another ifland, which had been difcovered about an hour and an half before, bore, at the fame time, N. 72 W. During the night we had a light breeze from the S. S. W., with which we ftood to the S. E.; but fo far were we from ftemming the current, that, at day-light on the following morning, Tuefday the 3d, the firft of thefe iflands bore by compafs S. 68 E., diftant fix leagues, and the fecond N. 17 W., 12 miles diftant. At fuch a rate had we been driven by the current between thefe iflands, that, notwithftanding we ufed every endeavour to preferve our fta-

tion

tion by keeping as the wind veered on the moſt advantageous tacks, yet, at noon, the firſt iſland bore by compaſs E. by S., at the diſtance of nine leagues, and the other N. N. E. ½ E., at the diſtance of 17 miles. In this ſituation the obſerved latitude was 1° 28′, longitude 267° 49′, by which the current appeared to have ſet us, ſince the preceding day at noon, ten miles to the north, and fifty miles to the weſtward.

In paſſing between theſe iſlands, which lie from each other N. 42 W. and S. 42 E., at the diſtance of twenty-one miles, we obſerved neither danger nor obſtruction; the ſouthernmoſt, which is the largeſt, did not appear to exceed four miles in circuit, and the northernmoſt about half a league; the former is ſituated in latitude 1° 22′ 30″, and longitude 268° 16′. Its north-weſtern ſide forms a kind of long ſaddle hill, the northern part of which is higheſt in the middle, and ſhoots out into a low point, which at firſt ſight was conſidered by us to be an iſlet, but was afterwards believed to be united. A ſmall peaked neck or iſlet lies off its ſouth-weſt ſide, which, like all the other parts of it, excepting that towards the north, is compoſed of perpendicular naked rocky cliffs. On the low north-weſt part we ſaw what we ſuppoſed to be trees, but we were by no means certain, for the iſland in general preſented to us a very dreary and unproductive

ductive appearance. The northernmoft ifland
rofe in naked cliffs from the fea, off which are
two iflets, or fmall rocks; that on its eaft fide is
remarkable for its flat table top, and for its being
perforated nearly in the middle. The fituation
of thefe iflands, the eafternmoft being nearly 5°
to the weftward of the meridian of the ifland of
Cocos, gave us at firft reafon to fuppofe them a
new difcovery, and not a part of the group of the
Gallipagos, as all the ancient accounts agree in
placing the Cocos due north from the wefternmoft of that clufter of iflands; but when we
took into confideration the very rapid currents
by which we had been controlled, they eafily
accounted for errors to which other navigators
muft neceffarily have been fubjected, who have
not, like ourfelves, been fo well provided with
the means of afcertaining the full effect of their
influence; which had, fince our leaving that
ifland, produced a difagreement of upwards of
two degrees of longitude in our dead reckoning.
The decifion of this point remained, therefore,
to be determined by our further progrefs to the
fouth; for, in the event of the firft or fouthernmoft, being Wenman's ifland, and the moft
northern, that called Culpepper's ifland, the
northernmoft of that group of iflands, little doubt
was entertained of our meeting with more of
them in purfuing our fouthern courfe; in doing

O 3 which

which we were not very expeditious the two
fucceeding days, as the wind between S. S. W.
and S. S. E. was very variable in point of ftrength;
and although we endeavoured to take every advantage it afforded, fo little progrefs did we make
againft the adverfe current, that on the 5th, the
moft fouthern of thefe two iflands was ftill in
fight, and at noon bore by compafs N. 31 W.,
diftant eight or nine leagues. The obferved latitude at this time was 59', longitude 268° 27',
by the dead reckoning 271° 24'; having, in the
laft twenty-four hours, been fet by the current
feven miles to the north, and forty-eight miles
to the weftward. As we were now approaching the equator, and as the fea was tolerably
fmooth, fome further obfervations were made on
the vertical inclination of the magnetic needle,
which fhewed

The marked end North face Eaft,   7°   8'
     Ditto   ditto   Weft,   8   3
     Ditto   South face Eaft,   7   28
     Ditto   ditto   Weft,   7   18
Mean inclination,   —   7   28
     The variation of the compafs, at
       the fame time,   —   8 eaftwardly.

We advanced fo flowly from thefe iflands, that
at fun-fet the foutherenmoft of them was ftill
within our view, bearing by compafs N. 12 W.
The wind was moftly at S. S. W. during the
                     night,

night, with this we ftood to the fouth-eaftward,
and at day-light on Friday morning the 6th,
difcovered a more extenfive land than the two
iflands we had juft paffed, bearing by compafs
from S. 10 E. to S. 35 E. This land appeared
to be very lofty, to be at a confiderable diftance
from us, and to be divided into three or more
iflands; but as we approached it the lefs elevated
parts were feen to be connected, fo that, in the
forenoon, it feemed to be only divided into two
portions, and even this divifion was rendered
doubtful, as we drew nearer to it, by the low
land rifing to view until about noon, when the
whole extended by compafs from S. 42 E. to
S. 10 E., with a detached rock S. 2 W. In this
fituation the obferved latitude was 28' north, the
longitude 268° 32'; having been fet, in the laft
twenty-four hours, by the current twenty-fix
miles to the weftward. This, however, appeared
to have taken place in the early part of that day,
as fince our having made the land in the morning, we had approached it with a light breeze,
without having apparently been influenced by
any current whatever.

In the afternoon a pleafant breeze fprang up
from the fouth-weftward, with which we ftood
clofe-hauled in for the land, and before fun-fet
faw very plainly, that what we had for fome
hours before confidered to be two iflands, was all

connected

connected by depreffed land on which was a
hummock, that had alfo appeared like a fmall
ifland; and beyond this low land, at a confiderable diftance to the fouthward, was feen an extenfive lofty table mountain. The land immediately before us formed alfo towards its eaftern
extremity a fimilar table mountain, and towards
its weftern point a very regular fhaped round
mountain, which, though not of equal height to
the others, was yet of confidsrable elevation, and
in this point of view feemed to defcend with
great uniformity. The eafternmoft, terminating
in a low point with fome fmall hummocks upon
it, at fix in the evening bore by compafs S. 47
E.; the wefternmoft, which terminated more
abruptly, S. 13 W.; and the detached rock,
which is fteep, with a flat top, S. 71 W. The
whole of this connected land appeared now to
form an extenfive lofty tract; and as I had no
intention of ftopping, the object for confideration
was, on which fide we fhould be moft likely to
make the beft paffage? The fouth-weft wind
from its fteadinefs, and the appearance of the
weather, feemed to be fixed in that quarter, and
as we approached the fhore we found a ftrong
current fetting to windward; I therefore did not
hefitate to ufe our endeavours to pafs to the weftward of this ifland, which under all circumftances
appeared to me to be the beft plan to purfue.

We

We drew in with the ifland until about nine at night, when we were within about a league of its fhores, and finding that the windward current was the ftrongeft near to the land, the night was employed in making fhort trips between the fhores of the ifland and the flat rock before mentioned, frequently trying for foundings with 100 fathoms of line without fuccefs. On Saturday the 7th, we were nearly up with the weftern extremity of the ifland, and as the weather was fair and pleafant with a very gentle breeze of wind, I wifhed, whilft the fhip was turning up along fhore, to acquire fome knowledge of what the country confifted, and for that purpofe immediately after breakfaft Mr. Whidbey, accompanied by Mr. Menzies, was difpatched with orders to land fomewhere to the fouthward of the weftern extremity of the land then in fight, which had been named Cape Berkeley. The part of the ifland we were now oppofite to, and that which we were near to the preceding evening forming its north-weftern fide, either fhoots out into long, low black points, or terminates in abrupt cliffs of no great height, without any appearance of affording anchorage or fhelter for fhipping. The furf broke on every part of the fhores with much violence, and the country wore a very dreary defolate afpect, being deftitute of wood and nearly fo of verdure to a confider-

able

able diſtance from the ſea ſide, until near the ſummit of the mountains, and particularly on that which formed nearly the north-weſtern part of the iſland; where vegetation, though in no very flouriſhing ſtate, had exiſtence.

The obſerved latitude at noon, being then within four or five miles of its ſhores, was $7\frac{1}{2}'$ north, the longitude 268° 29½'; in which ſituation the ſteep flat rock, called Rodondo rock, bore by compaſs N. 26 W.; the eaſternmoſt part of the iſland now in ſight, N. 78 E., and cape Berkeley in a line with more diſtant land, ſuppoſed by us to be another iſland, ſouth. As we advanced, the regular round mountain aſſumed a more peaked ſhape, and deſcending with ſome inequalities, terminated at the north-weſt extremity in a low barren rocky point, ſituated according to our obſervations in latitude 2' north, 268° 30' eaſt. From it the ſteep flat rock lies N. 2 W., diſtant 12 miles; and the ſhores of the north-weſt ſide of the iſland, ſo far as we traced them, took a direction about N. 50 E. ſixteen miles; the wind for the moſt part of the day continued light and variable between the weſt and S. W., but with the help of the current which ſtill continued to run in our favour, we paſſed in the afternoon to the ſouth of cape Berkeley, from whence the ſhores to the ſouthward of that point take a rounding turn to the eaſtward,

eaftward, and fhoot out into low rocky points.
The interior country exhibited the moft fhattered, broken, and confufed landfcape I ever beheld,
feemingly as if formed of the mouths of innumerable craters of various heights and different
fizes. This opinion was confirmed about five
in the afternoon on the return of Mr. Whidbey
and his party, from whom I underftood, that
about two leagues to the eaft fouth-eaftward of
cape Berkeley, a bay had been difcovered round
a very remarkable hummock, which feemed
likely to afford tolerably good anchorage and
fhelter from the prevailing winds; but as Mr.
Whidbey had little time to fpare, and as the
fhores afforded neither fuel nor frefh water, he
was not very particular in this examination, but
endeavoured to gain fome knowledge concerning
the general productions of the country. During
the fhort time the gentlemen were fo employed
on fhore, thofe remaining in the boat, with only
two hooks and lines, nearly loaded her with exceedingly fine fifh, fufficient for ourfelves, and
fome to fpare for the Chatham. Our opinion,
that this part of the ifland had been greatly fubject to volcanic eruptions, appeared by this vifit
to have been well founded; fince it fhould feem,
that it is either indebted for its elevation above
the furface of the ocean to volcanic powers, or
that at no very remote period it had been fo pro-
fufely

fufely covered with volcanic matter, as to render its furface incapable of more than the bare exiftence of vegetables; as a few only were found to be produced in the chafms or broken furface of the lava, of which the fubftratum of the whole ifland feemed to be compofed. Inftead of the different fpecies of turtles which are generally found in the tropical, or equatorial regions, thefe fhores, however fingular it may feem, abounded with that defcription of thofe animals which are ufually met with in the temperate zones, bordering on the arctic and antarctic circles: the penguin and feals alfo, fome of which latter I underftood were of that tribe which are confidered to be of the fur kind, were feen, as likewife fome guanas and fnakes; thefe, together with a few birds, of which in point of number the dove bore the greateft proportion, were what appeared principally to compofe the inhabitants of this ifland; with which, from its very uncommon appearance, I was very defirous to have become better acquainted; but we had now no time to fpare for fuch an inquiry, nor fhould I indeed have been able perfonally to have indulged my curiofity, as I ftill continued to labour under a very indifferent ftate of health, which in feveral other inftances had deprived me of fimilar gratifications.

At fun-fet the fteep flat rock bore by compafs

N. 5 W.

N. 5 W. and the land in fight from N. 56 W.
to S. 9 E.; the former, being the north-weft
point of the ifland, and the latter, the land that
was ftated at noon to be in a line with it, ftill at
a confiderable diftance from us; both of which
feemed to form very projecting points, from
whence the fhores retired far to the eaftward;
but whether only a deep bay was thus formed,
or whether the land was here divided into two
feparate iflands, our diftance was too great to
determine.

In the evening the wind frefhened from the
S. S. W. with which we plied to the fouthward,
and having ftill the ftream in our favor, we kept
near the fhore where the current continued to
be the ftrongeft. At midnight this breeze was
fucceeded by a calm, which lafted until day-light
the next morning, when, with a light breeze,
and the affiftance of the current, we made fome
progrefs along fhore. As we advanced, land further diftant, and apparently detached, was difcovered to the S. S. E.; at noon the obferved
latitude was 18½' fouth, the longitude 268° 23';
in this fituation we were oppofite to the land
mentioned the preceding day at noon. This
takes a circular form, and fhoots into feveral
fmall low projecting points. From the moft
confpicuous of thefe, called cape Douglas, the
adjacent fhores take on one fide a north-eaft-
wardly,

wardly, and on the other a foutherly, direction.
The above, being the neareft fhore, bore by compafs N. 78 E. diftant five miles; the fouthernmoft part of this land in fight S. 39 E.; the weft
point of the laft-difcovered detached land, which
is named Chriftopher's point, S. 28 E.; and cape
Berkeley N. 14 W. The land we were now
abreaft of bore a ftrong refemblance to that feen
the preceding day, equally barren and dreary
towards the fea-fide, but giving nourifhment to
a few fcattered vegetable productions on the
more elevated part, which rofe to a table mountain of confiderable height and magnitude, and
is the fourth mountain of this table-like form of
which this land is compofed.

The wind, during the afternoon and night,
blew a gentle breeze from the fouthward, but as
we continued to be affifted by the current fetting
to windward, we made fome progrefs in that direction, and were fufficiently to the fouthward
the next morning, Monday the 9th, to afcertain
pretty clearly that the laft-difcovered land, now
bearing S. 54 E. diftant nine leagues, was diftinct from the fecond difcovered land, or ifland;
and that its weftern part, Chriftopher's point, lies
from the fouth point of the fecond-difcovered
land, which is called cape Hamond, S. 13 E. at
the diftance of twenty miles.

Thus concluded our examination of thefe
fhores,

fhores, which proved to be thofe of the Gallipagos iflands. The wind now feemed to be fettled in the fouth-eaftern quarter, blowing a fteady pleafant gale ; and as the weather was fine, we were once more flattered with the pleafing hopes of having at length reached the regular fouth-eaft trade wind; we therefore made the beft of our way to the fouth-weftward with all fail fet, and at noon obferved we were in latitude 44' fouth. The longitude by the feveral chronometers, agreeably to their rates as afcertained at the ifland of Cocos, was by Arnold's No. 14,   267° 54' 30"

Ditto	176,	267	52 45
Kendall's,		267	52 30

But by the dead reckoning it ap-

peared to be   -   -   272   2   0

The variation of the furveying compafs was 8° eaftwardly, and the vertical inclination of the marine dipping needle was,

Marked End, North face Eaft,	-	2° 50'
Ditto ditto Weft,	-	2 45
Ditto South face Eaft,	-	2 30
Ditto ditto Weft,	-	2 30

Mean inclination of the north

point of the marine dipping needle,   2   29

The very exact correfpondence of the longitude by the chronometers, and which had uniformly been the cafe ever fince our departure from the ifland of Cocos, induced me to believe,

that

that at leaſt the relative poſition in point of longitude of that iſland with theſe would be found
correct; and I truſt, that the means adopted to
aſcertain the longitude of the former, will not be
found liable to any material error.

On reference to the relative poſition of the
land to which our attention had been directed
ſince the 6th of this month, the delineation of
its ſhores from our obſervations, will be found to
bear a very ſtriking reſemblance to that of the
weſternmoſt of the Gallipagos, as laid down in
Captain Cook's general chart; and although the
ſituation of Wenman's iſland does not correctly
agree, yet the correſpondence of the larger portions of the land with the above chart, is doubt-
leſs a further confirmation of their being the ſame
as is therein intended to be repreſented; from
whence I ſhould ſuppoſe,* that the firſt and third
portions of land ſeen by us conſtituted Albemarle
iſland, and that the ſecond was Narborough's
iſland. Theſe names were given by the Buc-
caneers, as alſo that of Rodondo rock to the ſteep
flat rock, and Chriſtopher's point to the weſt
point of the third land; and under this perſua-
ſion, this is the ſouth-weſt point of Marlborough
iſland, which is ſituated according to our obſer-

* This conjecture was on my return to England fully confirmed
by the information I received in conſequence of Captain Colnett's
viſit to theſe iſlands.

vations

vations in latitude 50' fouth, longitude 268° 34' eaft.

From thefe conclufions, all the objects I had had in view in fteering this fouth-eaftwardly courfe from Monterrey appeared to have been accomplifhed; fince I had not entertained the moft diftant intention of ftopping, to make furveys or correct examinations of any iflands we might fee. But as the fituation of thofe which were lying not far out of our track had been varioufly reprefented, I anxioufly wifhed to obtain fuch information as would place this matter out of all difpute for the future; and having been enabled to effect this purpofe to my fatisfaction, it was fome recompence for the very irkfome and tedious paffage we had experienced in confequence of the light baffling winds that had conftantly attended us after we had paffed cape Corientes; fince which time, to our ftation this day at noon, our progrefs upon an average had not been more than at the rate of 10 leagues per day.

I fhall now proceed to ftate, what little more occurred to my knowledge or obfervation refpecting that part of the Gallipagos iflands that we were now about to leave. The climate appeared to be fingularly temperate for an equatorial country. Since our departure from the ifland of Cocos the mercury in the thermometer had

VOL. VI.   P   feldom

feldom rifen above 78, and for the three preceding days it had moftly been between the 74th
and 76th degree; the atmofphere felt light and
exhilarating, and the wind which came chiefly
from the fouthern quarter was very cool and
refrefhing. The fhores appeared to be fteep and
bold, free from fhoals or hidden dangers; fome
riplings were obferved, which at firft were fuppofed to be occafioned by the former, but as
foundings were not gained when we were in
them, thefe riplings were attributed to the meeting of currents. The lofty mountains of which
this land is principally compofed, excepting that
which forms its north-weftern part, appeared to
us in general to defcend with much regularity
from a nearly flat or table fummit, and to terminate at the bafe in projecting points on very low
level land; fo that, at a diftance, each of thefe
mountains appeared to form a diftinct ifland.
This circumftance may probably have given rife
to the different ftatements of former vifitors concerning the number of this group of iflands; all
of them however agree in their affording great
ftores of refrefhment in the land and fea turtles,
in an abundance of moft excellent fifh of feveral
forts, and in great numbers of wild fowl. Our
having feen but few turtles whilft in the neighbourhood of thefe iflands, is no proof that thefe
animals do not refort thither; for in the fea we

faw

faw neither feals nor penguins, yet the fhores were in a manner covered with them; and in addition to this, the parts of the coaft that were prefented to our view confifted principally of a broken, rugged, rocky fubftance, not eafily acceffible to the fea turtle, which moft commonly, and particularly for the purpofe of depofiting its eggs, reforts to fandy beaches. With refpect to fifh, we had ample proof of their abundance, and of the eafe with which they are to be taken; but in regard of that great defideratum, frefh water, fome affert that the iflands afford large ftreams, and even rivers; whilft others ftate them to poffefs only a very fcanty portion, or to be nearly deftitute of it. This however is but of little importance, as, from their vicinity to the Cocos, where perpetual fprings feem to water every part of the ifland, veffels ftanding in need of a fupply, may eafily procure a fufficient quantity for all purpofes; and fince we faw in their neighbourhood many whales which we conceived to be of the fpermaceti kind, it is not unlikely that thefe fhores may become places of defirable refort to adventurers engaged in taking thofe animals. Notwithftanding that our vifit did not afford an opportunity for difcovering the moft eligible places to which veffels might repair; it neverthelefs, by afcertaining the actual fituation of the weftern fide of the group, has rendered the

tafk

talk of procuring fuch information more eafy to thofe, who may wifh to benefit by the advantages thefe iflands may be found to furnifh.

I fhall now take my leave of the Gallipagos iflands, and with them alfo of the North Pacific Ocean, in which we had paffed the laft three years.

CHAP.

CHAPTER V.

Proceed to the Southward—The Difcovery fprings her Main-maft—Scurvy makes its Appearance— Pafs the Iflands of Maffafuero and Juan Fernandez—Arrive at Valparaifo—Vifit St. Jago, the capital of Chili.

ON taking our final leave of the North Pacific Ocean, I could not avoid feeling fome regret in reflecting, that although I was convinced we had very effectually delineated its eaftern fhores, yet that the geography of a very large portion of that coaft which gives bounds to its weftern limits, ftill remained very imperfectly, and indeed almoft intirely, unknown to Europeans. The examination of thefe parts however had not formed an object of the prefent expedition; nor could we, without a complete re-equipment of both veffels in fome eftablifhed arfenal, have undertaken a fervice of that nature with any reafonable profpect of fuccefs, had it been within the limits of my commiffion. The length of time we had now been abfent from our native foil, the unpleafant intelligence we had

P 3   recently

recently received of the ftate of Europe, and the defire we had of adding our little ftrength to the means adopted for the reftoration of good order and tranquillity at home, all combined to reconcile us to any difappointment which the thirft for exploring or difcovering new countries might have infpired; and operated to fatisfy our minds as to the neceffity of making the beft of our way towards thofe regions, where our fervices in another line of duty might poffibly be more acceptable to our country.

Our progrefs however was not equal to our wifhes, for by Wednefday the 11th at noon, we had only reached the latitude of 2° 3′ fouth, when the vertical inclination of the magnetic needle was obferved to be,

Marked End,	North face Eaft,		0°	40′
Ditto	Ditto	Weft,	0	50
Ditto	South face Eaft,		0	30
Ditto	Ditto	Weft,	0	20

Mean inclination of the *north point*, 0   30

The variation of the compafs at this time was 7° 45′ eaftwardly.

The wind between S. E. and E. S. E. blew a fteady but very gentle breeze, and although the atmofphere was moftly free from clouds, yet the weather was temperate and pleafant; the thermometer night and day remaining between 75

and

and 76. On Thurſday the 12th, in the afternoon, the vertical inclination of the magnetic
needle was found to be as under;

Marked End, North face Eaſt,			1°	32'
Ditto	Ditto	Weſt,	1	38
Ditto	South face Eaſt,		1	40
Ditto	Ditto	Weſt,	1	17

Mean inclination of the *ſouth point*,   1   32
The variation of the compaſs, 7° 50' eaſtwardly.

The ſame light winds with pleaſant weather
continued until the following day, when, after
about ten hours calm, a breeze ſprang up from
the S. E. which gradually increaſed, and the
next day, Friday the 13th at noon, the latitude
was obſerved to be 4° 15' ſouth, longitude 265°
15'. The vertical inclination of the marine dipping needle was as follows:

Marked End, North face Eaſt,			5°	37'
Ditto	Ditto	Weſt,	5	32
Ditto	South face Eaſt,		5	55
Ditto	Ditto	Weſt,	6	3

Mean inclination of the ſouth point,   5   46
And the variation of the compaſs, 9° 7' eaſtwardly.

Since our departure from the Gallipagos iſlands
we had felt the influence of a current ſetting to
the weſtward, though this did not appear to be
of great ſtrength, as the error of the dead reckoning in longitude to this ſituation in the ocean
had not increaſed more than a degree.

The

The extremely bad failing of the Chatham had, throughout this voyage, very materially retarded the progrefs of our labours, but fince our laft departure from Monterrey the evil feemed to have much increafed; and confidering that our operations to the fouthward might acquire fome advancement from our preceding her, I informed Mr. Puget, that I fhould make the beft of my way with the Difcovery towards the ifland of Juan Fernandez; and in the event of his not arriving there before our departure, he was provided with further inftructions, which, with fuch as I might leave for him at that ftation, would be fufficient for his future government. After having made thefe neceffary arrangements, we made all fail in the Difcovery with a pleafant fteady gale from the S. S. E. Many oceanic birds and numbers of fifh ftill attended us, and we were now and then fortunate in taking fome of the latter. By the evening the Chatham was a confiderable diftance aftern, and by the next forenoon, Monday the 16th, intirely out of fight from the maft-head; fo that the diftance we had gained of her in twenty-four hours could not be much fhort of five leagues.

Our progrefs now was not only very expeditious, but very pleafant; the wind blew a fteady gale between E. S. E. and S. S. E; the fea abounded with a great variety of fifh, and was remarkably

fmooth;

fmooth; the weather, alternately clear and cloudy, with fome flight fhowers of rain, was very temperate and agreeable, the thermometer ftanding between 75 and 77.   On Saturday in fouth latitude 12° 43', longitude by

Arnold's No. 14,	-	255° 3½'
176,	-	255 0
Kendall's,	-	254 54

And by the dead reckoning, continued from the ifland of Cocos, 260° 32'.

In this fituation the vertical inclination of the magnetic needle was,

Marked End, North face Eaft,		23°	5'
Ditto	Ditto	Weft,	23	50
Ditto	South face Eaft,		23	58
Ditto	Ditto	Weft,	23	18

Mean inclination of the fouth point, 23   23
The variation of the compafs, 4° 55' eaftwardly.

As we advanced the wind decreafed in its force, and gradually inclined to the eaftward and northward of eaft, with nearly the fame pleafant weather.   On Thurfday the 26th, in latitude 19° 44', longitude 253° 45', the vertical inclination of the magnetic needle was found to be,

Marked End, North face Eaft,		36°	20'
Ditto	Ditto	Weft,	36	17
Ditto	South face Eaft,		35	23
Ditto	Ditto	Weft,	35	15

Mean inclination of the fouth point, 35   49
Variation of the compafs, 24° 5' eaftwardly.

The trade wind during the two fucceeding days was light and variable in the eaftern quarter, and on Sunday the 1ft of March we feemed to have reached the variable winds, having a frefh breeze, attended with a very heavy fwell from the north-weftward. The obferved latitude at noon was 23° 24', longitude by

Arnold's No. 14,	-	255°	3'
176,	-	254	52
Kendall's,	-	254	53
And by the dead reckoning,		260	25

The variation of the compafs was 4° eaft-wardly. In the afternoon we again reached the temperate zone; and notwithftanding that fince our departure from the Gallipagos iflands we had paffed under a vertical fun, the height of the mercury in the thermometer had at no time ex-ceeded 77 degrees.

The north-weft wind continued with fair pleafant weather until the evening of Monday the 2d, when it veered to the north, and became light and variable between the N. N. E. and E. N. E. On Wednefday the 4th, in latitude 26° 45', longitude by Arnold's No. 14, 258° 39', we paffed fome drift wood, and we had many birds and fifhes about the fhip. Some good lunar obfervations had been lately procured by fome of the officers, which fhewed the longitude to be about 5' to the weftward of Arnold's No. 14,

18'

18' to the eaftward of No. 176, and 3' to the eaftward of Kendall's chronometer; the dead reckoning at the fame time fhewing 264° 10'; the
variation was 4° eaftwardly, and the thermometer
from 73 to 75.

From this time our progrefs was much retarded
by the wind being adverfe, and varying between
fouth and E. S. E.; the weather however continued fair and pleafant until the morning of
Sunday the 8th, when the breeze frefhened, attended by fome fhowers and fmart fqualls; in one
of thefe, the heavieft we had experienced for a great
length of time, the head of the mainmaft was
difcovered to have been very badly fprung, about
five feet below the rigging and about feven feet
above, and oppofite to its former defective part.
The fails on the mainmaft were immediately
taken in, and on further examination of the
wound, the head of the maft was feen to be in a
very weak and fhattered condition. No time
was loft in relieving it of its weight, by getting
every thing down upon deck that was above the
top, and the carpenters were immediately employed in preparing two anchor ftocks as *fifhes* to
fupport the maft-head. At noon the obferved
latitude was 8°, the longitude 259° 32'; the variation of the compafs 5° 3' eafterly, and the
thermometer from 70° to 72°. The weather
was tolerably favorable for applying fuch remedies

to

to the defect in the maft as we poffeffed ; and on Monday afternoon, the 9th, it being as well fecured as was in our power, the mizentop-maft was fubftituted for a maintop-maft, that being as much as the weak ftate of the lower maft was capable of fuftaining, and the maintop-gallant-maft was got up for a mizen-top-maft. By this unfortunate accident our quantity of canvas was fo reduced, that our progrefs towards the appointed rendezvous was rendered very flow ; we however made the beft of our way, with winds very variable both in refpect to force and direction, though generally attended with moderate pleafant weather.

Without the occurrence of any circumftance worthy of recital, we paffed on until Saturday the 14th, when we found ourfelves in latitude 33° 13', longitude 262° 43', and variation 4° eaftwardly. At this time, to my utter aftonifhment and furprize, I was given to underftand from Mr. Menzies that the fea fcurvy had made its appearance amongft fome of the crew. This was a circumftance for which it was not eafy to account. The high ftate of health which every individual on board the fhip (myfelf excepted) had appeared to enjoy for fome months before, and the refrefhments we had been conftantly in the habit of procuring fince our arrival at Monterrey, together with the very pleafant weather that had

attended

attended us fince that period, all confpired to render the caufe of this unfortunate malady the more inexplicable, efpecially as there had not been the fmalleft abatement or relaxation in the meafures I had adopted at the commencement of our voyage; but on the contrary, the moft rigid obfervance had been paid to all thofe circum-ftances, which had been proved from experience to be the happy and effectual means of preferv-ing that moft valuable of all bleffings, health. All thefe precautions and falutary meafures on this occafion feemed to have loft their effect, for the number of our fcorbutic invalids increafed, and with them alfo my folicitude, which may probably be more eafy to imagine than to de-fcribe.   The baneful effects which feldom fail to be confequent on this diforder at fea, filled my mind with apprehenfions for the fafety of our patients ; and having prefumed that we had at length profited fo much by the experience and indefatigable labours of that renowned navigator Captain Cook, as that by due attention we could on a certainty protect feafaring people from the fatal confequences hitherto infeparable, under fimilar circumftances, from this malignant dif-order, the difappointment which I felt on this occafion was inexpreffible.   This was the fecond inftance in which it had appeared during the voyage.

voyage. The firſt was on our paſſage from Nootka
to the Spaniſh ſettlements in New Albion ; but
I was then in ſome meaſure able to account for
its appearance, our people having been for many
of the preceding months expoſed in a very arduous and fatiguing ſervice to moſt inclement
weather, with only the very ſmall portion of refreſhments we were enabled to procure during
that time. Theſe reaſons did not now exiſt,
and I remained in the greateſt uncertainty concerning the cauſe of its origin, until at length it
appeared to have been derived from a ſource
from whence I leaſt expected it : namely, from a
diſobedience of my poſitive injunctions and orders
on the part of the cook, who had been ſtrictly
forbidden on any account whatever to allow the
ſkimmings of the boiling ſalted meat to be eaten
by the people. Of this diſobedience, the ſhip's
cook, a ſteady, grave, and valuable man, came
aft on the quarter deck, and made a voluntary
confeſſion ; and ſtated, that he had not only
acted in direct oppoſition to my repeated injunctions in the preſent inſtance, but alſo on the
former occaſion ; though he had not been induced at any other time during the voyage, by
the importunities of the people, to tranſgreſs, in
giving to the crew the ſkimmings of the boilers
to mix with their pulſe, which at both thoſe
times,

times, but particularly the prefent, they had been able to procure in great abundance from their Spanifh friends.

On his examination it appeared that he had been lefs fcrupulous in complying with the demands of the people, in confequence of arguments that had been frequently urged and fupported by fome on board, who feemed to be acquainted with the opinions of the prefident of the Royal Society, and who ftated, that *he* conceived that pulfe with any kind of greafe was not only a wholefome food, but alfo very antifcorbutic.

When the great infipidity of peas or beans alone, without the aid of butter, or other qualifying material, is taken into confideration, it is not much to be wondered at that a deviation from reftrictive rules in thofe refpects fhould have taken place, with people fo totally indifferent and carelefs of themfelves as are the generality of feamen. The very unreferved and feeling manner in which the cook acknowledged his tranfgreffion, and the contrition he fhewed for having thus departed from his duty, intitled him to my full forgivenefs; on which he earneftly affured me, that he would in future attend ftrictly to my directions, and I had reafon to believe that he performed his promife. The cook's name was John Brown, which I feel a fatisfaction in recording,

recording, from his having beeen the means of eſtabliſhing a fact of ſo much importance to maritime perſons, by the two experiments which his honeſty compelled him to make known, at the riſk of a puniſhment for diſobedience of orders.

All our antiſeptics were reſorted to, but they did not ſeem to act ſo well as on the former occaſion; and ſince the number of ſcorbutic patients increaſed daily, I had reaſon to believe that the pernicious indulgence which had produced the diſeaſe, had been a very general practice amongſt the crew.

With the wind blowing a ſteady gale, chiefly between N. N. E. and N. W., attended with fair and pleaſant weather, we made as much progreſs as could well be expected in our crippled condition. In the courſe of the preceding week we procured ſeveral very good lunar obſervations for the longitude, which, when reduced by Arnold's No. 14 to Wedneſday the 18th at noon, ſhewed their reſults to be as follow:

The mean of 31 ſets taken by Mr. Whidbey,	273° 25′ 55″			
Ditto	18	ditto	Mr. Baker,	273 36 48
Ditto	30	ditto	Mr. Swaine,	273 32 30
Ditto	37	ditto	Mr. Manby,	273 13 37
Ditto	30	ditto	Mr. Orchard,	273 17 44

The mean of the whole 136 ſets collectively taken ſhewed what I conſidered the true, or nearly the true longitude, to be   -   273 25 30

By

By Arnold's chronometer No. 14, the longitude

was	-	-	-	273°	5' 30"
		176	ditto	272	7
Kendall's,	ditto		ditto	273	7 45

From thefe ftatements it fhould feem, that the chronometers were at this time materially gaining on the rate now allowed. The dead reckoning fhewed 280° 1'. The obferved latitude was 33° 50' fouth, and the variation of the compafs 9° 15' eaftwardly.

At day-light in the morning a ftrange fail had been difcovered at a great diftance aftern, or rather upon our weather quarter; fhe was foon found to be drawing up to us, although we had all the fail fet that we were able to carry; and as fhe appeared to be a brig, little doubt was entertained of her being the Chatham; the opinion of her being our confort was confirmed about four in the afternoon by her anfwering the private fignal, and as fhe had now evidently the advantage of us in point of failing, we did not fhorten fail, but left her to overtake us; which however was not effected until about nine o'clock on Friday forenoon the 20th, when Mr. Puget came on board, and I had the pleafure to underftand from him, that, like ourfelves, they had had very fine weather ever fince our feparation; and that on the 2d of March he had met with a large Spanifh merchant fhip named the Rofalie,

Vol. VI.   Q   Antonio

Antonio Joseph Valaro, master, laden with cocoa and jesuit's bark from Guayaquil, and bound round cape Horn to Rio de la Plata, and from thence to Cadiz; having quitted the former place on the 20th of the preceding January. The commander of this vessel mentioned the loss of the ship Edward of London, which had been unfortunately cast away at a place called Manquiva, and that several other British vessels, which had been very successfully employed in the southern whale fishery, had visited different ports on the coast of Peru and Chili, where they had been well received; and that the English were in high estimation in those countries. From this gentleman Mr. Puget became informed, that the anchorage at Juan Fernandez was considered as very bad and greatly exposed; that a Spanish frigate had lately been lost there; and that the island afforded but very few refreshments. On these accounts he strongly recommended, that in case the Chatham stood in need of any articles of naval stores, that she should repair to the port of Valparaiso, as being the most likely place on the coast of Chili for procuring such supplies.

After Mr. Puget had obtained this information, and exchanged with Sen.r Valaro some mutual, though trivial marks of civility, they parted, and each vessel pursued her course with a pleasant gale at E. N. E., which enabled the Chatham

the

the next morning to crofs the fouthern tropic in the longitude of 257° 40', about a degree and a half to the eaftward of our track acrofs that line, about forty hours before them. The winds had permitted the Chatham to fteer a more eafterly courfe than we had been enabled to do, which, with our reduced rate of failing, had contributed to form this early junction, and had obtained me a great degree of fatisfaction, as it had rendered our ftopping at Juan Fernandez intirely unneceffary.

The very unferviceable and damaged ftate of our mainmaft demanded, that we fhould without delay repair to fome port more eligible than this ifland was likely to prove for adminiftering to our neceffities, efpecially as the head of the maft, in addition to the former accident, had upon a more minute furvey been found to be very rotten. A defect of fo ferious a nature, admitting of no delay in the application of the moft effectual remedy, left no doubt in my mind refpecting the meafures that it would be moft defirable to purfue for the accomplifhment of that object.

In confequence of the ftrong injunctions contained in my inftructions, not to vifit any of the Spanifh fettlements on this coaft, excepting in the event of the moft abfolute neceffity, I deemed it expedient to fubmit to Mr. Puget, and the principal officers of the Difcovery, the ftate and condition of the maft from the carpenters written

Q 2 report,

report, together with that part of my fecret inftructions relative to the matter in queftion.
Thefe having been maturely taken into their
confideration, they were unanimoufly of opinion,
that for the good of His Majefty's fervice intrufted to my care and execution, and for the
prefervation of His Majefty's fhip, it was indifpenfibly neceffary that the Difcovery fhould immediately repair to the neareft port, for the purpofe of procuring a new mainmaft; fince the
difabled one, with every repair that it was poffible to give it, would ftill be very inadequate to
the fervice that might be demanded of it in thofe
boifterous feas, which at this feafon of the year
we muft neceffarily expect to encounter in paffing round cape Horn.

The port of Valparaifo feeming to be the moft
likely to fupply our wants, and being the neareft
to us, our courfe was directed thither with a
frefh northerly breeze, and fair and pleafant weather. At noon the obferved latitude was 33° 55′
fouth, the longitude by

Arnold's chronometer, No. 14,	277°	36′
	176,	276	31
Kendall's	ditto	277	32
And by the dead reckoning,		284	19

And the variation of the compafs was 10° caft-
erly.

About four o'clock in the afternoon the ifland
of

of Maffafuero was feen bearing by compafs
E. N. E., 11 or 12 leagues diftant. The wind
at this time blowing a frefh breeze rather to eaftward of north, our courfe was directed to the
fouthward of this ifland ; but from its diftance,
and the approach of night, we were unable to
fee much of it. At midnight we were paffing
within about 4 leagues of its fouthern fide, its
centre then bearing by compafs N. 15 W. The
latitude of the fhip by the log fince noon was at
this time 34° 3′ fouth, the longitude by Arnold's
No. 14, according to the laft rate was 278° 56′,
and by the lunar obfervations brought forward
by No. 14, allowing the fame rate, 279° 17′; but
as the chronometers were evidently gaining, and
that very materially, the true longitude of this
ifland was deduced from fubfequent obfervations,
which fhewed its centre to be in 279° 26′ eaft.
Its latitude from the preceding and following
days obfervations, which with the fhip's run
agreed exceedingly well together, was 33° 40′
fouth. This ifland did not appear to exceed three
leagues in circuit : its furface is hilly, rugged,
and uneven, and it appeared to terminate abruptly in rocky cliffs at the water's edge. During the night we had a frefh breeze with fome
fqualls, which continued the next morning, Sunday the 21ft, when the jury maintop-fail yard
was carried away ; not in confequence of a prefs

Q 3

of

of fail, but like many others of our materials, from being quite worn out and rotten. This was immediately replaced with another, of whose strength and qualities we had not a much better opinion. At about ten in the forenoon the island of Juan Fernandez was seen bearing by compass N. 60 E. The latitude was shewn by observations at noon to be 33° 56' south, longitude by

Arnold's No. 14,	-	280° 16' 30"
176,	-	279 18
Kendall's,		280 15

By the last lunar observations
brought forward by No. 14,   280 37 30
And by the dead reckoning,   286 51

The variation of the compass at this time 13° eastwardly.

We had sensibly felt the influence of a current during the last two days, setting to the eastward at the rate of ten miles per day. In this situation the south-west point of Juan Fernandez, or rather what we supposed to be Goat island, bore by compass N. 39 E., at the distance of 18 miles. In the afternoon we passed the southern side of Juan Fernandez, at the distance of about 14 miles, which was too indistinctly seen to attempt any delineation of its shores. Its south-west point appeared by our calculations to be situated in latitude 33° 45' south, and longitude corrected by subsequent observations, 281° 8' 47" east. Its

aspect

aſpect in this point of view was not very inviting;
the point terminates in a high ſteep bluff, its
eaſtern part ſeemed to be leſs elevated, and the
whole compoſed a group of broken irregular hills,
forming altogether as rude and groteſque a ſcene
as the imagination can well fancy.

The wind ſeeming now to be fixed in the
northern quarter, and being to the ſouthward of
our port, our courſe was directed to regain the
parallel of its latitude; this was accompliſhed by
Monday noon, being then by obſervation in latitude 32° 55′ ſouth, true longitude 285° 30′; the
wind was ſtill at N. N. W., with fair and pleaſant weather; the thermometer from 66 to 68,
and the variation of the compaſs 13° 42′ eaſtwardly. Having now got to the northward of
Valparaiſo, our courſe was ſo ordered as to pre-
ſerve that ſituation. This however proved to be
a very unneceſſary precaution, as towards midnight, in latitude 32° 51′, the wind, after becoming light and variable, was ſuccceded by a freſh
breeze at ſouth, that ſeemed to be equally ſteady
and fixed in its direction as the northerly wind
had been before; ſo that we had now again to
haul to the ſouthward, in order that we might
keep to windward of our port.

On Tueſday forenoon, the 24th, we gained a
diſtant view of the lofty coaſt of Chili to the
eaſtward. The obſerved latitude at noon was

Q 4   32° 53′

32° 53′ fouth. The land at this time was too far off to diftinguifh any of its particular parts. The wind blew frefh from the fouth, with which we made great progrefs towards the land, and by fun-fet the fhores were diftinctly feen to extend by compafs from N. 50 E. to S. 68 E., about 10 leagues diftant. In this point of view the fea coaft appeared to be compofed of hills of various fhapes and fizes confiderably elevated; behind thefe the interior country rofe to a very lofty range of ftupendous mountains wrapped in perpetual fnow. Thefe were the Andes, and when firft feen, which was fhortly after noon, were at the diftance, I fhould imagine, of nearly 40 leagues; but we had not an opportunity of making the neceffary obfervations for afcertaining that fact. We continued to ftand in fhore until ten at night, when, concluding we were within three or four leagues of the land, we tacked and ftood to the W. S. W. under as much fail as we could venture to carry, for the purpofe of fetching, if poffible, to windward of Valparaifo.

At two o'clock on Wednefday morning the 25th, we again ftood in for the land, which was very indiftinctly feen, owing to a denfe haze in which it was enveloped. The wind at S. S. E. was light, and it was not until about ten in the forenoon that we were in with the fhores; on which there was no one circumftance that could

indicate

indicate our being in the nighbourhood of Valparaifo, nor point out whether we were to the
north or fouth of that port, excepting our own
reckoning, which fhewed it to be in the former
direction. I did not think it prudent in our crippled fituation to rifk a difappointment, and for
that reafon we ftood off fhore until an obfervation for the latitude could be procured ; which
by the help of a double altitude, was accomplifhed
about eleven o'clock, when we bore away in latitude 33° 10′ fouth, for a point not far diftant
from the place where we expected to find the
bay of Valparaifo. At noon the above point,
which was the moft northern part of the coaft
in fight, and appearing like a fmall rocky ifland,
lying clofe to a low or moderately elevated projecting point of land, and terminating at the fea-
fide in a round hummock like a bell, bore by
compafs N. 43 E.; a rugged rocky iflet lying
clofe to the main land, near the fouth point of a
fmall fandy bay, being the neareft fhore, N. 64 E.,
two or three miles diftant; and the fouthernmoft
part of the coaft in fight, S. E. by S.

The view we had thus gained of the coafts of
the kingdom of Chili prefented but little to attract the attention, or excite the curiofity, of
ftrangers. Thofe parts immediately on the fea
fhore were compofed of rude cliffs and rocky precipices, againft which the weftern fwell broke

with

with unremitting violence. Above thefe cliffs
the country was varioufly broken by irregular
eminences, fome formed of naked barren rocks,
and others confifting of a reddifh fubftance almoft
equally unproductive, on which fome verdure
appeared here and there, with a few ftunted
fhrubs and bufhes, fome of which were at great
diftances from each other; but nothing like a
tree was to be feen, and the landfcape, bounded
by the frozen fummits of the lofty Andes towering above the lower barren mountains that defcend from them towards the fea coaft, exhibited
an extremely dreary, defolate, and inhofpitable
picture.

As we proceeded, a low fteep bluff point of
land, beyond that which terminated our northern view of the coaft at noon, was now feen
lying in a direction from it, N. 51 E. about three
leagues diftant, and which proved to be the weftern point of entrance into Valparaifo bay.

Our attention was now directed in queft of
the " great rock or fmall ifland" defcribed by
Sir Richard Hawkins in 1593, as lying " a league
" or better to the fouth of, and a good mark and
" fure fign of, the port." At firft I was at a
lofs to difcover which of the two noticed at
noon was Sir Richard's rock, as both are much
further from the bay of Valparaifo than he defcribes them to be; but as we advanced, I had no
doubt

doubt of the moſt northern being the " great
" rock or ſmall iſland." This lies upwards of
three leagues, in a direction S. 51 W. from the
point of Angels, which is the weſt point of Valparaiſo bay, and is rendered ſtill more conſpi-
cuous for pointing out the port, by being ſituated
cloſe to a very projecting point called by the
Spaniards Pr Quraumilla, from whence the ſhores
of the main land to the ſouthward take a direction ſome degrees to the eaſtward of ſouth, and
thoſe to the northward, as before ſtated, towards
Valparaiſo.   It is alſo the ſouth-weſtern point
of a ſpacious open bay bounded by a ſandy beach,
where anchorage might probably be found, but
which muſt be much expoſed ; and as ſeveral
rocks were obſerved lying at a very little diſtance
from the ſhore, the chance is that the bottom
may be compoſed of the ſame materials.   On
the north-eaſt ſide of this bay a houſe and ſome
ſmaller habitations near it were ſeen, and the
country in its neighbourhood appeared to be leſs
ſteril and forbidding than thoſe parts to which
we were oppoſite in the morning.   Its ſurface,
though unequal, was leſs broken ; and although
it could not boaſt of a luxuriant vegetation, yet
the naked, rugged precipices, that formed a barrier againſt the ocean on each ſide of the bay,
were no longer the general characteriſtic of the
interior country, which preſented a ſurface of
                                        ſome

fome foil, on whofe withered herbage both flocks
of fheep and herds of cattle were feen grazing,
on the fides of the hills.

Along thefe fhores, which feemed to be bold,
we paffed at the diftance of from half a mile to
half a league, without difcovering any danger
which is not fufficiently confpicuous to be
avoided; and, with the affiftance of a fine foutherly breeze, by two in the afternoon we were
abreaft of the point of Angels, off which fome
rocks extend to the diftance of about half a
cable's length. Thefe we paffed at about twice
that diftance, without gaining foundings. In
failing round this point, the country fuddenly
opened upon us, and prefented a fcene to which
we had long been intire ftrangers; the whole of
the bay was now exhibited to our view terminated by a fandy beach; near the upper margin
of which, and on the fides of the adjacent hills
was feen the town of Valparaifo; and although
from its fituation it could not boaft of much
pleafantnefs, yet in this point of view it appeared
to be neat, of confiderable extent, and built with
regularity; the churches rofe above the other
buildings, and the whole being defended by feveral forts, all confpired at once to announce,
that we were again approaching towards the
civilized world.

In the bay and near to the fhore rode feveral
fail.

fail of merchant fhips, engaged in their refpective
occupations; to and from which boats were paffing and re-paffing to the fhore, where a very
lively fcene was exhibited of men and cattle;
the whole exhibiting that fort of commercial intercourfe between diftant countries, that the arts
and civilization can alone carry into effect.   This
pleafing profpect of at length drawing towards
our native country, after fo long an abfence
amongft the rude, yet hofpitable, nations of the
earth, was however not unmixed with forebod-
ings of a painful nature, left the intelligence refpecting the diftracted ftate of Europe, which we
had but too much reafon to apprehend would
meet us on vifiting thefe fhores, fhould be of a
more melancholy complexion than we had anticipated.

The wind from the fouthward blowing directly out of the bay, obliged us to make fome
trips for the purpofe of reaching a proper fituation for anchoring, which was accomplifhed
about three o'clock in 10 fathoms water, muddy
bottom.

An officer was immediately difpatched to inform the governor of our arrival, of the occafion
of our vifit, and of the affiftance we required.
A fhip that had been feen in the offing in the
morning anchored foon after us, and, together
with the Difcovery and Chatham, made ten fail

of veffels riding in the bay; of thefe five fhips
and two brigs were Spanifh merchantmen, and
the other the Lightning of Briftol, a South-fea
whaler, commanded by a Mr. Cook; from whom
we received little encouragement to hope for
fuch a reception at Valparaifo, as we confidered
we had a right to expect, or as our fituation demanded.   Soon after we had anchored, however,
and during the abfence of Mr. Manby, who was
the officer fent to the governor, a Spanifh officer
came on board with congratulations on our arrival from Senr Don Lewis Alava, a colonel in
the army, governor of this port, and brother to
our friend of that name at Monterrey.

   This meffage was accompanied by the ftrongeft
affurances on the part of the governor of affording us every affiftance that we might require, and
which might be in his power to beftow, and with
hopes that he fhould foon have the pleafure of
feeing myfelf and officers on fhore, where we
might depend upon receiving every civility; adding, that the time we might remain at Valparaifo fhould pafs as agreeably as it was in the
power of himfelf and the inhabitants of the town
to render it.

   It was not eafy to reconcile two reports fo very
oppofite, though I did not hefitate to give more
credit to the latter than to the former, efpecially
as our firft impreffions were received from one

                                        not

not perfectly fober. Had I entertained any
doubts, my fufpenfe would not have been of long
duration, for on the return of Mr. Manby, every
thing the Spanifh officer had ftated was confirmed; and we now underftood, that if thofe
on board the Lightning laboured under any uncomfortable reftrictions impofed by the governor,
it was to be attributed folely to their own indif-
cretion and improper conduct, which had rendered fuch meafures on the part of the commanding officer indifpenfibly neceffary for the prefervation of good order.

Mr. Manby informed me that Sen' Alava had
ftated to him, that notwithftanding he did not
entertain the leaft doubt that Don Ambrofio
Higgins de Vallenar, the prefident and captain
general of the kingdom of Chili, would confirm
all the promifes which he then made ; yet it was
neceffary, before any material operations fhould
take place, to obtain his excellency's fanction
and approbation for their being carried into effect.
For this purpofe he fhould difpatch a courier
that evening to the capital, St. Jago de Chili, the
refidence of the Prefident, and where he now
was, and he hoped it would be convenient to me
to make fome communication to his excellency
by the fame conveyance, on the fubject of our
vifit, and the fuccours we required.

With this requeft of the governor's I inftantly
complied;

complied; the meffenger was then difpatched, and we were given to underftand that a reply might be expected on the Saturday or Sunday following; in the mean time there was no reftraint on the officers vifiting the town; the markets were open to us to obtain fuch immediate refrefhments as we might require; and we were equally at liberty to recruit our ftock of water and of fuel.

On thefe agreeable communications being made, the garrifon was faluted with thirteen guns, and on this compliment being equally returned, I waited upon the governor, whilft the veffels were mooring by the bower anchors in a N. N. E. and S. S. W. direction, a cable each way; the fouthern anchor in ten fathoms, the northern in fixteen fathoms water, on a bottom of ftiff muddy clay. The point of Angels bearing by compafs N. 35 W. diftant about a mile; the faluting fort on the weftern fide of the bay, N. 53 W. about half that diftance; the governor's houfe in another fort, S. 86 W. about three cables diftant; a rocky point running off from the town, being the neareft fhore, S. 7 W. one cable and a half diftant; a redoubt on a hill, S. 5 E.; a confpicuous white church in the village of Almandrel, S. 65 E.; the eafternmoft fort, N. 83 E.; a remarkably lofty, rugged, fnowy mountain, terminating partly in a flat, and partly

in

in a peaked fummit, being a part of the Andes, N. 61 E.; the eaft point of the bay, N. 57 E. about a league diftant; a more diftant point, N. 17 E. three leagues off; and the northernmoft part of the coaft in fight, N. 6 W.

On Thurfday morning the 26th, accompanied by Mr. Puget and feveral of the officers of both veffels, I paid my formal vifit to governor Alava, and had the pleafure of receiving every mark of polite and hofpitable attention from him, with repeated affurances that nothing fhould be wanting on his part to relieve our wants, or to render Valparaifo as pleafant and agreeable to us as its circumftances would allow. Thefe ceremonies being concluded we returned to the veffels, where our vifit was fhortly repaid by the governor, attended by moft of the principal officers and inhabitants of the town; and on their coming on board they were faluted with thirteen guns. From all thefe gentlemen we received the moft preffing intreaties to vifit their families; which civilities we did not fail to accept, expreffing our thanks for the cordiality with which they had been fo obligingly made.

The day was pleafantly fpent amongft our new acquaintance, who readily affifted me in making arrangements for procuring a fupply of the abundant refreshments which this luxuriant country

VOL. VI.   R   afforded.

afforded. In doing this, my firft care and principal object was, immediately to adopt the moft
efficacious meafures that could be devifed, for
eradicating the inveterate fcorbutic diforder
which now prevailed, and which had greatly increafed amongft the crews of both veffels. The
number of fcorbutic patients rendered incapable
of attending to their duty on board the Difcovery,
amounted to feventeen. On board the Chatham
their number was not fo great, though the difeafe was making a rapid progrefs; and I learned
from Mr. Puget, that on his making inquiry into
the caufe of it, he had found that the fame
pernicious practice had been indulged in on board
the Chatham, which had taken place on board
the Difcovery during our late long and tedious
paffage, that of permitting the fat fkimmings of
the boiling falt meat to be eaten by the people
with their pulfe, and to be ufed for frying their
fifh; but it did not appear that this unwholefome
indulgence had been carried to fuch an extent on
board the Chatham, as it had been on board the
Difcovery. In confequence of this information,
I deemed it expedient that the whole crews of
both veffels fhould, in addition to the regular allowance of frefh beef and greens, and new foft
bread from the fhore, be daily ferved with a quantity of grapes, apples, and onions; and I had foon
the

the happinefs of finding, that this falutary diet
was attended with the defired effect of intirely
eradicating the difeafe.

Whilft we were waiting for the return of the
courier difpatched to his excellency the Prefident,
my time was not unprofitably employed; for I
embraced that opportunity to vifit the feveral
warehoufes, and by fo doing obtained a complete
knowledge of the quality of the ftores and provifions they were capable of affording us.   When
this was done, I made the neceffary arrangements
for receiving them on board the inftant we fhould
be at liberty to accept them.   In the courfe of
my inquiries I had the mortification to learn, that
there was not a fpar, either at Valparaifo, or in
the country within our reach, of a fize fufficient
to be converted into a maft, for the purpofe of
replacing our difabled one on board the Difcovery.
This was a matter of very ferious concern; but
as a new maft could not here be procured, the
only expedient we had the power of reforting to,
was to ufe our beft endeavours to repair the old
one.   This I purpofed to do by turning the maft
end for end, by which means the moft defective
parts would fall below the deck; where, by the
addition of the *fifhes* we had on board by way of
further fecurity, I was in hopes, that with great
care and attention to the performance of the
work, we fhould be able to render it fufficiently

R 2   ftrong

ftrong to anfwer the purpofe of carrying the veffel to England.

The town of Valparaifo not affording any ta-
verns or places for the reception and accommodation of ftrangers, we were obliged to intrude
on the hofpitality of its worthy inhabitants for
fuch conveniences when we vifited the fhore.
Thefe civilities were conferred in fo handfome a
manner as at once to relieve us from any idea of
our being intruders; the pleafure that every one
manifefted in entertaining us, completely removed every fentiment excepting that of gratitude on our parts, for the repeated acts of kindnefs they fo very obligingly beftowed. Amongft
the firft to whom we were indebted in thefe refpects was Don Juan Barrara, the collector of the
king's duties, and Don Praeta, the captain of the
port. We firft became known to thefe gentlemen in their public capacity, and they had the
goodnefs to introduce us to many others of their
friends, all of whom treated us with the greateft
politenefs, attention, and hofpitality; but as their
houfes were not more than fufficiently large for
the accommodation of their own refpective families, a lodging on fhore was not to be eafily procured. The very indifferent ftate of my health
at this time however, required that I fhould avail
myfelf of this opportunity of fleeping on fhore,
and taking as much of the exercife of the country

try as my ſtrength would permit ; for this reaſon
I was induced to apply to the governor, to allot
apartments for myſelf and a few of the officers in
ſome of the public buildings of the town, with
which he very obligingly complied ; and in the
event of our equipment in this port meeting with
the approbation of his Excellency the Preſident
of Chili, of which there was little doubt, the
Caſa de Exercicios was appointed for our reception and reſidence. This building had been
erected ſome years ago as a chapel of eaſe, for the
purpoſe of accommodating the country inhabitants who came into the town on Sundays to attend divine ſervice, but who frequently could not
find room in the churches ; and it had likewiſe
been appropriated for the penitential acknowledgments of the women.

Our time on board was buſily employed in
making every thing ready to proceed in the ſervice we had to perform, the inſtant we ſhould
receive the ſanction of the preſident for ſo doing.
On Saturday evening the 28th, agreeably to our
calculations, the courier returned, and I had the
ſatisfaction to receive from his Excellency Senr
Don Ambroſio Higgins de Vallenar, preſident and
captain general of the kingdom of Chili, the
moſt ample confirmation of all the liberal offers
which had been made to us by Governor Alava;
together with a letter containing the moſt polite

R 3   congratu-

congratulations on our having thus far fafely accomplifhed the great object of our expedition,
and having at length arrived in a country where
nothing fhould be wanting within the reach of
his power to fupply, that could in any way contribute to the reftoration of our health, adminifter
to our future comforts, or tend to re-equip the
veffels, and repair the damages which they had
fuftained. Thefe obliging and friendly offers were
further accompanied by a communication to
governor Alava, ftating, that if myfelf and fome
of the principal officers fhould be inclined to
vifit the capital, we had his Excellency's permiffion to do fo; and in the event of our undertaking a journey to St. Jago, the governor was requefted by the Prefident to employ his good
offices, in feeing that we were properly provided
for the excurfion.

I embraced the earlieft opportunity to return
my moft grateful acknowledgments to the Prefident, for his extreme politenefs and liberality
towards us; and I loft no time in fetting hard to
work on the various fervices which now demanded our attention. My firft and principal
object was to get out the main-maft; for this
purpofe, on Monday morning the 30th, the fhip
was moved nearer in fhore, and moored in four
fathoms, to infure more effectually fmooth water
for performing that operation. After this was
accom-

accomplifhed, on the following morning, the
maft was hauled up on to the beach between
Valparaifo and the village of Almandrel, where
a tent was erected, and at the governor's exprefs
defire a guard of marines from the Difcovery was
pofted there, to prevent thefts, or other improper
conduct on the part of the inhabitants, as fome
of the pinnace's covering had been ftolen the
preceding night.

Whether this application from the governor
proceeded from a fentiment of delicacy towards
us, or whether he confidered that our marines
would be more adequate to the protection of our
property than the Spanifh foldiers, is not eafy to
decide; but it appeared to be a very unprece-
dented and extraordinary circumftance, that a
guard fhould here be requefted by the governor
from an Englifh man of war, to do duty in the
dominions of his Catholic majefty. The marines
however were landed with a ferjeant, and planted
as centinels, with pofitive orders from me, on no
account to hurt any of the inhabitants, even
though they fhould be detected in the very act
of thieving; but to fecure their perfons, that
they might be dealt with according to their own
laws.

On the maft being examined we had the mortification to find, that the damage it had fuftained was greater than we had fufpected, as it

R 4   was

was fprung nearly two thirds through, a little below the hounds. Some Spanifh carpenters, in addition to our own, were immediately fet to work upon it; and as both the veffels required much caulking, the artificers of the country were alfo hired for this fervice. Our fail-makers were employed in repairing the old and making fome new fails; the coopers in fetting up cafks for the reception of flour, and repairing thofe made ufe of for water; and the armourer was making the neceffary iron work for the repair and fecurity of the mainmaft and other purpofes, whilft thofe remaining on board were varioufly employed about the rigging, and in the hold for the reception of a quantity of fhingle ballaft. Not being yet pofitively determined whether our route home fhould be round cape Horn, or through the ftraits of Magellan, and our cables and hawfers being worn to the laft extremity, a fupply of each fort was ordered to be made for both veffels, according to the dimenfions we required; for although we had found an abundance of fmall white cordage in the warehoufes, there were no cables; there being little demand at Valparaifo for fuch ftores; nor was there any tarred rope of any defcription, the cordage from four inches in circumference downwards, being all white rope, fuch as the Spanifh trading veffels in thefe feas ufe for running rigging. Thefe feveral fervices

were

were all put into a regular train of execution;
but as the following day was the anniverſary of
our departure from Falmouth, and the commencement of the *fifth year* of our labours, all
work was ſuſpended, and the people as uſual had
the day to themſelves.   They were all ſerved
with a double allowance of grog, and an excellent dinner, compoſed of the various good things
that this country ſo abundantly afforded.

All our operations were cheerfully reſumed
the next morning, Wedneſday, April the 1ſt;
and on my viſiting the artificers employed on the
maſt, I had the mortification to underſtand, that
on framing the heel of the maſt for the purpoſe
of its becoming the head, that end, near to the
place where the cheeks were to be fixed on to it,
was found to be extremely decayed, and ſcarcely
in a better ſtate than the other extremity.   It
was however, though rotten, not ſprung, and
having no reſource but that of applying the beſt
remedy in our poſſeſſion, two ſtout *cheeks* made
of our ſpare anchor ſtocks, together with two
ſtrong *fiſhes*, were fixed to the maſt below the
partners of the main deck, and continued up to
its head; and even with theſe additional ſecu-
rities, it would be but a crippled ſtick to depend
upon: yet as we had no alternative, we were
compelled to make the beſt ſhift we could, which
would neceſſarily oblige us to be particularly

cautious

cautious, and to prefs it as little as poffible in our paffage homewards.

The obfervatory, with the requifite inftruments, was fent on fhore, and, as ufual, committed to the charge of Mr. Whidbey, for the purpofe of making fuch obfervations as were now become neceffary for afcertaining the rates and errors of the chronometers, and for finding the latitude and longitude of Valparaifo. Having made this and fome other arrangements for carrying into effect the re-equipment of the veffels, I determined to avail myfelf of the obliging permiffion of the prefident to vifit the capital of Chili, and ordered preparations to be made for an excurfion to St. Jago.

Our party was to confift of Mr. Puget and Lieutenant Johnftone of the Chatham, and Lieutenants Baker and Swaine, and Mr. Menzies of the Difcovery. I had already made known to governor Alava my intention of vifiting St. Jago, who very obligingly gave directions, as Valparaifo did not afford any travelling carriages, that we fhould be provided with a proper number of horfes and mules for the expedition; the former for our riding, and the latter for carrying our luggage.

I now had the pleafure of finding that his Excellency the Prefident, together with his polite invitation to the capital, had alfo fent two dragoons from St. Jago, who were natives of Ireland,

land, in his Catholic Majefty's fervice, for the
purpofe of being our guides and interpreters, and
for rendering us every other fervice that we
might require on the journey. Thefe people
had been long in New Spain ; they feemed to be
highly delighted with the charge now intrufted
to their care, and not a little proud of the power
and confequence that was attached to it ; for, as
on this occafion they bore the immediate order
of the Captain-general, they had authority to do
many acts from which, in the capacity of dragoons only, they were prohibited. This power,
amongft other things, permitted them to take
any horfe or horfes whatfoever, whether in the
ftables or at pafture, for the purpofe of facilitating
the fervice on which they were employed ; but
as our vifit to St. Jago was purely for recreation,
I would not permit any compulfory meafures to
be reforted to for our accommodation ; and a
fufficient number of horfes were procured, at
twelve dollars each, for the journey thither, and
back again to Valparaifo.

Every thing being prepared, we fet out early
on Friday morning the 3d, with a numerous
cavalcade ; for, notwithftanding this country had
been fettled a great length of time, we were
given to underftand that we fhould find no accommodation on the road between thefe two
principal towns of the kingdom of Chili, excepting

ing fuch as might be met with in the villages
through which we might pafs or occafionally ftop
at, and thefe would confift only of a fhed or uninhabited empty houfe.   A fupply of provifions
might be depended upon, but there were neither
beds, feats, tables, nor any fort of convenient or
neceffary articles or utenfils to prepare them for
our table; all thefe, with our cook, we were
obliged to take with us; and, left we fhould be
difappointed of the promifed fhelter, we were
provided with a tent, which was packed in convenient travelling trunks, and carried on the
backs of the mules, according to the ufual method
of travelling in this country.   I could not, however, help expreffing my concern that the poor
beafts fhould be fo much loaded, and I objected
to the weight propofed to be carried, efpecially
the poles of the tent, which I fufpected would
prove too inconvenient a burthen for them to
move under: indeed this circumftance produced
fome altercation between the muleteers and the
dragoons; but as there was no appeal againft the
injunctions of the latter, the muleteers and myfelf were obliged to acquiefce, and twelve mules
were completely loaded with our tent and baggage.   The horfes that had been hired we
thought rather too fmall, and not of fufficient
ftrength; for, befides the weight of their rider,
they had each a moft enormous heavy faddle to
carry;

carry; but our Irish guides undertook to answer
for their abilities, and the event proved that their
judgment was to be depended upon.

From the town of Valparaiso, which is situated
on a narrow tract of very uneven ground at the
foot of the steep rocky precipices, which, at no
great distance from the water-side, compose the
shores, there is no pass immediately into the
country but for foot passengers; for the main road
which leads into the interior parts of the country,
approaches the sea-shore through the village of
Almandrel, whither our route was necessarily directed. This village is pleasantly situated, and is
on a more extensive border of low land than the
town of Valparaiso; but it is bounded in a simi-
lar way behind, by steep and nearly barren hills.
The valleys and plains, however, in its immediate neighbourhood, are fertile, and large gar-
dens were both cultivated for profit, and decorated for amusement. From Almandrel a tolerably good, though rather steep, road had been
made, in a zigzag way, over a ridge of hills, of
considerable extent and elevation, the summit of
which occupied us full two hours in reaching.
The old road between these two towns being a
very bad one, and dangerous to pass, his excellency had determined that a new and more eligible line of road should be made; and for the
more immediate convenience of the inhabitants

of

of St. Jago and Valparaiso, this new road, which is about sixteen yards wide, had been begun from each place, and by that means an easier and more pleasant communication with the adjacent country had already been afforded to the inhabitants of each of these towns than they had hitherto enjoyed. We were informed by our guides, that the whole of the new road was not yet finished, but was at that time in a progressive state towards completion, and that we should meet the people employed upon it as we proceeded.

Under the present circumstances of this road, and whilst the dry season may continue, it is doubtless as commodious a pass as could have been well designed; but, from the looseness of the soil, and the acclivity of the hills along the sides of which it is carried, it appeared to us that it would be liable to great injury in the winter season; which, we were told, is frequently subject to extremely heavy rains, that must necessarily rush with great impetuosity down the sides of this steep mountainous country.

Having gained the top of the road, which passes over a depressed part of that ridge of lofty hills which bind the sea coast, we arrived in a spacious plain, nearly on a level with the summit of the hills we had now left behind us. This plain extended to a considerable distance, in a north-easterly,

easterly, easterly, and south-east direction, where
it finished at the base of another ridge of hills,
beyond which were seen other ranges variously
diversified, and rising in succession one after
another; until our view was terminated by the
hoary head of the lofty Andes, wrapped in undif-
solving snow.   Had the intervening plain, and
the surrounding rising hills, exhibited the verdant
productions of nature, assisted by the hand of
man, the landscape would have been beautiful in
the extreme, but this was not the case; and the
apparent sterility of the wide waste, that now
encompassed us on every side, rendered that
abundant supply of good things which we had
been daily accustomed to see in the market of
Valparaiso, a circumstance not easily to be accounted for.

Instead of numerous villages, fertile pastures,
and fields in high cultivation, which I had expected to find, after passing over the hills near
the sea shore, an extensive open desert now appeared before us, destitute of wood, and nearly
so of verdure; as a few stunted trees only, and
some grovelling shrubs, were scattered at a great
distance from each other; and, excepting near
the banks of the sluggish rills of water that crept
through the plain, vegetation was scarcely perceptible; whilst the few miserable inhabitants
that existed on its surface, lived in wretched little
hovels,

hovels, or huts, made principally of mud. The frames of thefe dwellings, of which we had feen about a dozen, were rudely conftructed of wood, and plaftered over with a thick coating of mud; this ferved as a wall, whilft the unfmoothed furface of the ground formed the floor, and little or no covering appeared on the roof; the whole feeming fcarcely to afford a fhade againft the fcorching rays of the fun; for againft wind and rain thefe humble manfions could afford no fhelter.

At one of thefe mean abodes, about fifteen miles from Valparaifo, we ftopped to dine. The infide of the dwelling more forcibly difplayed the poverty of its inhabitants than had been exhibited by its external appearance; for it hardly contained the moft common neceffaries to the exiftence of human life; a dirty table, a ftool, a wretched bed in one corner, and five or fix croffes, comprehended all its furniture; yet it was not without fome decorations of a religious nature; and what ftill more attracted our notice, thofe who refided in it not only indulged in the luxury of taking the *mattee*, which is an infufion of an herb imported from Paraguay, but to our furprize, the very few utenfils they poffeffed for their moft common domeftic purpofes were chiefly made of filver. The land about thefe miferable hovels was, like the wide furrounding wafte, waſte, in a perfect ſtate of nature, without the veſtige of any labour having been ever beſtowed upon it, not even in the cultivation of a garden. The few wretched people who inhabit this dreary wild, ſeemed to rely intirely on the bountiful hand of Providence for their daily ſubſiſtence; and to paſs away their lives, without entertaining a wiſh to procure the leaſt addition to their happineſs or comfort, at the expence of any exertion. Indolence and ſuperſtition appeared to influence the whole of their conduct, which was marked with a greater degree of uncleanlineſs and thoſe characteriſtics that diſtinguiſh the very loweſt order of ſociety, than I had before witneſſed amongſt any people who had ever had the advantage of living amongſt thoſe connected with the civilized world.

The mules which carried our luggage were on the road before us, making the beſt of their way to the place where we purpoſed to reſt for the night, excepting one ſumpter mule, which had accompanied us with ſome articles of proviſions and provender for the day ; and by adding to our own ſtores the ſupplies which theſe hovels were able to furniſh, conſiſting of poultry, eggs, potatoes, onions, and fruit, we made an excellent repaſt, whilſt our horſes were alſo refreſhed, and prepared to proceed with us over this extenſive deſert.   Having now travelled ſome miles be-

yond the extent to which the new road from
Valparaifo had been carried, we found the old
one infinitely lefs commodious, and the difference
between the two was very great indeed. Inftead of the fmooth regular furface over which
we had paffed from Valparaifo along the new
road, this could only be confidered as a beaten
track, fometimes leading along, or through, deep
and irregular ravines and gullies, deftitute of the
appearance of any labour having ever been applied
to reduce the inequalities of its furface, or to remove any of thofe impediments which continually interrupted our travelling.

The making of the new road had doubtlefs
been a work of great labour; and to a people who
are not very induftrioufly inclined, and who are
all bigotted to former practices and original habits,
it is no wonder that the manifeft advantages that
muft refult to the inhabitants of the country from
his Excellency's wife undertaking, fhould be
overlooked, or rather not feen by them; and that
the execution of his judicious plan fhould have
deprived him, amongft the lower orders of the
people, of much of his popularity. For as the
thought had firft originated with the Prefident,
rather than not indulge a contradictory fpirit,
which our guides informed us had fhewn itfelf
amongft the bulk of the people, the inhabitants
feemed to be more willing to facrifice their own

future

future intereft and comfort by oppofing this be-neficial defign, than to do any thing which might promote its fuccefs.

Little variation occurred, in the fcenery already defcribed, in our journey in the afternoon, as we faw few objects to attract our attention until to-wards the evening, when we arrived at the vil-lage of Cafa Blanco, or, the *white houfe*. Here our guides propofed we fhould reft for the night, and after travelling twenty-eight miles in a way to which we were little accuftomed, we all gladly agreed to the meafure.

Cafa Blanco is a hamlet, confifting of a neat church and about forty houfes in its neighbour-hood; which, with fome inclofures of land under cultivation, formed a pleafing contraft to the barren naked country through which our day's journey had been directed. The principal perfon of the village appeared to be the curate, who hav-ing been made acquainted with our approach, was prepared to meet us, and gave us a like hof-pitable reception with that which had been fo generally fhewn by all the good people of this country with whom we had hitherto met. In the exercife of his humanity and good wifhes, our reverend friend feemed to be much hurt that he had fo little to beftow; but as we fortunately did not ftand much in need of his affiftance, ex-cepting in one refpect, that of providing us with

S 2   a lodging,

a lodging, we foon relieved him from his embarraffment. This gentleman immediately furnished us with a houfe, over which he held fome authority; a manfion precifely of the defcription which, we had been given to underfland, we fhould find on the road for our accommodation.

This houfe, if the ftruCture could be entitled to fuch a name, was fituated nearly in the centre of the village, and was fo rudely formed, that it could hardly be confidered as the work of a civilized people. Its walls were made of dried pieces of earth cut fquare into the fhape of bricks, which had been laid on each other when in a wet ftate, and plaftered over with the fame fubftance; but by drying unequally the plafter had fallen off in many places. Its infide was open like a barn, and confifted of but one apartment, which contained nothing but our baggage, that had arrived fome hours before us; and had the weather been rainy, it would have afforded us but very imperfeCt fhelter. The floor was no other than the ground in its natural, unlevelled ftate; but though it was not remarkable for its cleanlinefs, it was fpacious, and in that refpeCt more fuitable to the purpofes of our party, than the tent we had brought with us. As it, however, was totally deftitute of all kinds of furniture, we were obliged to refort to our neighbours for fuch temporary conveniences as we fhould want, which they very readily

readily fupplied: and whilft our fupper was preparing we vifited the inhabitants in the village,
by whom we were received with the moft cheerful affability; particularly by the younger parts
of the fex, amongft whom we noticed feveral
faces which, even by the fide of our fair countrywomen, might have been confidered as pretty,
had not the intolerable nafty cuftom of painting
both red and white, deftroyed the natural delicacy
of their comprexion, and impaired the effect of
the agreeable affemblage of their features.   Their
affiduity to pleafe was however very engaging,
and the evening paffed fo pleafantly, that the
fatigue of the day's journey was, I believe, intirely
forgotten by moft of us. , The houfes of this
village being all white-wafhed, gave it a neat
appearance, which, as we approached, impreffed
us with a belief that we fhould find thefe dwellings infinitely fuperior to the wretched hovels
we had paffed in the courfe of the day; but we
had the mortification to difcover, on accepting
the invitations of the principal people, that the
fame want of cleanlinefs prevailed, and that
wretchednefs, indolence, and fuperftition was
exhibited here in as great a degree, as amongft
the cottagers on the fun-parched defert.   The
only difference that we could difcern, between
thofe people and the inhabitants of Cafa Blanco,
confifted in the fuperiority of the external habi-

liments

liments of the latter, who had evidently dreffed themfelves in their beft attire for the occafion.

Our time was agreeably engaged until fupper was ferved, when we were favoured with the company of every inhabitant, I believe, belonging to the village ; the principal perfons partook of our repaft, whilft the others feemed to be equally gratified in the opportunity that was afforded them, of fatisfying their curiofity with a fcene fo novel and unexpected in their country. The glafs went cheerfully round, and our new friends did not retire until a late hour. Our blankets were then fpread, but the night did not pafs fo pleafantly as the evening had promifed ; for our reft was moft tormentingly difturbed by the vermin, which had been generated by the former filth of our habitation, and which now took revenge upon us ftrangers, for having endeavoured to difpoffefs them of their ftrong holds by fweeping out the place. When we arofe in the morning we found ourfelves but little refrefhed, owing to the great annoyance we had fuffered from myriads of bugs and fleas. Early the next morning we again fet out, and foon arrived at the foot of that range of hills that gives bounds to the plain on which Cafa Blanco is fituated. Thefe hills appeared to rife with a quicker afcent, and to a greater height above the plain we were then quitting, than the firft ridge had feemingly done from

the

the fea fide at Almandrel. The new road here led acrofs the lefs elevated part of the ridge, notwithftanding which, it was fo fteep that it was neceffary to cut the road in the fame zigzag diagonal way as before, and in its courfe from the bafe to the fummit of the hills, it made twenty-five returns or angles.

On this intermediate part of the new road the labourers were at work; and we underftood from our guides, that as a fufficient number of people could not be procured to carry the whole of the defign into execution at once, his Excellency the Prefident (having the comfort, convenience, and intereft of the inhabitants much at heart) had, in order to facilitate the intercourfe between thefe two great towns, ordered the moft difficult and dangerous parts of the new line of road to be firft made paffable and commodious. The road here was of the fame width, and equally well made, with the part before defcribed; but as the foil confifted of the fame loofe fandy materials, it muft neceffarily be liable in the winter feafon to the fame difadvantage I have before ftated, from the defcending torrents of rain.

We had here for the firft time an opportunity of feeing the peafantry of the country in a labouring capacity, and we could not help remarking, that their inactivity in the performance of their work could only be equalled by the humble

means

means they poffeffed for carrying it into execution.   There were about fifty men at work
with common pick-axes and fhovels; and to
fupply the place of wheel-barrows for the removal of the earth from the higher to the lower
fide of the road, the hide of an ox was fpread
on the ground, and when as much earth was
thrown upon it as would require the ftrength
of two men to remove, the corners of the hide
were drawn together by each of them, and in
that ftate dragged to the depreffed fide of the
road, and emptied where requifite, to preferve
a gentle flope in the breadth; or elfe difcharged
over the brink, and fent down the fide of the
hill.   The rocky parts, which were frequently
met with, were blown up with gunpowder; and
the fragments, which fometimes were very large,
inftead of being beaten into fmall pieces for the
purpofe of making a more folid foundation for
the paffing of carriages, were all moved to the
lower fide of the road, and, like the earth, thrown
from thence down the hill.   By this injudicious
practice the earth from the higher fide, which in
moft places might have been contrived to have
made a parapet along the brink, was not only
carried down by thefe maffy fabricks of rock, but
in many places the ground was torn up by them
in their paffage down; and as it appeared to us
that the brink was to be left in this open ragged
ftate,

ftate, the defcending rains muft foon caufe gullies that will injure the road, and do it confiderable damage. The fuperintendents, however,
feemed to have been aware that the torrents of
water, defcending from the upper fide of the hill
above where the line of road paffes, might have
the effect in rainy weather of wafhing away the
loofe materials of which the road is compofed;
for a channel was cut along the fide of the road
neareft the mountain to receive fuch water, and
to carry it down its inclined plane; but it appeared to us to be too fmall, and too much like
a gutter to anfwer the purpofe for which it was
intended. The lower fide, or brink, had neither
bank of earth, nor rail of wood, as a fence; nor
did we underftand that any fort of protection
was defigned to be made, the want of which
gave it a very unfinifhed naked appearance, and
in fome places, where the lower fide paffed over
a fteep part of the hill, or over perpendicular precipices formed by the rock, it appeared to be
dangerous in a high degree; for in the night, or
in the event of a horfe taking fright, or falling
near this outer unprotected fide, there can be
little chance of the animal or its rider efcaping
unhurt. Indeed it did not appear to us to be
prudent to venture too near to this fide in the
day time, as the road had already crumbled down
the

the hill, and had fallen into deep holes in many places.

The labourers, I was informed, received their provifions, and a rial and an half per day, which according to the rate at which we received the dollar, (viz.) at three fhillings and nine-pence each, makes the amount of their daily wages about feven-pence fterling, and the value of their food cannot exceed a groat. Thefe circumftances made it appear to us very extraordinary, that in a country where the expence of labour did not exceed eleven pence per day, more perfons were not employed in agriculture, and other rural improvements; efpecially as the foil and climate feemed to be well adapted for cultivation, and the fituation of the country infured a ready market for every kind of produce; of which, there could be no doubt, an abundance would eafily be procured, to reward the labours of induftry. By the introduction of a greater proportion of the common neceffaries of life, and by the obtaining a few of its comforts, it is reafonable to fuppofe that a general fpirit for exertion would be diffufed amongft the lower orders of the people, who might be taught, by encouragement, to prefer a life of diligence and activity to that fupinenefs which at prefent difgraces the larger part of the community. The fubmiffive obedi-

cence

ence that is here paid to every regulation or re-
straint impofed by the priefts, gave us reafon to
believe that it might be within their power to
infift that each individual fhould employ himfelf,
or be employed by others, a certain number of
hours each day, either in his own garden, or in
the general hufbandry of the country; for which
certain rewards, proportionate to the exertion,
fhould be affigned as an incentive to a life of
induftry. This would foon produce an inclination for employment, which would not only promote the general happinefs of the people, but
would be the means of fecuring to every one, in
proportion to his diligence, the comforts that
would certainly arife from this change in the
prefent œconomy of their lives. Inftead of the
univerfal apathy to work that feemed to per-
vade the whole of the labouring clafs, who were
dragged to their employment, without any felf-
impulfe, like an ox to the yoke, their daily labour would be undertaken with alacrity; and,
in looking forward to the advantages that would
refult from their exertion, they might foon be
ftimulated to prefer the habits of induftry to
thofe of fupinenefs and indolence.

On reaching the top of this range of hills, we
could plainly difcern the neat looking village of
Cafa Blanco, which added greatly to the appearance of the country we had left behind. The

road

road forward to St. Jago defcends on the north eaft fide of thefe hills, but it had not fo many angles or returns in it as that by which we had afcended on the other fide, becaufe the intermediate valley, between this range of hills and the mountains before us which we had yet to pafs, was confideravly more elevated from the level of the fea, than the plain on which Cafa Blanco is fituated.

After breakfaft, we proceeded on our journey along a very narrow path, which, without a guide, might have been eafily miftaken, as there were many fimilar to it, in various directions, through a foreft of fmall trees, that continued for about four miles. About four in the afternoon we ftopped at a mud hovel, at the diftance of nearly five miles from the mountain of Praow. The country we had paffed through poffeffed little to entertain, and lefs to intereft, the traveller; its general character was fimilar to that over which we had paffed before, excepting that it was more wooded, without any objects to vary the fcene; and being much fatigued with our new mode of conveyance, and the heat of the weather, the advice of the dragoons to make this fpot our refting place for the night, was willingly acceded to by all parties. Some lamb and poultry were foon procured for dinner, which was dreffed by our cook, and both proved to be very good.

good. Our table was fpread under the fhade of
fome vines clofe to the hovel, where we were
attended by a few peafants brought thither by
curiofity, who conducted themfelves very re-
fpectfully. We retired very early to our blankets, which, as before, were fpread in the hovel
on the bare ground.

By the recommendation of our guides, we
were on horfeback at three the next morning,
that we might avoid the intenfe heat to which,
they ftated, we fhould be expofed in afcending
the lofty fummits of Praow ; we accomplifhed
this before fun-rife by the new road, which made
thirty-two paffes or returns on its fide, cut out in
a manner fimilar to the other parts of it over
which we had already travelled. In afcending
at this early hour, we found the air fo very cool,
that great coats or warmer clothing would have
been very acceptable ; and we all were of opinion, that the confideration which had tempted
our guides to recommend our travelling thus
early, was more to infure a refting place the next
evening amongft fome of their particular friends,
than to avoid the heat ; a meafure on which,
however, much of our comforts might very poffibly depend.

From the top of Praow the landfcape was very
interefting. To the eaftward ftretched the extenfive valley in which St. Jago is fituated, and
which

which was terminated by the lofty ftupendous Andes, whofe fummits exhibit perpetual winter. In the oppofite direction the view of the country was not lefs worthy of our attention; a great number of mud hovels were now difcerned, that had before efcaped our notice as we had travelled along, and we now underftood that the valley through which we had juft paffed was confiderably more inhabited, efpecially near Praow, than thofe parts of the country nearer to Valparaifo. The people are chiefly peafantry, whofe principal employment is to take care of fome oxen and fheep that feed in the vicinity of their feveral huts.

We defcended Praow to the north-eaft, by fewer paffes than we had afcended on its oppofite fide, as the valley in which St. Jago is built is much higher than the other two acrofs which we had travelled; the general character of the country being that of an inclined plane rifing towards St. Jago, although its furface is broken by the ridges of mountains before defcribed. The road ftill continued in an eaftern direction, and was here as well made and as broad as the turnpike roads in England. On either fide were feveral fmall orchards, and a few plantations with fome indifferent pafture land, on which cattle were feen grazing under the fhade of a few fcattered trees; but the general want of cultivation gave the face of the country a barren and wild appear-

appearance, deftitute of any feature that could indicate our approaching fo large and populous a city as that of ·St. Jago; the only people we faw were two or three travellers, and a few muleteers.

We ftopped to breakfaft about fifteen miles from the capital, whofe lofty fpires were now plainly difcerned, towering above the numerous houfes which the city appeared to contain. Notwithftanding our prefent vicinity to fo large a town, we found no other place for the accommodation of travellers than the mud hovel, where we were entertained in the fame way as we had been before; and where, like the others at which we had ftopped, there was no fign of any improvement whatever, either in the building, or in any other refpect that might add to the comfort of life; the fame want of cleanlinefs, and wretched condition which I have before had occafion to remark, continued here to debafe the character of the inhabitants, who, notwithftanding their external appearance of wretchednefs and mifery, wore neverthelefs a contented look, and together with a cheerful countenance poffeffed a difpofition to oblige that was extremely grateful to our feelings, though their exceffive indolence and inactivity created in us a mixed fentiment of pity and reproach. In addition to the ufual fupplies we had found on our journey, we we here procured some excellent water melons of luxuriant growth and in high perfection, which were very refreshing and acceptable.

Having finished our breakfast we again resumed our journey; the road was level, broad, and firm, and we had not travelled far, before on each side of it were seen plantations and vineyards, in each of which a neat white house was generally situated at a little distance from the road. The appearance of cultivation and fertility in these low lands, when contrasted with the stupendous summits of the Andes, produced a most agreeable effect, and rendered this part of our journey very pleasant and entertaining. After a smart ride of nearly two hours, we arrived at a house about a mile from the capital, where fatigue, and a journey of ninety miles, made it necessary that we should halt; not only for the purpose of taking some rest and refreshment, but also that we might equip ourselves for the visit of ceremony we were about to make to the Captain General. From hence I dispatched one of the dragoons who had attended us with a letter to his Excellency, announcing our arrival in the vicinity of the capital, and stating, that with his permission we would do ourselves the honor of paying our respects to him at the palace in the evening; and I gave further directions to the dragoon, to procure and send from St. Jago, carriages sufficient to convey

thither

thither the whole party. In the mean time our
dinner was provided and ferved, and it was our
intention as foon as that fhould be over to drefs
ourfelves in all our beft apparel, that we might
make as uniform an appearance on this occafion
as our feveral ftocks of clothing would enable us
to do; for the extreme length of the voyage had
deprived moft of the party of the principal parts
of their wardrobe, and we had fcarcely a coat or
hat that was fit for common ufe, much lefs for
an occafion like this. In the midft of our endeavours to make as fmart an appearance as we
could contrive, the dragoon returned, accompanied by an officer from the Captain General,
whom he fent for the purpofe of compliment-
ing us and congratulating us on our arrival,
and of defiring that we would immediately repair to the palace, on horfes which he had fent
for the purpofe of conveying us in a fuitable manner to the capital.

Although it was by no means my intention to
have made fo public an entry as this arrangement
of the Prefident's would neceffarily expofe us to,
yet it appeared to me that we could not decline it
without giving umbrage, or perhaps offence; we
therefore endeavoured to equip ourfelves in the
beft manner we were able, and in doing fo we
referved our uniforms, which were extremely rotten and unfit for any fervice on horfeback, for

the purpofe of appearing in on our vifit of ceremony to his Excellency. The frefh horfes which
had been fent from St. Jago, we had imagined to
be like thofe which had brought us from Valparaifo, but, to our great aftonifhment, thofe which
had now arrived from the Prefident under the
care and directions of another officer, feemed to
be very high-bred animals; and were all richly
caparifoned with fine faddles and bridles, and
faddle cloths richly decorated, and fringed with
gold and filver lace, according very ill with the
drefs in which we were under the neceffity of
appearing. All my former objections to a public
entry were now greatly increafed, and I became
very defirous that we might be permitted to vifit
St. Jago in a more private manner; but on re-
prefenting this to the officers, inftead of acceding
to the wifhes of myfelf and party, whips and
fpurs were inftantly produced, that nothing might
be wanting to complete our appearance on horfeback in every particular. The ufe of the fpurs
however was generally declined by us all, left
fome embarraffment or mifchance fhould take
place from their being unintentionally applied,
whilft our thoughts were engaged by the new
objects that were likely to attract our attention
as we paffed through the ftreets of the city.
Trivial as this circumftance may appear, yet to
the officer who had charge of this efcort it was
a matter

a matter of the firft importance. He not only ufed all his eloquence to perfuadeus to wear the fpurs, but even expoftulated with us on the impropriety of appearing without them, and the unreafonablenefs of our declining fo effential a part of drefs; all his intreaties were not, however, fufficient to overcome our objections, and to his great mortification we mounted without them, and proceeded towards the capital, with a true military ftep, attended by the two officers, and our former guides the dragoons.

The inconvenience we experienced on firft fetting out, from being equipped in this very extraordinary manner, was greatly increafed by the crowds of people who had affembled to fee our cavalcade pafs along, in which they were fully gratified by the flownefs of our pace, until we arrived at the palace; where, on our alighting, we were received by a guard which was turned out on the occafion, and were conducted in form to the audience chamber. Here we were received by his Excellency Don Ambrofio Higgins de Vallenar, with that fort of unaffected welcome in which neither ceremony nor flattery appeared, and which amply repaid us for all the little fufferings we had endured in the courfe of our journey. This polite and cordial reception we had indeed anticipated from the reports we had received, before our departure from Valparaifo, and

T 2

afterwards

afterwards on the road to St. Jago. His Excellency's character, not only in refpect of his
great attention and urbanity to ftrangers, but of
his parental care and conftant folicitude for the
general happinefs and comfort of all the people
who lived under his government, were the conftant topics of our converfation; and it is not to
be wondered at if, on this occafion, we became
inftantly impreffed with the juftice which report
had done to his virtues, by his congratulations
and hearty welcome to the capital of Chili, which
were delivered by him in our own language with
a fluency that greatly excited our aftonifhment,
when we were informed by his Excellency, that
he had now been refident in New Spain twenty-
four years, during which time very few opportunities had occurred to him for fpeaking Englifh.
We now learned from Don Ambrofio himfelf
that he was a native of Ireland, from whence he
had been abfent upwards of forty years, that at
an early period of his life he had entered into the
Englifh army; but not obtaining in that fervice
the promotion he had expected, he had embraced
more advantageous offers on the continent. His
firft commiffion in the fervice of his Catholic
Majefty was in the corps of engineers, from
whence he exchanged into the dragoons, and
was foon raifed to the rank of lieutenant-colonel;
in this fituation he ferved for fome time in Old
Spain,

Spain, and afterwards in this country, until he obtained the diſtinguiſhed poſt of military commander on the frontiers of Chili, and governor of Conception. In this ſervice he was employed twelve years, and had the good fortune, by the conſtant exerciſe of his humanity, and an uniform attention to the comforts of the native inhabitants of the country, ſo to ſubdue the natural fierceneſs of their diſpoſitions, as to induce them to ſubmit to the government of Spain. For this eſſential ſervice he was promoted about the year 1783 to the exalted ſtation he now fills; ſince which time he has been honoured with repeated marks of approbation and diſtinction by his Catholic Majeſty, who has been pleaſed to confer upon him the orders of Charles the Third, and St. James, with the rank of lieutenant-general in the Spaniſh army.

A room of conſiderable dimenſions was allotted to me in the palace, and a large apartment adjoining to it was appropriated to the uſe of Mr. Puget and the reſt of the officers, in which were a ſufficient number of ſmall beds for the party, covered with thin gauze, as a protection againſt the muſquitos. The two dragoons who had attended us from Valparaiſo were now appointed to be uſeful to us in the capacity of ſervants; and every other matter was attended to, ordered, and ſettled, that evening, which could in any way

T 3   contribute

contribute to render our stay at St. Jago, and our residence in the palace, as pleasant as possible. Nor did the politeness of the President end here, for, previously to the supper being announced, he introduced to our acquaintance Don Ramon de Rosas, the corrigidor, and Don Francis Cassada, a captain of dragoons, who received the President's directions to use his utmost endeavours in shewing us every thing in St. Jago worthy the attention of strangers, and to make us known to the principal families residing in the city.

The supper, consisting of a great variety of hot dishes, was served up on silver, at which no person was present but Don Ambrosio the President, Don Ramon de Rosas and ourselves; all sort of ceremony was now laid aside, and agreeably to the repeated intreaties of his Excellency, we considered and felt ourselves as much at home as if we had been partaking a repast in England with our most intimate acquaintances. The first part of our conversation was chiefly engrossed by inquiries respecting our late discoveries on the north-west coast of America. In this I was very happy to learn, that no part of our conduct, or transactions with any of the subjects of his Catholic Majesty, appeared to have given the least cause for jealousy, or complaint against our little community; and I was also much gratified by the very handsome compliments that were paid to

myself

myfelf and officers, on the fuccefsful labours of
our voyage. After the curiofity of the President,
and Don Ramon was fomewhat fatisfied on this
fubject, the former, with great indignation, re-
counted a circumftance which I cannot forbear
to mention, although, being a matter only of converfation, it may poffibly appear too extraneous.
At the time when his Excellency was the governor at Conception, and during the late American, French, and Spanifh war with England, an
enterprize was meditated and planned by the
Court of Great Britain againft that place, which
was then the feat of government in the kingdom
of Chili. When Sir Edward Hughes failed with
his fleet from England to the Eaft Indies, it was
generally believed that he was to have acted only
in defence of our eftablifhments in that quarter,
but before that admiral had reached the firft place
of his deftination in the Eaft Indies, the Prefident
ftated to us, that he was in poffeffion of a copy
of Sir Edward Hughes's orders, which had been
tranfmitted to him at Conception from Old
Spain, by which documents he became informed,
that an attack was purpofed to be made by that
fleet from the Eaft Indies on the Spanifh fettlements in South America, and that Conception
was the place againft which the enterprize would
firft be attempted. In confequence of this intelligence a general alarm took place throughout

T 4   all

all the eftablifhments on the coaft; the fortifications, which had been much neglected, were repaired and ftrengthened; the number of troops
attached to each were greatly augmented; and
every preparation was made for the purpofe of
acting vigoroufly on the defenfive; and to this
circumftance alone his Excellency attributed the
abandoning of the defign, that had been concerted
by the Britifh Cabinet.

Soon after fupper was ended, a number of ladies made their appearance at the iron grating
that protected the window of the palace, begging our acceptance of nofegays, and requefting
that we would join the reft of their party, affembled at a little diftance from the palace; but as
I thought it would be more refpectful to pay our
compliments to his Excellency in the audience-
room, which formality was fixed for the fucceeding morning, before we fhould vifit any one
elfe in the city, we declined their obliging invitation for the prefent, with a promife of acknowledging their civility the following day.

We did not retire until an early hour, when
we found our beds tolerably good, but we could
not help being much difgufted at the infufferable
uncleanlinefs of our apartments; the floors of
which, but more particularly that appointed for
the refidence of the officers, were covered with
filth and dirt. Application was inftantly made

to.

to the dragoons, to procure us fome brufhes or
brooms in order to fweep it out, but, to our
great mortification, they told us that fuch things
were not in common ufe at St. Jago; fo that the
only alleviation we could obtain was that of water to fprinkle the duft, which was fo thick in
the officers' apartment, that it would rather have
required a fhovel than a brufh for its removal.

Every Sunday morning the Prefident has a
levee, which is ufually attended by the military
people, and the principal inhabitants of the city
and furrounding country. For the purpofe of
being formally introduced at this levée, we made
ourfelves as fmart as the exhaufted ftate of our
refpective wardrobes would allow, and then repaired to the audience-chamber; this room,
which is fpacious, was neatly, but not extravagantly, furnifhed; the anti-chamber was large in
proportion, and the entrance to each was from
the ground, through large folding doors. In the
anti-chamber were the portraits of the feveral
prefidents of Chili, from the firft eftablifhment of
the Spanifh authority in this part of the country,
to the prefent governor, whofe portrait was one
of the number. The infide walls of thefe rooms
were covered with glazed tiles, refembling thofe
from Holland, for about eight or ten feet from
the floor, which had a good effect, and was a
great relief to the dead white plafter of the remaining

maining part up to the ceiling. At the upper
end of the audience-room was a ſmall ſtage, raiſed
a few feet from the floor, upon which was placed
the chair of ſtate, ornamented with a canopy of
red damaſk, and decorated with the portraits of
their Catholic Majeſties, which were placed on
each ſide of the Preſident's chair. The levee
was attended by about one hundred and twenty
perſons, the greater part of whom appeared in
the regimentals of the eſtabliſhed militia of the
country; and, in ſuch a well dreſſed company,
our thread-bare uniforms ſuffered much by compariſon. I had, however, taken the precaution
to apologize to his Excellency for the reduced
ſtate of our apparel, and he did not fail, on introducing us to his friends, to enumerate the
hardſhips we had undergone, to ſtate the length
of time we had been abſent from the civilized
world, and to conclude, on every occaſion, with
ſome panegyric on the laborious undertaking in
which we had been ſo long engaged. This very
polite and friendly attention ſoon relieved us
from any embarraſſment which, at firſt, it was
natural we ſhould feel in being thus unexpectedly thrown into a circle of gentlemen, who
made a very ſplendid appearance, and who ſeemed
to have great pride in conforming to the faſhion
of the day, and the etiquette of court parade.
From all the gentlemen, to whom we were made
known,

known, we received the moſt flattering congratulations on our arrival at St. Jago, accompanied
by very friendly invitations to their houſes ; and
every one appeared to be anxious to make our
time paſs as pleaſantly as the circumſtances of
the place would permit.   The ſpecimen we had
already received from our very hoſpitable friends
at Valparaiſo, left us no room to doubt the ſin-
cerity of theſe ſtrangers, whoſe kind ſolicitude
to gratify our inclinations on every trivial occaſion, was infinitely greater than could reaſonably
have been expected.   After we had ſeverally
paid our compliments to the Preſident, the levee
broke up, and we followed the reſt of the party,
accompanied by Don Ramon and Captain Caſ-
ſada, to the levee of the Biſhop of Chili, which
always commences on the concluſion of the Preſident's.   Here we were again received with the
ſame politeneſs and affability which had marked
our reception at Don Ambroſio's.   The Biſhop
is addreſſed by the title of *Illuſtriſſima*, and the
palace in which he conſtantly reſides, in point of
magnificence and ſhow, exceeded, in a great degree, every houſe in St. Jago, not excepting the
Preſident's, to whom the Biſhop is the next perſon in rank and conſequence.   The rooms here
were not ſo large as thoſe of the royal palace,
but they were ſufficiently capacious and well
proportioned; the walls were hung with yellow

ſilk

filk, feftooned at the top, the furniture was rather gaudy than elegant, yet every object befpoke the richnefs and exalted ftation of the illuftrious owner. The Bifhop was dreffed in a loofe clerical garment of purple filk, buttoned clofe, with a fort of apron that extended round his waift, and reached below his knees. This part of his drefs, I was given to underftand, is commonly worn in Spain by the dignitaries of the church.

The fame perfons who had attended the levee of his Excellency, repaired with us to the palace of the Bifhop; but their deportment here, in point of refpect, far exceeded that which had been fhewn to the Prefident. Many priefts attended the levee, one of whom always conducted to the Bifhop the perfon who was to be introduced, who when fufficiently near, bent one knee, and received in that fubmiffive attitude the benediction of the church. On this occafion, the Bifhop with one hand made the figure of a crofs over the head of the perfon introduced, whilft he prefented a ring which he wore on a finger of the other, to receive an additional homage, paid by touching it with the lips, as in the act of kiffing. This ceremony was not reftricted to a few, for we did not perceive any one in the group that did not go through it; and, as I had made it a conftant rule to conform, on all occafions, to the innocent manners and cuftoms

toms of whatever country we might chance to
vifit, I fhould not have hefitated to perform the
like ceremony on our introduction, had the
ftighteft hint been given, either by Don Ramon
or Captain Caffada, that it would be expected
from us; but, as their filence left us completely
to our own feelings, we each of us fimply made
our bow, which appeared to be as well accepted,
and to receive as gracious a benediction, as if we
had adopted the other cuftomary formality.

The Bifhop made many very pertinent inquiries refpecting the countries we had vifited, and
feemed to have great pleafure in the little information we were able to afford him ; for at this
time, we had not an interpreter with us, who fo
perfectly comprehended what we defcribed in
Englifh as to make a faithful tranflation of it to
the Prelate ; and I do not recollect that I ever felt
more real regret, than on this occafion, that I did
not fufficiently underftand the Spanifh language
to hold a converfation with this apparently intel-
ligent gentleman, who was pleafed to embrace
every opportunity of beftowing fome encomium
on our late refearches, and to offer his congratulations on our having fo happily concluded them.

From the Bifhop's palace we were conducted,
by our friends, to the houfes of the judges and
great officers of ftate, in all of which we experienced the fame cordiality and friendlinefs, and
received

received the same pressing intreaties to visit their families as had uniformly been offered by every person with whom we had become acquainted since our first arrival in this hospitable country. About two o'clock we returned to the palace, where we found the President waiting our arrival for dinner, which was served up on a plain deal ill constructed table, by no means corresponding with the magnificence of the dinner service, which was entirely composed of silver. The company consisted of the President, Don Ramon de Rosas, Captain Cassada, and ourselves; and the conversation turned chiefly on the late labours of our survey, and the discoveries we had made on the coast of North-West America, which were repeatedly honoured with the most flattering commendations from the Captain General, who appeared to be extremely interested in the events which we related.

After drinking coffee, which is always brought in as soon as the cloth is removed, every one retired to his private apartment, a custom which so generally prevails in this kingdom, that, between the hours of three in the afternoon and six in the evening, no person is seen in the streets, the shops are shut up, and the same stillness prevails as if it were actually night. Accustomed as we had hitherto been to a life of constant anxiety, and to be satisfied with little rest,

we

we were at firſt greatly at a loſs to diſcover how
we ſhould employ the hours which were thus
dedicated to ſleep by the ſociety in which we
were now living; but the exerciſe of the morning, the heat of the weather, the want of occu-
pation, and the natural inclination to ſleep after
a hearty meal, ſoon reconciled us to the practice
of the country; and we all indulged in a *fieſta*, (or
afternoon's nap) and enjoyed it I believe full as
much as the moſt voluptuous Spaniard in the
capital.

Accompanied by our new friends, we were introduced in the evening to the family of Senr
Cotappas, a Spaniſh merchant of conſiderable
eminence. A deſcription of this gentleman's
manſion will ſerve to convey an idea of the manner in which all the houſes in the city of St.
Jago are built. This, like moſt of the principal
habitations, formed a quadrangle, incloſing an
open area, or court-yard, of about thirty yards
ſquare, one ſide of which is a dead wall that runs
parallel to the ſtreet; and, as none of the houſes
are more than one ſtory in height, this wall totally obſcures every appearance of the buildings
within. The entrance into the fore-court from
the ſtreet, was through a gateway in this wall,
to which the houſe fronted, occupying the oppoſite ſide, whilſt the wings, or two remaining ſides

of

of the fquare to the right and left, were, as is
moft commonly the cafe, divided into offices for
fervants, and fleeping apartments. Sen[r] Cotappas's houfe confifted of an anti-chamber, a large
kind of dining-parlour, and bed-chamber. All
the rooms were very fpacious, the principal one
meafured about fixty feet in length, twenty-five
feet in breadth, and I fhould think the height of
it was about equal to the breadth. This room
was fuperbly, or rather finely, furnifhed; from
the ceiling were fufpended two glafs luftres, or
chandeliers; and on the walls were fome paint-
ings, the fubjects of which were taken from the
facred writings; at each end of the room were
large folding doors. The company we here met
were divided into two parties; the ladies were
feated on cufhions on one fide of the room, and
the gentlemen were fitting oppofite to them on
chairs, amongft whom we were inftantly furnifhed with feats. The entertainments of the
evening confifted in a concert and ball, in both
of which the ladies had the principal fhare, and
feemed to take great pleafure in excelling in both
the accomplifhments of mufic and dancing. The
whole of the concert was performed by the ladies; one led the band on the piano-forte, whilft
the others filled up the accompaniments on vio-
lins, flutes, and the harp; the whole was extremely

·tremely well conducted, and afforded us a mu-
fical treat, to which we had been long intire
ftrangers.

We fhould have been extremely happy to
have aviled ourfelves of the preffing intreaties of
Sen Cotappas to join with the ladies in dancing,
but as their country dances appeared to be very
difficult, and as no one amongft us could recollect the figures of any of thofe we had been accuftomed to in England, we were under the
mortification of acknowledging our ignorance,
and declining the intended civility of the mafter
of the houfe.   From this difappointment in the
pleafures of the evening we were, however, in
fome meafure relieved, by fome of the ladies,
who had retired from the dance, fending us a
meffage, requefting we would join their party on
the cufhions; with this we inftantly complied,
and confidered ourfelves greatly indebted for this
mark of condefcenfion, as it was departing from
the eftablifhed rules of their fociety on fuch occafions.   The generality of the ladies in St. Jago
are not wanting in perfonal charms, and moft of
thofe we had the pleafure of meeting this evening might rather be confidered handfome than
otherways; they are, in general, brunettes, with
expreffive black eyes, and regular features; but a
want of that neatnefs, which is fo much valued
amongft Englifhmen, and fo much the pride of

VOL. VI.   U   my

my fair countrywomen, was confpicuous in many
particulars, efpecially in the total neglect of their
teeth, which are fuffered to become intolerably
dirty.   This inattention was not only in a very
high degree offenfive, but it appeared to us in-
compatible with the pains that feemed to have
been taken in the decoration of their perfons;
for, at this affembly, they were all fuperbly
dreffed, agreeably to the fafhion of the country.
The moft fingular part of their drefs was a fort
of bell-hooped petticoat, that reached from the
waift to juft below the knees, though fome of
them did not wear them quite fo low; immediately beneath this external part of their drefs
appeared the under linen garment, the bottom
of which, as well as the taffels of their garters,
was fringed with gold lace.

The general deportment of the ladies was
lively and unreferved; and they very obligingly
loft no opportunity of relieving us from every
little embarraffment, to which the difadvantages
we laboured under, in not underftanding their
language, frequently expofed us; and I verily
believe that there were few occafions, during the
whole of our voyage, in which our want of
knowledge of the Spanifh language was more
fincerely regretted; as it deprived us of the pleafure of enjoying the lively fallies of wit which we
had reafon to believe occurred very often in the
female

female circles, by the laughter and applaufe that their converfation fo frequently occafioned. This was certainly an evidence of their natural ingenuity, though it did not amount to a proof of their minds having been duly cultivated; and it is not without concern that I ftate, from the teftimony of their own countrymen, that the education of the female part of the fociety in St. Jago is fo fcandaloufly neglected, as to confine the knowledge of reading and writing to a few of the ladies only. Some of them had the goodnefs to give us their names in writing, that we might the more eafily difcover and learn the true pronunciation of them; thefe were always written in large letters; but I do not mean from this circumftance, or from our having received but few of their names, to infer, that the education of the fex is as much confined as was reprefented to us; yet the circumftance of their being totally unacquainted with any other language than the dialect of the Spanifh fpoken at St. Jago, evinced that their education had been very little attended to.

Excepting the inftances which are unhappily to be found amongft the fex in England, the female part of the fociety poffefs a characteriftic delicacy of fentiment and expreffion; but here fuch a degree of levity is obfervable in the conduct of the ladies, not only in their converfation, but in dancing and on other occafions, as to give

a ftranger

a ſtranger, and particularly an Engliſhman, no reaſon to entertain a very exalted opinion of their virtue, but rather to impreſs him with notions prejudicial to the female character. I muſt, however, in juſtice to all thoſe ladies with whom I had the honour of being acquainted, and they were very many, beg leave to ſtate, that I diſcovered nothing that could impeach the fidelity of the married women, nor attaint the character of the ſingle ladies; notwithſtanding that the manners and cuſtoms of the country in which they live ſanction a freedom of ſpeech, and a familiarity of behaviour, that tended, in our opinion, to abridge the ſex of a portion of that reſpect from the men, of which, as Engliſhmen, we did not like to ſee them deprived. To them we were indebted for the moſt civil and obliging attention that can be imagined during our reſidence in the capital; their doors were always open to receive us; their houſes were in a manner our homes; their entertainments were formed for the ſole purpoſe of affording us amuſement; and no endeavour was omitted that could, in any way, contribute to the pleaſure we received in mixing with their ſociety. Nor were we leſs indebted to all thoſe gentlemen to whom we became known, who exerciſed the utmoſt of their powers to render our ſtay at St. Jago agreeable, by ſhewing us every thing worthy of our notice, and by communicating every information

formation that was either ufeful or entertaining. We were under particular obligations to Don Ramon de Rofas and Captain Caffada, for their unremitted attention, and goodnefs in introducing us to all the refpectable families refiding in St. Jago.

The time that we remained in the capital of Chili, paffed nearly in the fame manner as I have already defcribed, without the occurrence of any incidents to require a particular relation; for this reafon I fhall pafs over the feveral pleafant engagements we had in the different families during our refidence in this hofpitable place, and proceed to give fome account of the public buildings in the city, and to detail fuch other information as we were enabled to collect, and which, probably, may not be unacceptable to my readers. In doing this, however, I fhall not pledge myfelf for the authenticity of the facts, nor the precifion of the circumftances I am about to relate, becaufe I was not fufficiently acquainted with the Spanifh language to put the queftions that I wifhed to have refolved in a proper way myfelf, nor to acquire the information I fought for, in fo correct a manner as is defirable in inquiries of this nature: in addition to this difadvantage, I found it almoft impoffible, on a variety of occafions, to make our interpreters tranflate our queftions on fubjects on which they

U 3   were

were not converfant, fo as to obtain, from thofe
who were able to reply to them, fatisfactory an-
fwers.

The city of St. Jago, including the detached
houfes, or fuburbs, I fhould fuppofe, cannot be
lefs than three or four miles in circumference;
but this is only by eftimation, as I did not con-
verfe with any one who could, or did, anfwer me
this queftion; but as the ftreets run at right angles to each other, and fome of them are little
fhort of a mile in length, this computation cannot
be very erroneous. The city is well fupplied with
water from the river Mapocho, which has its
fource in the mountains, at fome diftance from
the capital, and is made to branch off in fuch a
manner, on its approaching the town, as to pafs
through the principal ftreets. This, in a hot climate, cannot but be fuppofed a very great luxury,
and as conducing extremely to the health of the
inhabitants; but the fame want of cleanlinefs
that pervades the infides of the houfes, here manifefted itfelf in the open air, and inftead of this
ftream becoming the means by which the ftreets
might have been kept conftantly fweet, it is rendered a moft infufferable nuifance, by the prodigious quantity of filth which is emptied into
it from the houfes. As no care was taken that
a fufficiency of water fhould be brought down
to carry the foil and naftinefs away, nor to remove

move it in places where it formed obftructions
to the current, and produced the moft offenfive
exhalations; and as the ftreets, which are narrow,
are partially paved with fmall ftones in the middle, and with only a few flag-ftones for foot paf-
fengers on the fides, our walking about the town
was, from thefe circumftances, rendered very unpleafant.

The river before mentioned, from whence the
city is fupplied with water, overflowed its banks,
in the month of June, 1783, in confequence of
an inundation, and rufhed down towards St. Jago,
with fuch impetuous fury, that it demolifhed
almoft all the dams that defended the country,
did confiderable damage in the town, and filled
every individual with fear and confternation left
a fecond inundation fhould fucceed; in which
cafe, from the extremely defencelefs ftate in
which thefe torrents had left the city, there was
great reafon to apprehend that not a fingle edifice
would be left ftanding in the capital. The prefent Captain-General gave immediate orders that
plans fhould be made by the moft able and experienced engineers and architects, for the purpofe of replacing a wall, or dam, that had principally defended the city from the river, and
which had been deftroyed, at this time, by the
inundating force of its waters; but, notwithftanding that the defign he had in view was for

U 4   the

the protection of St. Jago and the furrounding country, and to infure the fafety, interefts, and comforts of the inhabitants, yet, a popular party was made againft him, as in the inftance of the new road, which he projected, and is now carrying into execution between this place and Valparaifo, and, after experiencing much fatigue, perplexity, and expence, it was not until the month of January, 1792, that he effected his purpofe fo far, as to begin the excavation for the new wall, or dam, againft the fide of the river, This will long remain a monument of his patriotifm and perfeverance, and he has now the gratification of hearing many of thofe who had before oppofed the undertaking, acknowledge this valuable defign to be an effectual protection againft any future danger.

The wall is faid to have a foundation fourteen feet below, and to rife as many feet above, the furface of the water; it appeared to be a very ftrong work, well executed, and capable of refifting any force or weight of water that may come againft it. It not only affords complete fecurity to the town, but ferves as an agreeable walk for the recreation of the inhabitants. On the fide next to the water a parapet wall is raifed, fufficiently high to prevent any accident in walking; it is about a quarter of a mile in length, and, at convenient diftances, flights of eafy and commodious

dious ftairs are judicioufly placed to afcend the
wall, from whence a commanding view is obtained of St. Jago and the adjacent country.   The
whole is built with brick and lime-mortar, and,
on the firft ftone being laid, an obelifk, in imitation of that in St. Peter's fquare, and many
others in Rome, was erected, on the pedeftal of
which is the following infcription, in Spanifh :

D. O. M.

In the reign of Charles the Fourth :

and

During the Government of this Kingdom,

by

Don Ambrofio Higgins

de

Vallenar ;

Who ordered

Thefe dams to be conftructed

in the year

1792.

There were two very fumptuous fabrics erecting in St. Jago, which, when finifhed, as I was
informed by the Prefident, would be unequalled
in New Spain ; the one is the Caffa de Moneda,
or the *money-houfe*, and the other is the cathedral.

At the diftance of about five quadras* to the
fouthward of the principal fquare, is erecting, by

* Thirty-fix quadras make a mile.

order

order of his Catholic Majesty, the Money-House, or Mint. The situation is open, healthy, and well chosen for this extensive and spacious building, which appeared to be constructing upon the plan of the public offices contained within Somerset-House in London, though the structure is by no means equal to that edifice, either in size or magnificence. It is intended for the residence of all the officers and people belonging to the Mint. The apartments for the former are large and commodious, and the rooms for the latter are very convenient. To these are added a sort of hospital for the sick, and a chapel for divine service. Large places are to be fitted up for the reception of the materials and implements used in assaying the precious metals, and separating them from the ore. The walls are built with large bricks, and the cement, or mortar, is from lime procured by the calcination of shells. Part of the inside was plastered with a most delicate white substance, that had the appearance of being very durable. Most of the iron-work used in the building, and such as is necessary for the implements, &c. used in the business of coining, is imported from Old Spain. Patterns for the balconies, balusters, and rails, have been transmitted from St. Jago to Biscay, which have been sent back in iron, most perfectly and satisfactorily executed. All the wood made use of in this fabric

bric is oak, excepting for the doors and windows, which are made of cyprefs. The principal front is to the north, and is about one hundred and fifty yards in length. Befides the door, or grand entrance, which is adorned with eight columns, there are eighteen inferior windows, and eighteen fuperior balconies. The two other fronts look to the eaft and to the weft, and are each of them one hundred and feventy-eight yards in length; thefe are decorated in the fame manner as the principal front, with pillars and balconies, between which are various efcutcheons, with devices alluding to the purpofe for which the building is erected. The court-yard is forty-five yards fquare, the whole adorned with columns, architrave, frize and cornice, which extend round the court at fome little diftance from the building. The principal entrance leads into a fpacious faloon; on the right are the apartments deftined for the fuperintendent, and on the left are to be thofe of the auditor; befide thefe, in the other two fronts, are the public offices, the hall for drawing bills, the office for weighing gold and filver, the treafury, auditory, chapel, hofpital, &c. &c. After paffing through the court-yard towards the fmelting-offices, we entered a paffage, fourteen yards wide, which led round all the workfhops and offices of labour: the whole of the edifice is of the Doric order, and the

diftribution

diftribution of the offices and apartments appeared to have been well confidered and judicioufly appropriated. The communications were
likewife commodious, and well concerted to facilitate the bufinefs between one office and another, and the whole together was a ftructure
well deferving our attention.

The architect is profeffor Don Joa. Joefca,
difciple of the lieutenant general Don Francifco
Savatini, firft architect to his Catholic Majefty.
Don Joefca undertook to finifh and complete
this building for feven hundred thoufand dollars,
and the Captain-General, impreffed with a juft
idea of the ufe and importance of fuch an eftablifhment, was induced to give his confent to the
undertaking, as the calculation of the expence
bore, in his eftimation, no proportion to the advantages it would afterwards infure, or the convenience it would afford. The architect, however, feems to have been greatly miftaken in the
money which he ftated the building would coft,
as the Prefident affured me, he was clearly of
opinion, that it would require a million and an
half of dollars to be expended on the edifice before it could be completely finifhed.

There is a fmall hill, about twelve quadras
diftant from the principal fquare, in the grounds
belonging to the religious of the Dominican
order, which is called St. Domingo. This hill
                                        contains

contains a quarry of freeſtone, of a whitiſh colour, ſoft, and eaſily worked by the chiſſel. The vicinity of this hill to the city, and the facility with which the ſtones were to be procured from the quarry, induced the Biſhop Don Juan Gonzales de Melgarego to begin the laborious undertaking of building a cathedral; for which purpoſe he gave forty-three thouſand dollars towards its erection, and laid the firſt ſtone of the edifice on the firſt day of July, 1748. At this time there was not an artiſt in the kingdom of Chili to whoſe ability a work of this deſcription could be entruſted, for which reaſon no particular plan was adhered to, and the architecture ſeems to be a medley of whatever occurred to the perſons who ſuperintended its conſtruction. The principal front is to the eaſt; that ſide which communicates with the epiſcopal palace is to the ſouth, and the north front runs parallel to the ſtreet. The length of the building is about one hundred and twenty yards, its breadth is not leſs than thirty-five, and the height of the middle aiſle is eighteen yards.

It was not until after thirty years were expired, that application was made to Madrid for a ſkilful profeſſional perſon to ſuperintend the completion of this edifice. In the year 1775, Don Joeſca, the architect employed in building the money-houſe, was appointed to this office, and, fortunately,

nately, at this time, the principal front was not begun. The plans he drew were submitted to the then prelate, Don Manuel de Alday; and, on the first day of March, in the year 1780, this artist took upon himself the charge of the building, which, at this time, wanted only five arches to reach the line of the principal front; the elevation of which, I was given to understand, is a close imitation of St. John de Lateran, and according to the designs of the famous Barromini. There are three doors in this side, embellished with columns of the Ionic order; within is a handsome staircase, that leads to light and elegant towers, which add greatly to the beautiful appearance of this front. The cathedral contains ten altars, and, though they appeared to have been constructed without regard to any rule of proportion, yet they are well worthy of attention. The columns and pilasters of each are an excellent imitation of jasper; these are green, the pedestals are red, the cornices yellow, the bases and capitals are gilt, and the whole together produces a very good effect. The colour of the stone, with which this edifice is built, resembles that of the Portland stone of England; but whether it is of the same durability, or not, time only will determine. The workmanship of the mason appeared to us to be ill executed, as few of the edges of the stones were so neatly wrought

as

as to fit with exactnefs.   Spires and other church ornaments, we were given to underftand, were intended to be erected, but the time when the building would be finifhed was not afcertained; the priefts, however, faid mafs in one part of it, which was fufficiently completed for that purpofe.

A very large church is alfo conftructing, under the direction of the fame architect; this ftructure is built with bricks, its front is of the Doric order, with two large towers, in which confiderable knowledge of beauty and proportion feems to have been difplayed.   The infide of this church is of the Ionic order, it contains three aifles and feven chapels.

The gaols of the city having fallen into decay fome years ago, and becoming infecure for the confinement of prifoners, a large building, of the Tufcan order, was erected, and appropriated to this purpofe.   This ftructure has rather a magnificent appearance and the diftribution of the cells and apartments it contains feems to have been made with confiderable judgment.   The centre of the building is occupied by a grand tower, in which is the city clock; and the bell, which ftrikes the retreat at nine o'clock; after which, it becomes the duty of the watchmen to fecure all perfons of fufpicious appearance, or fuch as are found in the ftreets with unlawful weapons.

Befide

Befide thefe public buildings, about half a quadra from the principal fquare is a houfe belonging to Sen' Don Jofe Ramirez de Saldana, perpetual regidor of St. Jago, and one of its moft opulent citizens. The porch, which is in the centre of the principal front of this manfion, is decorated with Doric columns, and many pillars of the fame order are with confiderable tafte arranged on each fide of it. This building is reputed to be the only one in the city in which the rules of architecture have been ftrictly obferved; and, on that account, it is highly efteemed by thofe of the inhabitants who have any knowledge of the art, or tafte for regular compofitions.

A very good houfe was erecting about fix quadras from the fquare before mentioned, after a defign of Inigo Jones, as a country refidence for Sen' Don Jofe Antonio Aldunate, the Provifor General of this bifhoprick, who is juftly extolled for his polifhed manners and literary abilities.

At the diftance of fourteen quadras from the fame fquare a chapel was building, at the expence of the friars belonging to the order of St. Francifco. The Doric prevails in the external compofition of this edifice, but within the pillars are of the Corinthian order. It contains ten diftinct chapels, is dedicated to our Lady of Carmin, and is called the Little Convent.

Having given fome account of the moft confpicuous

fpicuous public and other buildings, that were either finifhed or erecting, in St. Jago, I fhall now proceed to ftate fuch information refpecting the population and commerce of this city as I was enabled to procure.

St. Jago, the capital of Chili, is ftated to have been founded on the 12th of February, 1541. This city is the refidence of the Prefident, who is Captain-General of the whole kingdom, and Governor and prefiding Judge of the audience chamber, or court of juftice.   It is faid to contain thirty thoufand five hundred inhabitants; and, if my eftimation of its extent be not very incorrect, it muft be confidered as populous.   The fubordinate cities in this great kingdom are, Coquimbo, Chillan, Conception, and Valdivia; and the principal towns are Valparaifo, Capiapo, Vallenar, St. Francifco de Borja, St. Raphael de la Rofa, La Ligua, Quillota, Los Andes, Melipilla, St. Jofeph, Anconcagua, St. Ferdinand, Curico, Talca, Linares, Nueva, Bilboa, Caugeres, and others of lefs importance.

The kingdom of Chili is ftated to extend, in a northern and fouthern direction, from the uninhabited parts of Atacama, which divides it from the vice-royalty of Peru, to the ftraits of Magellan; and, in a weftern and eaftern direction, from the ocean to the foot of the Cordilleras, which divides it from the vice-royalty of Buenos

Vol. VI.   X   Ayres;

Ayres; but I cannot help being of opinion, that the kingdom of Chili does not extend further south than the southern extremity of the isles de Chiloe, as I should confider the American coast, to the southward of those islands, to be that of Patagonia. It is divided into two bishopricks, or provinces, St. Jago and Conception, each of which are under the immediate care and direction of an Intendant; Brigadier Don Francisco La Mata Linares has the charge of the latter; and the further title of Chief Intendant of the province of St. Jago is added to the rest of the posts of honour and places of emolument enjoyed by the present Captain-General Don Ambrosio Higgins de Vallenar; the value of whose appointments amount, annually, to thirty thousand dollars, whilst those of Don La Mata Linares do not exceed ten thousand dollars. These provinces are each subdivided into small districts, which originally were known by the name of Corregimientos, but are now called Subdelegaciones.

There is about a million of specie coined at St. Jago every year, which is the fund from whence the salaries of the state officers, the military establishment, and other incidental expences of the government, are defrayed. The army consists of a battalion of infantry in Conception; two squadrons of horse, one company of dragoons, and two of artillery. The cavalry of

of this country are all well mounted, and extremely expert horfemen, and were they as fkil-
ful in the ufe of fire-arms as they are in the management of the fword and the lance, they would
not be inferior to any troops of this defcription in
Europe.   I was given to underftand, that in cafe
of an attack upon Valparaifo, the principal fea-
port of the kingdom, an army of eight thoufand
men, confifting of cavalry and militia, could there
be affembled for its defence in twenty-fours hours.

The country, to the fouthward of the river
Biobio, in the province of Conception, is inhabited by a nation of very fierce Indians, who
formerly committed great depredations on the
frontiers under the Spanifh authority, and lived
in a continual ftate of hoftility with their civilized neighbours; but, in confequence of the humane, judicious, and political arrangements which
have been made, from time to time, by Don
Ambrofio Higgins, the number of the turbulent
fpirits has been much reduced, and the natives
now ceafe to be regarded with any apprehenfion
by the Spaniards.   In the diftrict which they
occupy, I was given to underftand, there were
ten thoufand warriors, a robuft and hardy race of
men; but fo far had the wife adminiftration of
the prefent Captain-General fucceeded, in fub-
duing the natural ferocity of thefe Indians, and
in bringing them over to fupport the authority

X 2   and

and interefts of the crown of Spain ; that Don
Ambrofio did not entertain the leaft doubt of
their co-operating with the forces of His Catholic Majefty, fhould it be neceffary to call them
forth againft the invafion of a foreign enemy.

Independently of the warfare which thefe
people had, for many years, carried on againft
the Spaniards, they were fubject to continual in-
furrections and internal commotions amongft
themfelves. During the time that Don Ambrofio had the chief military command on this
frontier, he happily fucceeded in terminating the
feuds which had fo long prevailed amongft the
feveral tribes compofing this great nation, and
had introduced amongft the ferocious inhabitants
of this country, a fpirit of induftry, and a defire
to excel each other in the cultivation of the
ground, the breeding of cattle, and other peaceful arts ; but upon his being promoted to the
elevated fituation which he now fills, with fo
much honor to himfelf, and benefit to the country, he was under the neceffity of leaving the
guardianfhip of thefe children of nature, and of
repairing to the capital. Soon after his departure from the frontiers, frefh animofities, and
new caufes for jealoufy, arofe amongft the different tribes, which ended in a war, that was fu-
rioufly carried on by all parties. Their peaceful
and domeftic occupations no longer engaged their
attention,

attention, and their agriculture and breeding of
cattle, which had become the fources from whence
they were enabled to derive many comforts,
were abandoned and totally neglected. Don Ambrofio, with the fame warmth of heart and intereft for the happinefs and profperity of the Indians, which, during his refidence amongft them,
had produced fo valuable an effect on their tem-
pers and difpofitions, reprefented to the Court of
Madrid the commotions that continued to exift
amongft the Auraucan and other tribes on that
frontier ; and, at the fame time, propofed fuch
meafures as, in his opinion, were moft likely to
reconcile the differences, and eftablifh a perma-
nently good underftanding between the contending chiefs of the four Butalmapus, which are the
four diftricts into which this nation of Indians is
divided.

In confequence of this reprefentation, and the
meafures recommended by the Captain-General,
he was directed by the Spanifh court to repair to
the camp of Negrete, and there to hold a convocation, for the purpofe of hearing and redreffing
thofe grievances which were ftated by the feveral
chiefs to be the caufes of all their difcontents:
and, as the preliminary fpeech of the Prefident,
on this occafion, tends greatly to exhibit the natural character and general difpofition of thefe
people, I have been tempted to infert a tranfla-

X 3   tion

tion of it from the Indian language, under the impreffion that, to thofe of my readers who may be curious in tracing the gradations of the human character, from a favage up to a civilized ftate, it may not be unacceptable.

" The fpeech of Field-Marfhal Don Ambrofio Higgins de Vallenar, Prefident, Governor, and Captain-General of the kingdom of Chili, to the Auraucan and other Indian nations, met in convocation in the camp of Negrete, on the 4th day of March, 1793.

" Chiefs, my antient and honourable friends ; full of joy and fatisfaction that I now meet upon this happy ground of Negrete, as formerly on that of Longuilmo, the great chiefs and principal leaders of the four Butalmapus, into which this valuable country is divided, that ftretches from the fouth of this great river Biobio to the outer parts of the moft fouthern continent, and from the Cordilleras to the great ocean ; I falute you all with joy, and with the utmoft fincerity of my heart. I am ordered by the king, my mafter, to falute you in His Majefty's name, and to congratulate you on the felicity of this aufpicious day, which, through my mediation, on account of the love I bear you all, has reftored the ineftimable bleffings of peace to the four Butalmapus.

" With

" With the utmoft precifion and difpatch, I
have taken care to remove every obftacle that impeded the attainment of this moft welcome object. I have alfo been indefatigable in difpofing
the minds of thofe to peace who were reftlefs and
prone to revenge, or to take great umbrage on
little occafions; and I have been unwearied in
all the conferences I have had with the feveral
chiefs, fince my arrival at the fort of Angels, and
in this encampment, during the time that I have
waited for the arrival of thofe more diftant leaders, who are now collected with the other mem-
bers of this affembly. I have patiently and fully
examined the complaints of fome, and heard the
excufes of others, on the diftreffing fubject of
your diffentions, your animofities, and your wars,
fo that nothing now remains for me to learn of
all their direful caufes. To-day, however, the
fun fhines bright, and I fee, with heart-felt joy,
that on my once again drawing nigh unto you,
a friendly difpofition appears in all, to terminate
the unhappy differences which long, too long,
have fubfifted amongft you; and I perceive that
you are prepared, once more, to unite in thofe
facred bonds of peace, in the full enjoyment of
which I left you, on my feparation from you,
and departure for St. Jago. I rejoice that you
all wifh to bury, under the fod of this encampment, all your animofities, heart-burnings, dif-

putes, and differences; and may the prefent meeting be a commencement of perpetual felicity to all the children of man who refide in the countries that extend from Biobio to Chiloe.

"Recollect your fituation, O my friends, when I was appointed by His Majefty to the military command of this frontier, and deftined to fit down among you. There are many amongft you, who can remember the miferable ftate in which I found the whole country; it was deftroyed on both fides the river, it was defolate and laid wafte, and all its inhabitants were fuffering the dreadful calamities of unceafing furious wars, brought on by their own intemperance and unruly paffions; many of whom were obliged to retire, with their women and children, to the mountains, and were reduced at laft to the neceffity of feeding on their faithful dogs that followed them! The great chiefs and Indians of the Butalmapus were witnefs of thefe things. Before I left you, however, (on his Majefty being gracioufly pleafed to promote me to the prefidency of the kingdom) your houfes were rebuilt, your fields fmiled with a yellow harveft, and your paftures were richly decorated with the herds of your cattle. Your women provided you with comfortable garments; the high-minded and unruly young men obeyed the voice of the chiefs; and none of thofe exceffes were practifed, which,

since

fince my departure, have exceeded the cruelties
and profligacy of your antient barbarifm; to
which you would probably have altogether returned, had it not been for the zeal of your Commander General, who reported your proceedings
to me, and happily fufpended, until I fhould be
fent amongft you, the fatal effects of your dif-
cords.

"I do not, however, wifh to fupprefs the
merit to which you have a juft claim, or to con-
ceal, that, in the midft of all thefe difturbances,
you rigoroufly obferved the promifes you made
me in Longuilmo. The Spanifh fettlements,
fituated on the fouthern fide of this great river,
have been, by you, moft fcrupuloufly refpected,
their perfons have been held facred, their cattle
have not been difturbed, and in no one circumftance have you broken the faith and goodwill
which you pledged yourfelves to maintain. Of
all this have I been made acquainted, from time
to time, by the feveral commanders on the frontier; and for this honourable part of your conduct I give you all due thanks. What I then
promifed I likewife have ftrictly performed; I
have recommended the four Butalmapus to the
protection of the king; I have fupplicated him
to continue to them his paternal affiftance; and
His Majefty, with that greatnefs of foul, and
piety

piety of heart, which so eminently distinguish his
royal character, has been pleased to order, that
you shall be supported and protected so long as
you may deserve the blessings of his favor, by
adhering to the good, separating yourselves from
the bad, and evincing, by the general tenor of
your conduct, your subordination and obedience."

The humanity, good sense, patience, and per-
severance, of the Captain General, very conspi-
cuously appear upon this occasion; and it is not
less pleasing to observe, that, even amongst these
untaught nations of the earth, their political engagements are scrupulously fulfilled; and that
the distresses consequent on intestine warfare,
have not the power to make them violate their
treaties, or to break those promises which they
solemnly pledge themselves to perform.

The territorial possessions of such of the Indians as have submitted to the authority, and
placed themselves under the protection, of the
Spanish crown, have been all confirmed to them
by treaty; to be used, cultivated, or disposed of,
agreeably to their own wishes or determinations;
and, as an incitement to their future industry
and repose, I was informed by Don Ambrosio,
that he had purchased from them a large tract
of land, which he had divided, and laid out ad-
vantageously, for the purposes of agriculture and
breeding

breeding cattle; and had left it in their poffeffion, under the direction of proper perfons to fee.
his defigns carried into effect.

Whilft we were under the hofpitable roof of
the Prefident, I had an opportunity of feeing a
chief and fix of the Indians, who had come to
the palace to pay an annual vifit of refpect to the
Captain General. Thefe people were of a mid-
dling ftature, they were ftout and well made, of
regular features, and not unlike the North-Weft
American Indians; they were dreffed after the
Spanifh fafhion of the country; but if an opinion
can be correctly formed of the tribe they belong
to from fo fmall a fample, they would, by no
means, anfwer the expectations I had formed of
their prowefs and military character. Thefe Indians were accompanied by a Spanifh gentleman,
who refides amongft them in one of their villages, and is called Captain of Indians; and I
underftood, that to each tribe an officer, of
fimilar rank, is attached, who prefides over their
interefts, correfponds with the Captain-General,
and, on all occafions, acts as their advifer and
interpreter.

The exterior commerce of the kingdom is
principally carried on from the fea-ports of Conception, Coquimbo, and Valparaifo; but the latter has the greateft fhare of trade, arifing from
its central fituation, and its vicinity to the capital:

tal: the diſtance from St. Jago was formerly thirty leagues; but it will be decreaſed, when the new line of road is complèted, to twenty-two leagues.   From St. Jago, to the top of the firſt hill towards Valparaiſo, a diſtance of about ſix leagues, the road is finiſhed; between the foot of the hill and the city there are three bridges built with bricks over three ſwampy places, which before were frequently almoſt impaſſable, and in many other parts, where the road is depreſſed, it is paved acroſs, to give a free courſe to the rain waters, and at the ſame time, to prevent any damage from their paſſing over the looſe materials of which the road is compoſed.   This extent of road is now become the general reſort of the inhabitants, either for walking, riding on horſeback or in carriages; and the valuable character who firſt projected it, whenever the multiplicity of his buſineſs would allow him to take any recreation of this nature, is conſtantly attended thither by a numerous company of the inhabitants, and on ſuch occaſions he derives a conſiderable degree of ſatisfaction in proving how eaſily he can travel up the firſt hill from St. Jago in his coach, with the aſſiſtance of four mules only.

The meaſured diſtance between St. Jago and Buenos Ayres I could not learn, but I underſtood

that

that the poft travels from thence to the capital of Chili in twenty days; and that the country, from Buenos Ayres until it reaches the foot of the Cordilleras, which run in a northern and fouthern direction, and pafs to the eaftward of St. Jago, is one intire defert, without trees or any other fort of vegetation; and that it is fo completely a level plain, that even a hillock does not appear on its furface.

The neareft filver mine to St. Jago is at the diftance of about feven leagues, and the neareft gold mine is to the north-eaft of the city, at the diftance of about thirty leagues.

The value and importance of this rich country to Old Spain is fully exhibited in the feveral ordinances, rules and directions, which, from time to time, have been iffued to the Intendants of the provinces, and enforced by the fupreme council of the Indies, at the exprefs command of His Catholic Majefty. Thefe are comprehended under diftinct titles, or heads, as they have reference, or apply to, the ecclefiaftical or civil government of the kingdom. The principal obfervances are thofe refpecting the tenths and contributions for the endowment of the churches, and the fupport of the religious orders; the collection of the public revenues, the appropriation of the royal eftates, the adminiftration of juftice, the regulation

tion of the internal police, and the delegation of powers and authority in the event of foreign wars or domeſtic inſurrections.

I was ſo fortunate as to obtain a tranſlation of moſt of theſe rules by which the archbiſhops and chief officers of ſtate regulate their conduct; and as it does not appear to me, that I can ſhew the rigid attention which is, and has ever been, paid by the Spaniſh court to the intereſts of theſe wealthy eſtabliſhments, ſo well, as by quoting ſome few of the royal commands, I have extracted three for this purpoſe.

" Number 150.

" By the Bull of Alexander the VIth, dated the 16th of November, 1501, and confirmed ſince by ſucceſſive ſupreme pontiffs, the TENTHS OF THE INDIES belong to my royal crown, and half of a year's ſalary on the benefices conferred by me; with full dominion, abſolute and irrevocable, to aſſiſt the churches with a ſufficient ſum annually, for the decorous maintenance of the divine law, and for a competent ſalary to the prelates and other miniſters of the holy goſpel, who ſerve at the altar. In virtue of which, the fundamental diſpoſition of the ritual has been promulgated, that theſe objects may be duly fulfilled. My crown remains under the obligation of ſupplying, at the expence of the reſt of the rents of its patrimony, the ſum deficient to which

theſe

thefe, annually, may not amount, for the endow-
ments and other holy purpofes; and therefore it
is incumbent upon all thofe acting under my
royal authority to be watchful over, to have good
difcretion in the adminiftration of the decimal
productions, and to divide them amongft the
parties interefted, with due exactnefs and inte-
grity, that the holy churches, parifhes, and hofpitals, under the immediate fovereign protection,
may not feel any injury or wrong, nor my royal
exchequer be called upon for its pledged refponfibility. I therefore command, that the royal
officers do affift at all the public fales and accounts of the tenths, and that they likewife attend
to the erections and repairs of the churches, and
duly examine the expence of each, and that they
ultimately prevent all frauds and impofitions, to
the end that the participants may have their
right, and that my royal eftates may not be
charged with any refponfibility for deficiencies.
Having confidered that the new eftablifhment
and fyftem of intendancies may offer doubts, on
the method propofed for carrying the feveral regulations into effect, I have thought proper, con-
formably to the true fpirit of the laws already in
being, to annex the following commands, for the
purpofe of facilitating the new arrangement, and
to infure the moft exact execution of all the matters it contains."

Here

Here follow directions for the calling of meetings, and a lift of the officers commanded to attend them, with a great number of rules for fecuring to the government a due adminiftration of their feveral functions. And it will be feen, by the following extracts, that the happinefs of the people, the prefervation of good order, and the improvement of the country, are objects not lefs regarded by the Spanifh monarchy, than the eftablifhment of its religious perfuafion, or profiting by the immenfe wealth which South America is capable of yielding.

" Confiding in the care and attention which has been manifefted by the Intendants of provinces, I command that they do, by means of themfelves, or fubaltern judges, gain a thorough knowledge of the lives, inclinations, and cuftoms of the people fubject to their government; that they chaftife the lazy, and thofe of bad intentions, who, far from fupporting the good order and police of their refpective towns, caufe inquietudes and fcandal, disfiguring, with their vices and lazinefs, the good face of things, defpifing the laws, and perverting the defigns of thofe amongft them who are virtuoufly difpofed. They are not, however, under colour or pretext of their authority, to be inquifitive, or to meddle in the life, genius, private purfuits, or domeftic concerns of individuals, nor to take cognizance

of

of reports or uneftablifhed accufations that cannot influence the good example of the people, nor difturb the tranquillity of the public government.

" For the due adminiftration of juftice, and the circumftances which have already been provided for by the foregoing articles, it appears, that whatever may conduce to the happinefs or profperity of my vaffals, fhould and ought to be diligently attended to and obferved by the magiftrates and officers of police. For this efpecial purpofe, I order that the Intendants do procure, from engineers of the greateft renown and abilities, topographical maps of their refpective provinces, in which are to be diftinguifhed their boundaries, mountains, woods, rivers, lagoons, and all other matters worthy of note; and to this end, the engineers fo employed are to execute their commiffions with all the promptitude, exactnefs, and punctuality of expreffion poffible; they are to become acquainted with the temperature and qualities of the feveral foils, and of the natural productions, not only of the animal and vegetable, but of the mineral, kingdoms; of the mountains, valleys, paftures, and meadows; of the rivers which are capable of being widened, made navigable, and ultimately to communicate with the ocean; the expence of fuch undertakings, and the benefits that would refult to my

fubjects

fubjects from carrying fuch works into effect.
They are to make themfelves perfectly fatisfied in
what places new channels or aqueducts might be
made, which would be ufeful for the watering
of the lands under cultivation, and for the purpofe of reducing labour by the erection of mills.
To report the ftate of the bridges; pointing out
thofe which require repairing, and the paffes over
which additional ones ought to be thrown.
What roads can be amended, improved or fhortened; what protection or guards are neceffary for
their fecurity.   In what parts are growing timbers, ufeful for fhip-building in the provinces, or
valuable in the European arfenals; they are to
certify and report upon the induftry and commerce of the diftricts; the fea-ports capable of
fheltering veffels, which from their fituation and
utility ought to be kept open, and fuch as are
prejudicial that had better be fhut.   The Intendants will alfo inform themfelves of the means
of bettering the condition of my people, by aug-
menting their comforts, and by conferving the
happinefs and profperity of my dominions. With
thefe objects before them, they are to take efpecial care, that, in the towns or villages, within
their refpective provinces, they do not allow of
vagabonds without deftination, nor people without inclination to work ; but that they make
the fturdy, and of competent age to manage
arms,

arms, inlift into my royal regiments, engage in my marine fervice, or on board fhips of commerce; or elfe that they order fuch perfons to be employed in the repairing or erecting fuch public works, as fhall be judged moft proper, according to the circumftances of each individual's cafe. Should any fuch perfons be unfit for work, and mendicants by profeffion, they fhall be taken up, put into hofpitals, and there be employed each according to his ftrength; but if it can be proved that they are reftlefs unquiet fubjects of no refponfibility, and bad character, the penalties eftablifhed by the laws of the Indies are to be inflicted, and fuch vagrants are to be fent to hard labour in the mines, or to the Prefidios."

Thefe ordinances are alfo the firft of a great number of regulations, which follow for the encouragement of induftry, the cultivation of the furface, and extending the mineral property of thefe kingdoms, in which is difplayed no lefs zeal and concern for the profperity and comforts of all the inhabitants, whether of Spanifh extraction or the native Indians, than for the intereft which the Spanifh crown poffeffes in fecuring to itfelf the monopoly of this valuable part of its extenfive empire. For as the kingdom of Chili cannot but be regarded as capable of producing great wealth, as well from its furface as from its inex-

hauftible

hauftible mineral productions, it may fairly be esteemed as one of the richeft territories belonging to his Catholic Majefty. In order, however, to promote the growth of the greateft quantity of corn and number of cattle, encouragement fhould be given to the lower orders of the people to become induftrious, and to prefer the pleafant purfuits of cultivation to that fupine and inactive way of life to which they have been fo long accuftomed; for if a fpirit of induftry were generally diffufed amongft them, and due rewards held out for working the valuable metals, the prefent habits of indolence would probably be overcome; and as there does not exift any phyfical impediment to exertion, either from climate or any local circumftance, it is not poffible to afcertain what might be the fum of the return from the productive labour of this highly favored country, when fuch labour fhould be properly directed to the feveral fources of its latent wealth. The influence of the ecclefiaftical orders over the minds of the people, and the preference which is given by them, and the generality of the inhabitants, to an ufelefs unworthy life of lazinefs and begging, will continue to operate againft any change; and it is much to be apprehended, that nothing but a totally new modification of their prefent fcheme of fociety, can infure to the indi-

viduals,

viduals, and to the ftate under which they are protected, the advantages that a reform in their political fyftem promifes in future to beftow.

Confidering that the time we had now been abfent from the veffels had been of fufficient length to accomplifh the feveral fervices I had left to be performed, preparations were made for our return to Valparaifo; and after expreffing our moft grateful acknowledgments for the weighty obligations conferred upon us, by the unremitting attention to our prefent comforts, and anxious concern for our future welfare, which on every occafion had been exhibited by his Excellency the Prefident, and making offer of our beft thanks for the friendly, hofpitable, and polite entertainment we had received from other individuals during our ftay in the capital, we took our leave, and proceeded from St. Jago toward Valparaifo. The fame mode of conveyance as that to which we had before reforted, was now adopted for our journey back to the fea coaft. Neither the road we had to retrace, nor the country on either fide of it, prefented any thing in the courfe of our travelling worthy of remark, that I have not fufficiently noticed on our journey to St. Jago, excepting that the road, which from the loofenefs of the materials with which it is formed, had fuffered, as I fufpected it would, very much by the defcending waters

from

from the mountains, and in many places it was greatly injured by the rain that had fallen during our refidence at St. Jago; and it is much to be feared, unlefs fome means can be adopted for its fecurity, and to prevent the injurious effects of the defcending torrents, that this valuable defign projected by Don Ambrofio will in a great meafure be defeated.

On our arrival at Valparaifo I found moft of our bufinefs in a ftate of forwardnefs; the mainmaft had been repaired and was got on board, but on our attempting to rig the main-yard, on Thurfday the 16th, it was found to be rotten nearly half through in the middle of it, and in this ftate intirely unfit for fervice; this was a mortification I did dot expect to have met with, and as there was no poffibility of procuring at this place a fpar of fufficient fize to replace it, the only means we had of repairing the defect was by making a temporary yard out of a fpare maintopmaft, with the addition of the yard arms of the yard which was decayed, and which I was extremely forry to obferve were by no means in a perfectly found condition.

Although a further detention at Valparaifo was now unavoidable, yet that was not the only circumftance which produced me concern on this occafion; for this additional difafter was of fo ferious a nature, that when I came to reflect

on

on the difabled condition of our main-maft, and
that our main-yard would be in *three pieces*, I
was under the cruel neceffity of giving up all
further thoughts of recommencing our furvey of
the coaft to the fouthward of the iflands of Chiloe,
and to determine on making the beft of our way
from this port round cape Horn to St. Helena.
I could not, however, avoid having fome apprehenfion left our very crippled ftate fhould prove
infufficient to preferve the veffel amidft the boifterous feas we had to encounter in this paffage,
notwithftanding that every precaution within
our power that could be devifed was reforted to,
for the purpofe of making the maft and yard as
fecure as poffible.

The regret I felt in being thus compelled to
abandon the examination of this almoft unknown,
yet interefting part of the coaft, is not to be defcribed; becaufe I had anxioufly hoped that I
fhould have been enabled by our re-equipment at
Valparaifo, to have carried into effect the whole
of the commiffion which his Majefty had been
pleafed to entruft to my execution; but under
all the circumftances of both the veffels' condition, I did not confider myfelf warranted to indulge my inclinations at the hazard of his Majefty's fhips under my command, and at the rifk
of the lives of fo many valuable men, who had
cheerfully endured the fatigues of our former fur-

Y 4   vey,

vcy, and who, after fo long an abfence from their native country were intitled, in a peculiar manner, to every care and protection that were in my power, for the purpofe of infuring them a fafe return to their families and friends.

The main-yard was fent on fhore, and the carpenters were immediately employed upon it; but as I could not flatter myfelf that it would be in a ftate fit to be received again on board in lefs than eight or ten days, I employed this interval in examining the ftores and provifions with which we had been fupplied, in attending to the repairs of the veffels, vifiting the obfervatory on fhore, and making fome obfervations on the harbour and town of Valparaifo; with which, and the refult of the aftronomical and nautical obfervations made during our ftay, 1 fhall conclude this chapter.

The caulkers were yet bufy on the decks and other parts of the Difcovery, and the rigging demanded infinitely more repair than I had fuppofed it would have required, owing to the very rotten and decayed ftate of almoft every rope on board. In thefe effential fervices the artificers were conftantly engaged, whilft the reft of the crew were employed in procuring a full fupply of water, and fuch a ftock of flour and other provifions as I confidered would be neceffary until we fhould arrive at St. Helena.

Ships

Ships deftined to the port of Valparaifo, fhould endeavour during the fummer months to make the coaft well to the fouthward of the bay, in order that a fair wind may be infured for entering the bay. The foutherly winds, which in general extend from 60 to 70 leagues from the coaft, moftly prevail until the month of May; and from the middle of that month during all the months of June, July, Auguft, and September, I was given to underftand the prevailing winds were from the north. Thefe winds are commonly attended with great quantities of rain, and very foggy weather, but they do not often blow with much violence. As foon as the wind returns to the fouthward the dry feafon commences, and fo it continues with little variation during the remainder of the year. Thefe winds, however, frequently blow very ftrong, fo as to break veffels adrift, though well fecured by anchors on the fhore, near to the town of Valparaifo. Within four or five leagues of the point of Angels, which is the weftern point of the bay, is a low rocky point, near to which is a detached high barren rock; thefe points lie from each other S. 51 W. and N. 51 E. To the northward of the above low rocky point, are fome fcattered rocks, that lie about two miles from the point, and about a fourth of that difdiftance from the fhore, and to the northward of

thefe

thefe rocks is a fandy bay, on the north eaft-fide
of which is a houfe. In this bay I was led to
believe that anchorage might be had, though
the fituation is certainly very much expofed.
The point of Angels, (off which are alfo fome
rocks lying very near to it,) may be approached
by failing at the diftance of half a league from
the fhore, and as foon as the point is paffed the
town of Valparaifo is inftantly difcovered. About
feven miles to the north-eaft from this point is a
clufter of rocks lying at fome diftance from the
fhore, on which the fea breaks violently; but
we had no opportunity of afcertaining their fituation with any degree of precifion. The bay is
about four miles wide, and about a mile deep;
apparently free from any fort of danger; but as
it is greatly expofed to the northerly winds, the
trading veffels conftantly moor with two good
anchors and cables in that direction, and with
other cables faft to anchors on fhore, in five or
fix fathoms water, foft fandy bottom, near to the
euftom-houfe; by which means it is expected
that the officers of the revenue may be enabled
to prevent any contraband trade, by vigilantly
attending to their duty in the day time, and by
a rowing guard during the night. The depth
of the water gradually increafes with the diftance
from the fhore to 35 fathoms, and the bottom
becomes more tenacious. In the depth of fixteen

teen fathoms, in which we took our ftation, it was a very ftiff clay. Here we moored a cable each way to the northward and to the fouthward, the point of Angels bearing by compafs N. 35 W., the fort in the town N. 86 W., the redoubt on the hills S. 5 E., the church at Almandrel S. 65 E., the eaft fort N. 83 E., the eaft point of the bay N. 57 E., and the neareft fhore S. 7 W., a cable's length diftant.

On the top of a hill, on the eaft fide of the bay, is an open or barbet battery, lately erected with ftone and brick, and capable of mounting ten guns; this battery commands all that fide of the bay, the beach, and the village of Almandrel. On the fummit of another hill is a ftone redoubt, of a circular form, with eleven embrafures; thefe command the beach and village of Almandrel to the eaftward, the bay to the northward, and the town and harbour of Valparaifo to the north-weftward. Although this fortification was in a moft neglected and ruinous condition, we were given to underftand, that the principal magazine was inclofed within its ruins. The largeft and moft confiderable fortification is in the middle of the town, within which is the refidence of the governor. It is fituated on a fmall eminence, one fide of which is open to the fea, and is fepa-rated from it only by a very narrow pafs. The height of the lower wall, which is ftrong, and

well

well built with mafonry, is about fifteen feet to
the embrafures ; of which, there are fix that front
the fea, two face the ftreet to the eaftward, and
two look into the market-place to the weftward.
The upper part of the hill is furrounded by another ftrong ftone wall, about ten feet in height,
and half way up the hill ; a third wall croffes it,
which fhews three embrafures to the fea, immediately over the fort, and the governor's houfe
below. At the place where this wall terminates,
which is near the fummit of the eminence, the
fide of the hill falls perpendicularly down into a
deep gully, by which the fort is encompaffed, and
which might be the means of rendering this fortification unaffailable, and a place that might
long be maintained, were it not for other hills
within mufket-fhot, which command every part
of it. The fpace inclofed by the lower wall is
about four hundred yards in length, and in fome
places about one hundred in breadth ; here are
the barracks for the troops, and at the upper end
is a building, in which a court is held, for the
regulation of the police of the town. A door, in
that fide of the wall which faces the market-
place, is the only entrance, and leads by a wind-
ing ftair-cafe to different parts of the fortification.
There is one other fortification, about half a mile
from the fort, fituated on the weft fide of the
bay, at the foot of a high hill, and but little ele-

vated

vated above the level of the fea. This fhews a face of five embrafures to the eaft, and in that direction commands the weft fide of the bay; three embrafures to the northward are fo difpofed, as to be able to open upon any veffel the inftant fhe paffes round the point of Angels; whilft two others to the fouthward, command the fhips lying in the harbour or the bay. We computed that thefe feveral places contained about feventy pieces of cannon, many of which were without proper carriages, and fome were lying difmounted under the walls of the lower battery in the town.

From the weftern fort fome rocks extend into the bay, and the bottom is too foul for veffels of any force to anchor nearer to this fortification than about four hundred yards; but they may approach and anchor in a very eligible fituation, within about two hundred and fifty yards of the garrifon or principal fortrefs; and neither of thefe places, in their prefent fituation, would be able to refift a well directed fire even from two or three frigates.

It appeared to us to be very extraordinary, that, under the exifting circumftances of Europe, and during a war between Spain and France, the fortifications at Valparaifo fhould remain in fuch a neglected, ruinous, and defencelefs ftate, and that no meafures fhould either be reforted to, or appear to be in contemplation, for putting them

into

into a more refpectable condition : efpecially as
it is from this port that the kingdom of Peru
principally depends for its fupply of grain ; in
return for which fugar, tobacco, indigo, and fpirits, are imported into Valparaifo. Tar we found
not only to be a very fcarce but dear article, as
the expence of the quantity which was neceffary
for our new cables, was nearly equal to that of
the workmanfhip and raw material of which
they were compofed.

The houfes in Valparaifo, on account of the
earthquakes which frequently happen in South
America, like thofe at St. Jago, confift of the
ground floor only ; the walls are built with mud,
and plaftered over with a preparation of lime ;
they are convenient, well adapted to the climate,
and are in general handfomely furnifhed. In the
town and in the village of Almandrel there are
fix churches, within the diocefe of the archbifhop
of St. Jago, but under the direction of a vicar,
who refides at Valparaifo, and is amenable for
his conduct to the archbifhop. The town and
its neighbourhood are under the jurifdiction of
the governor, who receives his appointment, with
a falary of four thoufand dollars per annum, from
the king of Spain ; but he is neverthelefs under
the immediate orders and controul of the Captain-General. All civil and military caufes are
heard at St. Jago. Capital offences are feldom
committed ;

committed; a man was found guilty on a charge of felony, and hanged about three years before our arrival, a punifhment that, we underftood, was feldom known to be inflicted.

I could not afcertain what were the revenues of the king of Spain on the exports and imports at Valparaifo, the collection of which is an important part of the governor's bufinefs : nor was I able to fatisfy myfelf as to the amount of dollars which are annually fent from this port to Old Spain, but I had reafon to believe it was not lefs than one million and an half. The quantity of gold and filver coined into money at Mexico is prodigious ; I obtained an account of the coinage there, from the 1ft of January to the 31ft of December, 1793, by which it appeared that the total amount was as under :

In gold.	In filver.	Total.
pefos, or hard dollars,	pefos,	pefos,
884,262.	23,428,680.	24,312,942.

This, however, was the greateft quantity of fpecie ever known in one year to have been coined in the money-houfe at Mexico.

In anfwer to a letter, which by the defire of Senr Don Ambrofio I had written to him, acquainting him with our fafe return to Valparaifo. he had the goodnefs to exprefs the moft ferious concern for the decayed ftate in which I had the misfortune to find our main-yard; and in a let-

ter

ter to Governor Alava, he directed him to ufe his utmoft endeavours to fupply us with a new one, by fcarching amongft the traders in the port; and ftating that he had underftood from the fhip Mercury, a main-yard for the Difcovery might be procured. Although we could not on this occafion avail ourfelves of the Prefident's kind attention, yet thefe letters breathed not only fo much friendlinefs and anxiety for the prefervation of our little community, but exhibited fuch earneft folicitude for the fafe return of our expedition to Europe, left the important information we had to communicate fhould be loft to the world, that I cannot refift noticing this circumftance as an additional proof of the goodnefs and magnanimity of his Excellency the Prefident of Chili.

The wind, which had been generally in the fouthern quarter, blowing gently, and fubfiding into a calm towards the evening of Thurfday the 23d, changed to the north, and was accompanied by a very heavy rain, that continued with little intermiffion all the following day, Friday the 24th. After the rain ceafed, the weather was cloudy and unpleafant until Saturday the 25th, when the wind returned to the S. S. W. with fair and moderate weather, notwithftanding which the Chatham's fmall bower cable, in confequence of its being completely worn out, broke, which obliged Mr. Puget to warp the

vefel

veffel nearer in fhore, and to moor to an anchor
on the beach ; after which the anchor, with the
remainder of the cable, was recovered. On the
Monday following, (the 27th) the carpenters
finifhed the main yard, and it was got on board
and rigged, the caulkers had nearly finifhed their
bufinefs ; and, as I was very anxious to take our
departure, I gave orders for the obfervatory and
inftruments to be received on board, and the veffels to be made ready for proceeding to fea the
firft favourable opportunity. It was not, however,
until Tuefday the 5th of May, that we had fufficient wind to encourage us to unmoor, which
was done about fix in the morning, with a light
breeze of wind from the fouth ; but this foon
dying away, we returned nearly to the place from
whence we had come. On a frefh breeze fpringing up, about noon the next day, from the fouth
and S. by W., we unmoored, and after faluting
the fort with thirteen guns, (which were equally
returned) and taking our leave of Governor
Alava, and the reft of our very hofpitable friends
at Valparaifo, we made fail from the port, in
company with the Chatham and a Spanifh brig
and fchooner.

The trade of this port is carried on in fhips
from two hundred and fifty to feven hundred
tons burthen ; in which is annually exported to
Lima about fifteen thoufand tons of wheat and

wheat-flour, large quantities of fmall cordage, dried falt fifh, and apples, pears, and peaches, in great abundance. All goods imported are landed on a foft fandy bank lying before the cuftom-houfe, and from thence carried into the ware-houfes, or removed to diftant parts of the country on the backs of mules ; by which conveyance the articles for exportation are in like manner brought down to the fhore. Moft kinds of vegetables, and a great variety of fruits, as well thofe of the northern parts of Europe, as thofe common in the tropical countries, were here procured in great plenty, were all excellent of their kinds, and were very cheap: the water was extremely good, though the mode of obtaining it was fomewhat tedious, as we were obliged to fill our cafks from pipes of a fmall bore, through which it was conducted from the refervoir in the market-place down to the water-fide. Although there was no perceptible current in the bay, the rife and fall of the tide was evidently about three feet.

Aftronomical and Nautical Obfervations.

On the 27th of March, 1795, Kendall's chronometer, according to the laft rate, fhewed the longitude to be   —   287° 46′ 50″
Arnold's No. 14,   —   287 53 35
Ditto   176,   —   286 30 50

The

The true longitude, as afcertained at the obfervatory, by 39 fets of lunar diftances, was 288° 28' 52".

By which it appears, that Kendall's chronometer was 42' 2"; Arnold's No. 14, 35' 17"; and Arnold's No. 176, 1° 58' 2" to the weftward of true longitude.

By equal altitudes, taken on the 26th of April, 1795, Kendall's chronometer was found to be faft of mean time at Greenwich, on that day at noon,   —   — 10^h 59' 23" 15'''

And to be gaining on mean
    time, per day, at the rate of   29 34
Arnold's No. 14, faft of mean
    time, at Greenwich, ditto   6 15 10 15
And to be gaining on mean
    time, per day, at the rate of   25 10
Arnold's No. 176, faft of mean
    time at Greenwich, ditto   13 28 33 15
And to be gaining on mean
    time, per day, at the rate of   58 57
The latitude of the obferva-
tory, by twelve meridional
altitudes of the fun was found
to be   —   33° 1' 30"

The variation, by two different compaffes, and by fix fets of obfervations on each, 14° 49' eaftwardly.

The

The vertical inclination of the magnetic needle :

Marked end North,	face East,	44° 57'
Ditto,	ditto,	West,	44	40
Ditto,	South,	face East,	43	45
Ditto,	ditto,	West,	43	40

Mean inclination of the marine dipping needle,   —   44 15

CHAP.

CHAPTER VI.

Quit Valparaifo—Proceed to the Southward—Pafs to the South of Cape Horn—Ufelefs Search for the Ifla Grande—Part Company with the Chatham— Arrive at St. Helena—Join the Chatham there— Leave St. Helena—Capture the Macafhar Dutch Eaft Indiaman—Proceed to the Northward— Difcover a Number of Veffels under Convoy of his Majefty's Ship Sceptre—Join the Convoy, and proceed with it to the Shannon—Difcovery proceeds from thence to the River Thames.—Aftronomical and Nautical Obfervations.

HAVING appointed with Mr. Puget our next rendezvous to be at St. Helena, with a frefh breeze varying between S. S. W. and S. by E. we left the bay of Valparaifo, Thurfday the 7th, and paffed the point of Angels, fteering to the W. S. W. The weather was clear and pleafant, yet a heavy fwell from the S. S. W. indicated very boifterous weather in that quarter; the wind, however, continued to blow a gentle gale from the fouth-weftern quarter, with which we made confiderable progrefs. From the extremely worn-out ftate of our fails, the foretop-

Z 3   maft

maft ftayfail fplit, and on a furvey of our other fails and cables, we were under the neceffity of condemning a beft bower cable, a foretopfail, and maintopmaft ftayfail, which were unbent, and replaced by others that could fcarcely be confidered to be in a much more ferviceable condition.

The obferved latitude, on Saturday the 9th, was found to be 33° 21' fouth, the longitude, by Arnold's chronometer, No. 14, 282° 5'; by No. 176, 282° 36' 30"; by Kendall's, 282° 6' 45"; and by the dead reckoning 282° 25'; the variation of the compafs 13° 15' eaftwardly. The wind veered for a few hours to the north-weft, and blew a frefh gale, with which we directed our courfe towards the S. S. E. until it returned to its former fouth-weftern quarter, when we fhould have been able to have made great progrefs to the fouthward, had we not been repeatedly under the neceffity of fhortening fail for the Chatham, which was far a-ftern. Some petrels, and fix or eight pintados, were feen about the fhip on Tuefday the 12th, and two days afterwards feveral large albatroffes were obferved at no great diftance. The weather continued to be pleafant until Tuefday the 19th, when the wind changed to the north-weft, and was attended by very thick difagreeable fqually weather. Our courfe was again directed to the S. S. E.; and

and it gave me concern that we were not able
to avail ourselves of this favourable wind, without
risking a separation from the Chatham; for,
notwithstanding the additional quantity of ballast
which she had taken on board at Valparaiso, she
did not appear to be improved in her sailing:
about noon her signal was made with a gun to
make more sail.   The wind increased from the
west and north-west, accompanied by very heavy
squalls of hail and rain; in the course of the
night false fires were burnt, to denote our situation to our consort, and on the next forenoon,
Wednesday the 20th, her signal was again repeated to make more sail; but as we still kept
increasing our distance from her, about noon I
ordered the mainsail to be hauled up, and a reef
taken in each of the topsails.   At this time, in
latitude 50° 50' south; longitude, by Arnold's
No. 14, 280° 33' 45"; by No. 176, 281° 32' 30";
by Kendall's chronometer 280° 25' 30"; and
by the dead reckoning 281° 11'; the variation
of the compass was observed to be 17° eastwardly; and cape Noir to bear by compass, according to the Spanish charts, S. 42 E. distant
100 leagues, but, by our calculations, it bore by
compass S. 46 E. and was at the distance of 107
leagues.

   As we proceeded to the southward the weather
gradually changed for the worse, and the wind,

which,

which, with little interruption, had hitherto been
agreeable to our wifhes, now became turbulent,
and blew at times in very heavy fqualls; in one
of thefe, about three o'clock on Friday afternoon,
the 22nd, we carried away the maintopfail fheet:
this obliged us to take in the fail; on the gale
increafing the foretopfail was furled; and, fearful
of any ferious accident, either to our main-yard
or maft, I directed the mainfail to be taken in,
and the topgallant yards and mafts to be ftruck,
in order that the weak parts might be ftrained
as little as could be helped; about an hour afterwards, the ftarboard bumkin was alfo carried
away, and the wind at W. S. W. continued to
blow with great violence until midnight, when
it became fomewhat more moderate, and we
were enabled to fet the mainfail and ftorm ftayfail. Falfe fires were burnt during the night as
fignals to the Chatham. Towards the next
morning, Saturday the 23d, after lowering the
topfails, and hauling up the mainfail, in a heavy
fquall of wind and hail, we wore the fhip,
to wait for our confort. In the afternoon, although the wind continued nearly from the fame
quarter, the weather became more moderate, and
we were able to get up our topgallant yards and
mafts, and to make the beft of our way towards
the fouth, directing our courfe as much to the
eaftward as the variation of the wind would permit.

mit. This favourable change, however, was not
of long duration; for, in the afternoon of Monday the 25th, on the wind veering to the weft
and north-weft, we were obliged to clofe-reef the
fore and maintopfails, and take in the mizen-
topfail. The gale continued to increafe with fo
much violence, that, by feven o'clock on Tuefday morning the 26th, we were under the neceffity of handing our topfails, and getting the
topgallant yards and mafts down upon deck, to
relieve the mafts, and to make the fhip as fnug
as poffible. The obferved latitude at noon was
56° 4' fouth ; by Arnold's chronometer No. 14,
the longitude appeared to be 285° 52' 30"; by
No. 176, 286° 55' ; by Kendall's, 285° 32' 15";
and by the dead reckoning 286° 33'. According
to obfervations which had been procured in the
two preceding days, it appeared, that the dead
reckoning had erred thirteen miles in latitude,
and twenty-five miles in longitude, the fhip
having been fet fo far to the north-eaftward.
The wind continued to blow very hard, varying
between W. S. W. and W. N. W. until towards
the evening, when it altered to the eaft, and
E. S. E. brought with it a very heavy fall of
fnow, and blew fo violently, that our weather
maintopfail fheet gave way, and obliged us to
take in the fail. About fix o'clock the next
morning, Wednefday the 27th, the wind again
changed

changed to the S. W. and the weather became
fufficiently moderate and clear to get up the
topgallant yards and mafts, and to fet our reefed
topfails. Notwithftanding that at this time there
was no great preffure on any part of the rigging,
fo extremely rotten and decayed were our principal ropes and fails, that our ftarboard maintopfail fheet broke, the gib-boom fnapped fhort off
about the middle, and the wind fplit the mizen-
topfail. Juft before nine o'clock in the forenoon,
an ifland was feen bearing by compafs N. 15 W.
which at firft we fuppofed to be Diego Ramirez;
but as that is reprefented by former navigators to
be a fingle ifland in the latitude of 56° 38' fouth,
longitude 291° 34'; as the land in fight foon put
on the appearance of being much broken; as we
had foundings about two in the afternoon at the
diftance of three leagues in the depth of eighty
fathoms, in the latitude of 56° 28' fouth, longitude 291° 23'; and as captain Cook had paffed
between the iflands of St. Ildefonfo and Tierra
del Fuego, in the latitude of 55° 53' fouth, longitude 290° 19'; I had every reafon to believe
that we had been miftaken, and that the land we
had feen at nine o'clock was St. Ildefonfo's ifles,
which at this time bore by compafs W. S. W.
the wind was lefs boifterous on the fucceeding
day, Thurfday the 28th, but the weather continued to be unpleafant, being very dark and
gloomy,

gloomy, with frequent heavy fhowers of fnow. About eleven o'clock at night, in a fquall of hail, rain, and fnow, the maintopfail was fplit and was replaced by another, which although whole and the beft we had, was in a very unferviceable condition.

Notwithftanding the fnow continued to fall fo very heavily that no obfervation for the latitude could be procured, yet by four double altitudes of the fun taken by two perfons with different inftruments, the latitude was found to be 56° 57'; the longitude carried on by the dead reckoning, and corrected by Arnold's chronometer No. 14, appeared to be 293° 39', and the variation of the compafs 23° eaftwardly.

Confidering that we were now fufficiently advanced to the fouthward to avoid any inconvenience or interruption from the iflands which lie off cape Horn, I determined to fhape fuch a courfe to the north-eaftward, as we proceeded in our route to St. Helena, as might afford me an opportunity of feeing and determining the fituation of the Ifla Grande, the fouthern point of which is ftated to be in latitude 45° 30', longitude 313° 20'. On Friday the 30th we were again vifited by ftrong gales and heavy fqualls of wind from the weft and north-weftern points, which frequently reduced us to our courfes; as we proceeded towards the north-eaft, the latitude

by

by an indifferent obfervation appeared to be 55°
28′, and the longitude at noon brought forward
by Arnold's chronometer No. 14, was according
to the dead reckoning 299° 9′.

On Monday the 1ſt of June, about ſix in the
morning, I ordered the foretopſail to be taken in,
for the purpoſe of allowing the Chatham to come
up with us, as ſhe was at this time far aſtern.
At day-light the next morning, Tueſday the 2d,
ſhe was in ſight from the main top, but not from
the deck.

Our latitude on Thurſday the 4th, by the
dead reckoning ſince the preceding day being
46° 16′, and the longitude brought forward by
Arnold's chronometer No. 14, 310° 8′, it was
reaſonable to conclude, as we had a freſh breeze
from the weſt and ſouth-weſt, that we were approaching very rapidly towards Iſla Grande; and
as I was very ſolicitous to examine the ſpace allotted to this iſland, I continued our courſe to the
northward, that we might fall into its parallel
ſome leagues to the weſtward of the ſpot aſſigned
to it; but in the afternoon we were again viſited
by a very furious ſtorm at firſt from the N. W.
but ſoon afterwards from the S. W. which
obliged us to ſteer to the eaſtward, under the
foreſail and cloſe-reefed maintopſail on the cap,
in order that we might keep a-head of the ſea
which ran exceſſively high, and broke with great
violence.

violence. Under this reduced canvas, we outfailed the Chatham fo much as to lofe fight of
her. The fouth-weft gale continued to blow
very hard until the morning of Friday the 5th,
when it moderated, and was attended by clear,
though feverely cold weather. We now ftood to
the northward, and had the pleafure of rejoining
the Chatham. At noon our obferved latitude
was 45° 30', longitude 312° 55'; in this fituation
I efteemed it to be a very fortunate circumftance
that the weather was fine, and that the horizon
was remarkably clear in all directions, excepting
between the N. W. and N. N. E.; fo that had
any land been above our horizon within the dif-
ftance of from ten to twenty leagues, it could not
poffibly have efcaped our notice. Between the
limits above-mentioned, which were occupied by
a haze, we could alfo have difcerned land at the
diftance of five or fix leagues, and as it was in
this direction that we were fteering, we muft
have fallen in with it had any land there exifted.
From noon our courfe was directed about N. by
E. which by eight in the evening brought us to
the latitude of 45° 4', longitude 313° 3'. The
weather continued to be tolerably clear until the
clofe of the day, but no land was within our view,
nor had we the leaft reafon, from any of the
ufual indications, to fuppofe ourfelves in its vicinity,

nity, excepting from the numbers of birds that
were about the ship.

According to Mr. Arrowsmith's comprehensive
chart, (in which the Isla Grande is placed agreeably to the assigned situation of it by Mr. Dalrymple,) the track of Dr. Halley is laid down
about a degree to the westward of our path, cros-
sing the same parallel in the longitude of about /
311° 55'; from which circumstance it is probable, that those on board that vessel saw a considerable distance to the westward of them.
Since therefore we met with no drift wood, nor
other circumstance to indicate our vicinity to
land; (and had any been near to us in a west-
wardly direction, such indications most likely
would, from the generally prevailing winds, have
been presented to us), I was led to conclude,
that if M. La Roche did discover any island
under the parallel of 45° south, that such land
must have been to the eastward of our track.
Under this persuasion, about eight in the evening, as the weather had the appearance of being
fine, and the wind moderate, I steered a more
eastwardly course, with an intention, should the
winds prove favorable, to continue about this
parallel until we should pass the meridian of
South Georgia; from the shores of which island,
it is with great reason supposed, La Roche steered

to

to the north, and in that route fell in with Ifla Grande. It is therefore moft likely, that if any fuch land has exiftence, it will be found not very far remote from the fituation affigned to it by Captain Cook; a fact I was very defirous of eftablifhing.

On Saturday morning the 6th, although the weather was gloomy, with the wind from the north, yet it admitted of our feeing diftinctly all around us for feveral leagues; we continued to ftand to the eaftward until four in the afternoon, when in latitude 45° 6' fouth, longitude 314° 50', the atmofphere was fufficiently clear to have feen any land above our horizon at the diftance of fix or eight leagues, but nothing of the kind was within the limits of our view. The wind now veered to the N. E. and eaft, and blew a frefh gale, with which we ftood to the north, in the night to the S. E. and on the following morning, Sunday the 7th, to the S. S. E. and fouth, fo that we were unable to regain the parallel of 45° without employing more time than I had now to appropriate to this examination; being, from the extremely bad condition of our fails and rigging very anxious to loofe no opportunity of making the beft of our way to St. Helena; and for this reafon I gave up all further thought of fearching for Ifla Grande, and continued our courfe towards the N. N. E.

This

This fhort inveftigation, however, will ferve to fhew that no fuch ifland exifts in or about the latitude of 45° fouth, between the meridians 312° and 315° 20′ of eaft longitude; and that, as I have already mentioned, Dr. Halley moft likely determined the fame point, namely, that there was no fuch ifland, a degree further to the weftward.

At midnight the Chatham was clofe along fide of us, but by four o'clock the next morning, Monday the 8th, fhe was nearly out of fight aftern of the Difcovery, our mainfail and top-gallant-fails were therefore taken in to wait for her nearer approach; at day-light fhe was feen about three miles aftern, and having at this time a fteady frefh gale with fair weather, her fignal was made to make more fail, and repeated with a gun feveral times until about ten o'clock, when the Chatham neither making fail, nor ex-hibiting any reafon indicative of her wanting affiftance, I concluded that fome caufe of no very ferious nature had retarded her progrefs; and juft as we had fet our ftudding fails, I had the plea-fure to fee her employed in the fame bufinefs alfo.

Shortly after noon the wind veered to the S. W. and having increafed our diftance from the Chatham very confiderably, we fhortened fail to wait for her coming up, concluding that

fhe

fhe would foon overtake us under our then reduced quantity of canvas.   In thefe expectations
however we were difappointed; at ten at night
the wind had again frefhened from the N. N. W. ;
we now burnt a falfe fire to denote our fituation
to our confort, but this was not anfwered, and
by two the next morning, Tuefday the 9th, the
wind veered to the weftward, and blew a very
ftrong gale, during which, left we fhould lofe
the Chatham, we hauled up the mainfail and
clofe-reefed the topfails ; but as at day-light fhe
was not in fight from the maft-head, and as I
did not know in what direction to fearch for her,
I could not but confider the inferiority of her
failing had at length completed our feparation,
and in the hope that we fhould meet all well at
St. Helena, our next rendezvous, we made the
beft of our way thither, by continuing our courfe
to the north-eaftward.   The obferved latitude
at noon was 36° 45', longitude according to Arnold's chronometer No. 14, 324° 43', and the
variation of the compafs 6° eaftwardly.   The
wind continued to blow very hard at times, attended by heavy rains, and thick cloudy fqually
weather, in which our fails frequently fplit, and
our topfail-fheets and other effential parts of the
rigging gave way, until Saturday the 20th, when
it became more moderate, and in latitude 34 38'
fouth, longitude 347° 10', brought forward by

Arnold's chronometer No. 14, the ſhip appeared to have been ſet twenty-five miles of latitude towards the north, and thirty-four miles of longitude towards the eaſt of the reckoning.

About half paſt five o'clock on Sunday morning the 21ſt, Richard Jones, one of the ſeamen, unfortunately fell overboard from the main chains and was drowned. The accident had no ſooner happened than a grating was thrown overboard, and the ſhip was inſtantly hove to, for the purpoſe of affording him every aſſiſtance; but this was to no effect, for the poor fellow ſunk immediately, and was never more ſeen. By this melancholy event the ſervice loſt a very able ſeaman, and his comrades a good member of their ſociety. On the following day at noon, Monday the 22d, in latitude 32° 3' ſouth, longitude 351° 15', it appeared that the ſhip was nine miles of latitude to the northward, and twenty-five miles of longitude to the eaſtward of our reckoning; and that the variation of the compaſs by two ſets of azimuths was now 11° 20' weſtwardly. The eaſtwardly variation ſeemed to have ceaſed about the 16th of June, as in latitude 35° 43' ſouth, longitude 232° 5', it had decreaſed to 16', and ſince that period the weſterly variation had been gradually increaſing as we proceeded to the northward.

No circumſtances of importance, or ſuch as

are

are worthy to be recorded, took place, until about two oclock in the afternoon of Thurfday the 2d of July, when after experiencing tolerably plea- fant weather for the preceding ten days, the ifland of St. Helena was difcovered bearing by compafs N. by E.; about eight in the evening we fhortened fail, and hauled our wind on the ftarboard tack, as the ifland now extended by compafs from N. 3 W. to N. 35 W. at the dif- tance of about five leagues; at day-light the next morning, Friday the 3d, we made fail for St. Helena bay, and about fix o'clock we had the happinefs of difcovering the Chatham in the fouth-eaftern quarter. As we were now faft approaching a port from whence it was reafonable to expect that opportunities would frequently occur, dur- ing the time of our re-equipment there, to com- municate with our friends in England, I deemed it expedient that the order fhould be publicly read, which I had received from the Lords of the Admiralty, directing me to demand the log books and journals which had been kept, and the charts, drawings, &c. which had been executed by the officers, petty officers, and gentlemen on board the Difcovery; and directing alfo, that I fhould enjoin them and the whole of the crew not to divulge where they had been, until they fhould have permiffion fo to do: and a copy of this order was fent to Mr. Puget, with my directions to enforce the fame on board the Chatham alfo.

As we approached the bay of St. Helena, I had the mortification to fee a fleet of large ships ftanding out, and apparently bound to the northward. This fleet I confidered to be from the Eaft Indies, and that it was moft probably bound to England, under the protection of which I fhould have been happy to have performed the remainder of our voyage; for we were in no fituation to contend with the enemy's ships of equal force, nor to have efcaped from thofe of fuperior weight of metal. At half paft eight o'clock we anchored in 16 fathoms water, and moored with a cable each way. In the bay of St. Helena we found the Arnifton Eaft Indiaman, and an American bring. After faluting the fort with thirteen guns, which were returned, accompanied by Mr. Puget, I paid my compliments to the governor, and underftood from him, that the fleet of ships which we had feen depart from the ifland as we had approached it in the morning, was, as I had imagined, a fleet of Eaft Indiamen, together with feveral fail of Dutch prizes under the convoy of His Majefty's ship Sceptre, commanded by Captain Effington.

I was received by the governor of St. Helena with his accuftomed politenefs, and having underftood from him that hoftilities had taken

place

place between the Court of London, and the United States of Holland, I sent an officer on board a Dutch East Indiaman which I had perceived to be coming into the bay, and took possession of her as a prize.

The great plenty of excellent refreshments with which we had been supplied during our residence amongst our very hospitable friends at Valparaiso, had not only eradicated every appearance of the scurvy, before our departure from that port, but had so completely re-established the health of every individual on board (myself excepted) that although we had now been fifty-eight days at sea, during which time we had experienced much bad weather, particularly in that part of the passage as we had approached the western coast of Patagonia, and until we had passed round cape Horn and proceeded some distance to the north-eastward; and had also been obliged to make great exertions, and to endure great fatigue, owing to the repeated accidents that had befallen our sails and rigging, and the additional labour at the pumps consequent on the leak in the fore part of the vessel; I had the inexpressible happiness of seeing all my officers and men return to a British settlement, after an absence from England of more than four years and a quarter, perfectly well in health, and with constitutions apparently unimpaired by the extremely

A a 3

tremely laborious fervice in which they had been
fo long employed, and to which without a mur-
mur they had, at all times, and in all weather,
uniformly fubmitted with great zeal and alacrity.

Notwithftanding that I had the additional fatisfaction to hear, from Mr. Puget, that the crew
of the Chatham were now in a convalefcent
ftate, yet I was much concerned to become acquainted that their health, as well as that of the
officers, had fuffered very materially indeed in
their late paffage from Valparaifo. Although,
previoufly to our departure from that port, every
precaution within our power had been taken to
make both veffels as equal as it were poffible to
the tafk which they had to perform at the then
advanced feafon of the year, through fo tempef-
tuous and inhofpitable a region ; yet the fmall-
nefs of the Chatham had made her more liable
to the influence of the bad weather than the
Difcovery, and this will ferve to account for her
progrefs having been fo very frequently interrupted. For fixteen days together Mr. Puget
had been under the neceffity of keeping in the
dead lights, and from the violence of her motion
her decks and fides had become open and fo
leaky, that his people were conftantly in a wet
humid ftate when they retired from the deck, on
which, previoufly to their making cape Horn,
five

five men only in a watch were able to do duty;
the reft being rendered incapable of it by rheu-
matic complaints. Veffels of the Chatham's fize
fhould certainly make choice of the fummer feafon to infure a good paffage round the fouthern
promontory of America; for although the prevailing winds in the winter months of May, June,
and July, may expedite their voyage, yet this advantage is more than counterbalanced by the
fhortnefs of the days, the feverity of the climate,
and the very ftormy weather which is attendant
on this time of the year; this Mr. Puget reprefented as having had the effect of keeping the
Chatham, comparatively fpeaking, almoft under
water during the greater part of the paffage, in
which he ftated, that nothing of importance had
occurred fince the period of our feparation, and
that the reafon why our laft fignals were not anfwered on the night of the 8th of June, was,
that the fupply of falfe fire on board the Chatham
was at that time totally expended. From Mr.
Puget I alfo underftood, that in and about the
latitude affigned to La Roche's ifla Grande, the
Chatham, like the Difcovery, had been vifited
by a great number of birds, which, with fome
fea weed, were the only indications he had noticed of the vicinity of land.

My firft care was to take fuch precautions on our
arrival at St. Helena, as were moft likely to prove

efficacious

efficacious in preferving to the crews of both veffels that ineftimable bleffing, health, of which, on board the Difcovery, we were in fuch complete enjoyment.   For this purpofe fome frefh provifions were procured from the ifland, and occafionally ferved to both fhip's companies, with a plentiful fupply of efculent vegetables; the convalefcents from the Chatham were fent on fhore, and fuch regulations were adopted as appeared to be, in my judgment, moft likely to infure this defirable object; which, at all times, and on all occafions, throughout the voyage, had been a confideration with me of the firft neceffity and higheft importance.

After thefe arrangements were made, the obfervatory, as ufual, was committed to the charge of Mr. Whidbey; and now that the fhip was ftationary, the carpenters were employed in fearching for the leak in the fore part of the veffel, which, at times, during our late paffage from Valparaifo, had greatly increafed our labours, by our efforts to keep the fhip free from the great quantity of water which it admitted.   Notwithftanding that our main yard had, by great care and attention, brought us fafely thus far, yet, as I found it would be poffible to procure a new one at St. Helena, meafures were inftantly taken for replacing it with one, on which we could more fecurely depend; whilft other parts of the crew

crew were employed in the neceffary duties about the fhip, and in obtaining a full fupply of water.

According to our reckoning, this day was *Monday the 6th of July*, but at St. Helena we found it (agreeably to our calculations) to be only Sunday the 5th of July : for, by our having failed round the world, in an eaftern direction, we had, fince our departure from England, gained *one day* ; but as it was now become expedient that we fhould fubfcribe to the eftimation of time, as underftood by Europeans and the reft of the civilized world, to which we were now faft approaching, our former reckoning was abandoned, the day we had gained dropped, and after noon this day, we recommenced *Sunday the 5th of July*.

His Majefty's fhip the Sphinx, commanded by Captain Brifac, arrived on Tuefday, charged with difpatches from Admiral Sir George Keith Elphinftone, (now Lord Keith,) to General Clarke at St. Salvador, on the coaft of Brazil, who, with his army, was waiting at that port, until he fhould receive inftructions from Sir George that might enable him to co-operate with that admiral in the reduction of the cape of Good Hope. A convoy, I underftood, was foon expected to fail from St. Salvador, and as I had reafon to believe the Chatham's re-equipment would not take more than a week, I determined

to

to fend her thither for the purpofe of going with the firft convoy which fhould fail from thence to England, and that I would be content to remain here until fome Britifh veffel of force fhould touch at St. Helena in her way home, or that the next convoy from the Eaft Indies fhould arrive, under the protection of which, I fhould hope fafely to arrive in England in the courfe of the autumn. As the fervice which Captain Brifac had to perform required the utmoft difpatch, our boats, affifted thofe of the Sphinx in recruiting her water, after which, on the following day, Tuefday the 7th, fhe immediately failed for the coaft of Brafil.

Underftanding that our field-pieces would be of ufe to His Majefty's forces on the coaft of Africa, and confidering that the purpofe for which they had originally been put on board the Difcovery was now completely ferved, and that they could not be of the leaft poffible fervice to us in performing the remainder of our voyage to England, I availed myfelf of the Arnifton being engaged to carry troops from St. Helena to the fquadron under Admiral Sir George Keith Elphinftone, to confign, by that conveyance, the four pieces of ordnance, and the remaining parts of the ammunition we had on board, to the commanding officer of the expedition deftined againft the cape of Good Hope; and, on Friday the

the 10th, I was made happy on this occasion to
have it also in my power to assist with our boats
in the embarkation of the troops on board the Arniston.

The leak was soon discovered to be in the
bows of the Discovery, and our carpenters were
immediately employed in using their best endeavours to stop and prevent any further inconvenience from it.

On Sunday morning arrived the Orpheus of
London, commanded by Mr. Bowen, to whom
were entrusted duplicates of those dispatches
from Admiral Sir George Keith Elphinstone,
with which Captain Brisac had failed on the 8th,
with directions to the governor of St. Helena to
use his utmost endeavours to forward them immediately to General Clarke at St. Salvador.
The Chatham at this time being nearly ready
for sea, I considered that it would be furthering
his Majesty's service to charge Mr. Puget with
the care of these duplicate dispatches, with which,
after receiving the following order from me, he
departed for the coast of Brasil the following day,
Monday the 13th.

" Considering it to be expedient, and for the
good of His Majesty's service, that you should
proceed immediately to St. Salvador, in order to
carry some dispatches from Rear Admiral the
Honourable Sir George Keith Elphinstone, to
Major

Major-General Clarke, commander of his Majefty's forces, deftined to act with the faid rear-
admiral; and the faid major-general having
been directed to rendezvous at St. Salvador; you
are hereby required and directed to proceed,
without lofs of time, to the faid port, in order to
deliver the inclofed difpatches accordingly; and,
after having performed that fervice, you will
communicate to the commanding officer of his
Majefty's naval forces at that port, the nature of
the fervice on which you have been employed,
and that you have my directions, after deliver-
ing the faid difpatches, to ufe your utmoft exertions, for the purpofe of immediately proceeding to England, that you may be enabled to
carry into effect fuch further orders as you have
received from me. But fhould you not meet
with any naval officer, fenior to yourfelf, at that
port, you will inform Major-General Clarke,
that I conceive it to be a matter of great moment, that as little detention as poffible fhould
take place to retard your proceeding to England,
as before expreffed. If, before your arrival at the
port of St. Salvador, the faid troops and fquadron
fhould have departed, you are to ufe the utmoft
precaution not to promulgate the caufe which
carried you thither, but having, with all expedition, completed your water, &c. &c. you are
to proceed to England as already directed: and,

as

as it is of the utmoſt importance to prevent theſe orders, diſpatches, and private ſignals, from falling into the hands of the enemy, you are to keep the ſame in a leaden box, in order that they may be thrown into the ſea, in caſe of capture. And that you may avoid, as much as poſſible, falling in with the enemy's cruizers, on your approaching the coaſt of Europe, you will conſider, as circumſtances may point out, of the propriety of proceeding round the north part of Ireland, either to the firſt convenient port on the coaſt of Scotland or England, which you can make; from whence you will immediately repair to the Admiralty office, and there deliver the diſpatches with which you are charged.

" But in the event of your reaching St. Salvador before General Clarke ſhould have arrived, and finding no other Britiſh officer there with whom you may judge it proper to entruſt the diſpatches committed to your care; you are to continue there fourteen days, and after the expiration of that time you are to proceed as herein before directed; for which this ſhall be your order. Dated on board his Majeſty's ſloop Diſcovery, in St. Helena bay, this 12th of July, 1795.

GEORGE VANCOUVER."

To Lieutenant Peter Puget,
commanding His Majeſty's armed tender Chatham."

Previously to Mr. Puget's departure from St. Helena, we were given to understand, by Mr. Bowen, that it had been decreed, by the national assembly of France, that the Discovery and Chatham should pass the seas unmolested by the French cruizers, notwithstanding the existing war between the two countries. This agreeable intelligence induced me to alter the plan which I had formed of waiting at this island for convoy. The East India ships, under the protection of the Sceptre, had not yet been sailed so long from St. Helena, as to divest me intirely of the hope that we might overtake them, before they should have reached those latitudes in which we should be likely to meet with any thing unpleasant from the enemy's ships of force, in consequence of their commanders being unacquainted with the national decree in our favor, or in the event of any new matter having arisen between the powers at war to cause its being revoked. Every effort was therefore now made to expedite our re-equipment; the main yard, by the assistance of the carpenters belonging to the Arniston, was likely to be ready in the course of a day or two, in which time, I had reason to believe, our own artificers would have stopped the leak in the ship's bows; and as I entertained hopes that, soon after this service should be performed, the Discovery would, in all other respects, be fit for

sea,

fea, I determined to fail immediately, and not to wait for the uncertain arrival of any other veffel, which might afford us protection during the remainder of our voyage to England.

The fupply of vegetables which St. Helena afforded us was very ample; but fruits of all kinds were found to be extremely fcarce, owing to the want of rain. So fevere and continued had been the drought for the three preceding years, that moft of the trees, which were not indigenous to the country, had withered and fallen into decay, and amongft the exotics that had died were fix plants of the bread fruit, which had been left by Captain Bligh on his return in the Providence from the iflands in the Pacific Ocean. The lofs of thefe valuable plants was very much regretted, as they appeared to thrive, and it was hoped, would have come to perfection. The herbage had fuffered alfo in the fame proportion, and, in the courfe of the period above mentioned, upwards of fixteen hundred head of cattle had died upon the ifland. The fheep were very lean and poor, and the quantity of frefh provifions that could be obtained was by no means equal to the fupply I could have wifhed to have procured.

On Tuefday the 14th I had the pleafure to behold our new main yard in fuch a ftate of forwardnefs that it would be ready to be got on board and rigged the following day, and I had the

additional

additional fatisfaction of feeing, that by the unremitted attention of the refpective officers who
had the fuperintendance of the feveral fervices
which had become neceffary to be carried into
effect, little elfe now remained to be done than
to prepare the veffel for our departure.

Much of my time, fince our arrival at St.
Helena, had been employed about the concerns
of the Dutch prize Macaffar, and in making the
beft arrangements within my power, to fecure a
fafe paffage for her to England. The fhip was
in a very bad leaky condition, and although we
were able to give her fome repair, yet it was totally out of our power to refit her, and put her in
a proper ftate for fo long a voyage, efpecially as
there was little chance of her reaching any Britifh port before the commencement of the winter.

Having, from long experience been convinced
of the fkill and refources which Lieutenant Johnftone poffeffed, and which, on many trying occafions throughout the voyage, he had eminently
difplayed, I derived great fatisfaction in com-
mitting the charge of the Macaffar to his care.
For this efpecial purpofe he received my directions to quit the Chatham previoufly to her departure for St. Salvador; and in addition to the
people that were to be engaged at St. Helena, to
navigate the prize home, I fpared, from the crew
of the Difcovery, feventeen able feamen, on whofe
exertions

exertions I could with confidence rely, to carry
Mr. Johnſtone's orders, with promptitude, into
effect. With this ſupply of men on whom he
could depend, and with the kind aſſurances which
I received from Governor Brooke, that no aſſiſtance in his power ſhould be wanting in the man-
ning and re-equipment of the prize, I entertained
great hope that, under the protection of the firſt
convoy that ſhould arrive at St. Helena bound
to England, little danger was to be apprehended
of the Macaſſar's ſafe arrival, in ſome port of
Great Britain.

In the bay of St. Helena, on the 4th of July,
the chronometers ſhewed the following longitudes:

Arnold's No. 14,	–	354°	1′	35″
Ditto, 176,	∹	355	20	5
Kendall's,	–	352	35	5
The true longitude,		354	11	0

By which it appeared that Arnold's chronometer, No. 14, was 9′ 25″, and Kendall's 1° 35′ 25″
to the weſtward, and that Arnold's No. 176
was 1° 9′ 5″ to the eaſtward of the true longitude: and, by altitudes taken on this day, the 14th
of July, Arnold's No. 14 was found at noon to be
ſlow of mean time

At Greenwich,   –   17^h 10′ 42″ 50‴

And to be gaining on mean
time, per day, at the rate of   24   50

Arnold's No. 176, flow of
mean time at Greenwich,   9^h 18' 29" 50'"
And to be gaining on mean
time, per day, at the rate of   57
Kendall's flow of mean time
at Greenwich   -   12 15 3 20
And to be gaining on mean
time, per day, at the rate of   . 28 22

On Wednefday the 15th I had the pleafure of receiving our new main yard on board, it was immediately rigged, and the fhip in every other refpect made ready to proceed to fea. After paying my refpects to the governor, and returning him my beft thanks for his hofpitality and obliging attention to the neceffities of our little community whilft at St. Helena, I left Lieutenant Johnfton on board the Macaffar, with full directions in writing, by which he would be enabled to govern himfelf in conducting the veffel, of which he was put in charge to England, and about fix o'clock on the following evening, with a light breeze of wind from the S. E. we directed our courfe to the north-weftward, anxioufly looking forward to that happy hour which fhould once more land us amongft our refpective friends, from whofe fociety we had fuffered fo long and fo painful an abfence.

The weather continued to be very pleafant, and we made great progrefs to the north-weftward.

On

On Saturday the 25th we croſſed the equator in longitude 21° 35′ weſt from Greenwich, where the variation, by two ſets of azimuths, was found to be 9° 20′ weſtwardly. From this time no-thing occurred worthy of remark until Wedneſ-day the 5th of Auguſt; when one of the Cape de Verd iſlands was ſeen, bearing by compaſs N. 16 E. The weather had continued to be very pleaſant, and although the winds, ſince the concluſion of the preceding month, had veered from the ſouth-eaſtern to the weſt and north-weſtern quarters, yet we had not been prevented from making our north-weſtern courſe good, agreeably to my wiſhes.

Our people, ever ſince our departure from St. Helena, had been occaſionally employed in mend-ing the ſails and rigging, and, on all ſuitable op-portunities, they had exerciſed with the great guns and ſmall arms; whilſt the extremely plea-ſant weather which had attended us, had greatly contributed to our becoming well acquainted with the management of both.

About four o'clock in the afternoon of Thurſ-day the 20th, three veſſels were diſcovered to the northward, and at eight in the evening eight ſail were ſeen from the maſt-head, bearing by com-paſs N. 80 W. All our canvaſs was immediately ſpread, in the hope of our being able to overtake them; being in great hopes that the veſſels in

B b 2   ſight

fight would prove to be the convoy which had left the bay of St. Helena on the morning of our arrival there; in the event of which, I fhould be happy to avail myfelf of the protection we fhould derive by accompanying fo ftrong a fleet to England. At day-light the next morning, Friday the 21ft, five fhips only were in fight from the maft-head, but at feven in the morning nine fail of large veffels were fo clearly difcerned as to leave in my mind no doubt of their being a part of the fleet for which we had kept fuch an anxious, though hitherto unfuccefsful, look out, under convoy of his Majefty's fhip Sceptre, commanded by Captain Effington. About five in the aftertoon a boat, from the General Goddard Eaft-Indiaman, came on board, and confirmed us in the opinion we had at firft formed, and which every hour fince had ferved to ftrengthen, that the fleet before us was a convoy confifting of twenty-four fail of Indiamen, under the protection of the Sceptre. Upon receiving this information, I ordered a boat to be hoifted out, and I waited upon Captain Effington, by whom I was received with that unaffected hearty welcome, and unreferved fincerity, which are known by every one who has the happinefs of his friendfhip, to be the true type of his valuable character.

After putting myfelf under Captain Effington's orders, and receiving fuch inftructions as were

deemed

deemed to be neceffary by him, for the regulation of his Majefty's floop under my command, now attached to the fleet which he was convoying to England; I repaired on board the Difcovery, and by fpreading an additional quantity of canvafs, we foon had the pleafure of joining company with the Sceptre.

The fatisfaction I experienced, in the protection we had derived by overtaking and uniting our little force with fo powerful a fleet, was greatly increafed by my now underftanding from Captain Effington, that he was of opinion the agreeable tidings communicated to me at St. Helena, by Mr. Bowen, of a French decree having paffed the national affembly, in favor of the Difcovery and Chatham, was premature, and that, in the event of our having unfortunately met with an enemy of fuperior force, to whom of neceffity we muft have yielded, we fhould have had little chance of efcaping the horrors of a French prifon, in addition to the cruel mortification of lofing to our country much of the information which had been collected during the voyage. This reflection had the effect of reconciling my mind to the flow progrefs which I was now well aware would neceffarily be attendant on the conclufive part of our paffage to England. Having been fo fortunate hitherto, as to have loft *only one man out of both veffels in confequence of difeafe,* and as few by

accidents

accidents as I could reafonably have expected, when I duly confidered the length of our abfence from home, and the nature of the fervice on which we had been fo long employed ; I do confefs that, under the peculiar circumftances of our defencelefs fituation, I fhould have regarded it as a very painful tafk to have been compelled to the neceffity of expofing my excellent officers and valubale crew, who were now, comparatively fpeaking, almoft within reach of the welcome embraces of their neareft and deareft affections, to a conflict with an enemy, whofe fuperiority in point of force we had not originally been fitted out to meet, nor were we but in a very humble way prepared to refift, and from whom, in point of failing, when I adverted to the fhattered condition of our mafts and rigging, I entertained no hope of our being able to efcape.   I was, therefore, reconciled to the delays unavoidable in efcorts of this nature, though they became greatly augmented by the deplorable condition of many of Captain Effington's Dutch prizes, fome of which, I underftood, had been with great difficulty prevented from foundering.

Although our progrefs was neceffarily much retarded, yet our time paffed pleafantly away, by having at length regained the power of devoting it, on all fuitable occafions, to the comforts of a friendly intercourfe with our furrounding countrymen,

trymen, from the pleafures of whofe fociety we had been fo long eftranged.

Nothing very material occurred until Tuefday, 1ft of September; when, after contending with a frefh gale from the north and north-weftern quarters, which had commenced the preceding day, and had been attended with fome heavy fqualls of wind and rain; about nine o'clock in the forenoon, in about the latitude of 46° 12' north, longitude 29° 32' weft, one of the Dutch prizes made a fignal of diftrefs: we immediately hove to, and I fent the cutter to her affiftance, but fhe was found to be almoft a wreck, and in fuch a deplorably bad condition that it was impoffible to fave her, and fhe was therefore abandoned, by order of Captain Effington, and fet on fire about fix o'clock in the evening. After performing this fervice our cutter returned to the fhip, and in the act of hoifting her on board fhe was by accident ftove intirely to pieces.

I do not recollect that my feelings ever fuffered fo much on any occafion of a fimilar nature, as at this moment. The cutter was the boat I had conftantly ufed; in her I had travelled very many miles; in her I had repeatedly efcaped from danger; fhe had always brought me fafely home; and, although fhe was but an inanimate conveniency, to which, it may poffibly be thought, no affection could be attached, yet I felt myfelf under

fuch

such obligation for her services, that when she was dashed to pieces before my eyes, an involuntary emotion suddenly seized my breast, and I was compelled to turn away to hide a weakness (for which, though my own gratitude might find an apology) I should have thought improper to have publicly manifested.

The wind changed on Saturday the 5th, from the north-west to the opposite quarter, and blew a very hard gale, with squalls chiefly from E. by S. about six in the evening another of the Dutch prizes was observed to have made the signal of distress. We were directed to give her assistance; and the relief we were enabled to afford her was very salutary, and had become essentially necessary, as we found her in a very leaky state, and her crew in a very disabled sickly condition. The wind again veered to its former direction, and though it continued to be squally and unpleasant, it had been more moderate during the two last days; in one of these from the north-west, on Tuesday morning the 8th, about seven o'clock, we sprung our maintopmast, an accident that might have been attended with the most serious consequences, had we not been in a situation that afforded us the most ample protection, and which I had no doubt we should be able to maintain until we should arrive in some port of Great Britain, although our quantity of

canvass

canvafs fhould hereafter be materially reduced, as we had been repeatedly obliged to fhorten fail for the convoy. All the upper fails were taken in, the maft ftruck, and the carpenters immediately employed to remedy and provide for the difafter in the beft manner we were able; this bufinefs was completed about noon, and a topmaft with the topgallant rigging was again fet up. Notwithftanding that the weather was not very favourable to aftronomical purfuits, Mr. Whidbey procured fix fets, and Mr. Orchard three fets of lunar diftances, by the mean refult of which the true longitude, at noon, was found to be   —   —   20° 13' 0" weft

By Arnold's chronometer.

No. 14,	20	14	5	weft
Ditto,	176,	19	48	30	weft
By Kendall's,	—	20	0	30	weft
The obferved latitude	51	2	0	
Variation of the compafs,	22	wefterly.		

By our courfe having judicioufly been directed far to the weftward, it was moft probable that the coaft of Ireland would be the firft land in the Britifh dominions with which we fhould fall in. For thofe fhores, as the wind and other circumftances had allowed, we had been fteering for feveral days, and as our diftance from England every day and every hour decreafed, fo our happinefs became augmented in the grateful anticipation

ticipation of once more breathing our native air, once more repofing in the bofom of our country and expecting friends. Every breaft, as may be naturally imagined, was alive to fenfations of the moft pleafant nature, infeparable from the fond idea of returning home, after fo long an abfence, in an adventurous fervice to promote the general good, when unappalled by the confcioufnefs of deferved reproach. In the midft of thefe agreeable reflections, however, prefages of a melancholy caft would frequently obtrude upon the mind, and damp the promifed joys in contemplation. Few of us had been bleffed with any tidings from our families or friends fince our laft feparation from them; and in the courfe of fuch a lapfe of time what changes might not have taken place, what events might not have happened to difappoint our hopes; rob us of our prefent peace; or cloud the funfhine of our future days! Thefe were confiderations of a moft painful nature, and tinged our joyful expectations with folicitude and apprehenfion!

At length, about five o'clock on Saturday morning the 12th, a fignal was made by one of the headmoft fhips, that denoted fhe was within fight of land, and foon afterwards, from our maft-head, the glad tidings were announced that land was plainly to be feen, bearing by compafs E. S. E. At eleven in the forenoon it was known

to

to be the weftern coaft of Ireland, and arrangements were immediately made by the Sceptre for
keeping the fhips together, and for entering the
Shannon; where Captain Effington propofed to
remain with his convoy until a force more equal
to the protection of the valuable fleet he had
thus fafely brought into his Majefty's dominions,
fhould arrive, to efcort it from thence to England.   Having communicated to Captain Effington fuch parts of my orders from the Lords of
the Admiralty, under which I had failed, as applied to the government of my conduct on the
prefent occafion, I received his orders to repair
immediately to London; and the following day,
Sunday the 13th, after having feen the Difcovery fafely moored, with the reft of the fleet, in
the Shannon, and giving fuch inftructions, as
circumftances demanded, to my firft lieutenant
Mr. Baker, in whofe zeal for the fervice, and
abilities as an officer, a long experience juftified
me in implicitly confiding; I refigned my command of the Difcovery into his hands, and with
fuch books, papers and charts as had been previoufly felected, as being effential to the illuftration of the fervices we had performed, I took
leave of my officers and crew; not, however,
without emotions which, though natural, on
parting with a fociety with whom I had lived fo
long, fhared fo many dangers, and from whom I
had

had received fuch effential fervices, are yet more eafily to be imagined than I have the power to defcribe : and in the courfe of a few days I arrived at the Admiralty, where I depofited my feveral documents.

Before I bid farewell to the Difcovery,* I muft beg leave to arreft the attention of my readers for a few minutes, for the purpofe of taking a fhort view of the geographical knowledge which had been obtained of the earth, previoufly to the expedition which I have had the honour to command, and the happinefs of bringing thus to a conclufion ; and alfo to notice fuch parts of the globe as yet remain to be explored to make that fpecies of information complete. The effecting a paffage into the oriental feas round the cape of Good Hope, the difcovery of America, and the opening of a communication between the Atlantic and Pacific Oceans, by paffing either through the ftraits of Magellan, or round the iflands lying off the fouthern extremity of Tierra del Fuego, engaged the minds and utmoft exertions of the moft illuftrious navigators during the three laft centuries. Thefe enterprizes have been duly appreciated and juftly celebrated for the important lights they have thrown upon the fciences of geography and nautical aftronomy ; for the improvements they have caufed in the arts ;

* Arrived all well in the Thames the 20th of October, 1795.

for

for the commercial intercourfe which, by their means, has been opened and eftablifhed with all the maritime parts of the world; and, laftly, for the happy introduction of civilization amongft numerous tribes of our fellow creatures.

In the firft attempts to accomplifh thefe extenfive objects, Great Britain took no part; but no fooner did fhe perceive the importance of which they were likely to be to her confequence and profperity as a maritime ftate, than her fpirit for the attainment of fuch valuable acquifitions to fcience became roufed. In the courfe of a very few years, no fuch effential benefits have been fecured to mankind, nor has fo much geographical knowledge been acquired, as fince the commencement of DISCOVERY undertaken, and fuccefsfully accomplifhed, by the unremitted labours of Britifh navigators; whofe primary confiderations have been to direct their inquiries to objects of an ufeful nature, and to inveftigate and fupport the truth, by a plain narrative of thofe facts, which fell within the fphere of their obfervation, rather than to give encouragement, by the obtrufion of fpecious opinions, to hypothefes, however ingenious. In confequence of a ftrict adherence to this principle, the geography of the earth is now placed beyond the influence of conjecture, and is determined by fuch incontrovertible evidence, that the fmall fpaces that yet

remain

remain unexplored in the Pacific or Indian oceans are too infignificant to become an object of enterprize : there are, however, parts of the coafts, both of Afia and America, which would yet afford employment for the labourers in the fcience of DISCOVERY.

The Afiatic coaft, from the latitude of about 35° to the latitude of 52° north is at prefent very ill defined ; and the American coaft, from about the latitude of 44° fouth, to the fouthern extremity of Tierra del Fuego, is likewife very little known ; and I entertain no doubt, had not our late examination on the coaft of North-Weft America, fo delayed our return to the fouthern hemifphere, as to prevent my carrying the orders I had received into effect, that I fhould have derived great fatisfaction from a furvey and inveftigation of the fhores of that interefting country. If, however, by that portion of his Majefty's commands, which I have had the honour to execute, it fhall appear that a decifion may as juftly now take place, refpecting any navigable communication between the waters of the Pacific and Atlantic oceans, within the limits of our furvey, as on the hypothefis which gave as a counterpoife to the globe *a fouthern continent*, and which the indefatigable diligence of Captain Cook completely fubverted, I fhould hope that the purpofe for which his Majefty commanded
the

the expedition to be undertaken, will not be confidered as having failed for want of zeal or perfeverance, though it fhould hereafter be found incomplete for want of judgment and ability.

There were few objects to which I had paid more attention, or had more fincerely at heart, than that of obferving fuch a conduct, at all times, towards the feveral tribes of Indians, with whom we fhould frequently meet, as fhould prevent the neceffity of our reforting to any meafures that might endanger the lives of a people, whofe *real* intentions were always likely to be mifunderftood, from a want of knowledge in us of their refpective dialects or languages. After having refided, as it were, amongft them for more than two years, without having had the leaft occafion to fire a fhot in anger, I had fondly hoped that I fhould have been enabled to have completed our refearches in thofe before untrodden regions, without the lofs of life to a fingle individual belonging to the countries we might yet find it neceffary to vifit. In this my anxious concern for the great caufe of humanity I was, however, difappointed. The number of Indians from Traitor's cove which fell in the unprovoked attack upon our boats, on the 12th of Auguft, 1793, could not be afcertained; but, independently of this unfortunate affair, I do not know of more

than

than two men who afterwards loft their lives in confequence of our expeditions, from the Difcovery or Chatham. Thefe unlucky events did not, however, fail to produce in my mind much forrow and regret, from which I could find no relief but in the confoling reflection, that nothing but the moft urgent neceffity, for our own prefervation, would have compelled us to have adopted coercive meafures.

From the firft moment of my appointment, to the hour in which I refigned the ftation I had fo long held, the health of every individual under my command had been my firft care; and I had now the unfpeakable happinefs of beholding the fame perfons return on board the Difcovery to the river Shannon, in perfect health, as had failed with me from the river Thames, excepting fuch of the officers as had officially been fent home, or had been promoted in the Chatham; the feventeen feamen left at St. Helena, to affift in navigating the Macaffar to England*, and the undermentioned individuals, who were unhappily loft in the courfe of the expedition.

John Brown, carpenter's mate, drowned by accident, in the execution of his duty, off the fouth Foreland, 3d of February, 1791.

Neil Coil, marine, died of the flux, communi-

* Arrived all well the 22d of November, 1795.

cated

cated to the Difcovery, at the cape of Good
Hope, by an infected fhip from Batavia, 7th of
Auguft, 1791.

Jofeph Murgatroyd, one of the carpenter's
crew, miffing at fea the 21ft of January, 1793.

John Carter, feamen, poifoned by eating muf-
cles, in Poifon cove, 15th June, 1793.

Ifaac Wooden, drowned by accident, in the
execution of his duty, off Wooden's rock, the
24th of Auguft, 1794.

Richard Jones, drowned by accident, in the
execution of his duty, between the port of Valparaifo and the ifland of St. Helena, 21ft of
June, 1795.

By this lift it will appear that, from the 15th
of December, in the year 1790, to this 13th day
of September, 1795, comprehending a fpace of
four years eight months and twenty-nine days,
we had loft out of our complement of one hundred men, only one man by difeafe: and at the
time of our parting with the Chatham* at St.
Helena, fhe had not, in the courfe of the whole
voyage loft a fingle man, either in confequence
of ill health, or from any accident whatever.

The unfortunate lofs of thefe five men from
the Difcovery produced in me infinite regret, but
when I adverted to the very dangerous fervice in
which we had been fo long employed, and the

* Arrived all well 17th of October 1795.

many perilous fituations from which we had providentially been extricated, with all poffible ado-
ration, humility, and gratitude, I offered up my
unfeigned thanks to the GREAT DISPOSER OF
ALL HUMAN EVENTS, for the protection which
thus, in his unbounded wifdom and goodnefs he
had been pleafed, on all occafions, to vouchfafe
unto us, and which had now happily reftored us
to our country, our families, and our friends.

END OF THE JOURNAL.

NOTES

NOTES

AND

MISCELLANEOUS OBSERVATIONS.

SINCE my return to England I have had feveral converfations with Captain Colnett,
relative to the capture of his veffel at Nootka, and
the treatment that himfelf, officers, and crew,
received from the Spaniards during the time they
remained at that place, and afterwards whilft
they were prifoners at St. Blas; from the whole
of which it will appear, that he had been extremely ill ufed, and that no dependence is to be
placed on the accounts given to Sen' Quadra, or
myfelf, by the American commanders, who are
ftated to have been eye-witneffes of moft of the
tranfactions. The documents and papers which
Captain Colnett has fince produced to me, fully
prove that the Americans wilfully mifreprefented
the whole affair, to the prejudice of his character,
and the intereft of his Britannic Majefty's fubjects, engaged in commercial purfuits on the coaft
of North Weft America.

Having been particularly careful to ftate all
the important circumftances that came to my

knowledge

knowledge during my negociation with Senr Quadra, whether they were such as tended to establish the claims, or militate against the pretensions, of the British crown to the territories at Nootka, I have thought it proper, in addition to what has been already related, to give the following brief account of the capture of the Argonaut, as represented to me by Captain Colnett.

The settlement which Captain Colnett had in contemplation to make at Nootka, had been concerted at Macao, in November, 1789, at the time he entered into copartnership with several English gentlemen resident at that place.

On this occasion, Captain Colnett made it his particular business to become informed with respect to the property which those gentlemen held in the two vessels, the North West America and Ephigenia, then on the coast of Nootka; for as to the land, he entertained no doubt of its belonging to Great Britain, as the subjects of that state were the first European people who had discovered the country; and he was further well satisfied, that no other power whatever had a right to dispossess the gentlemen with whom he had engaged, of their property at Nootka, because he and they considered it to be exclusively their own. The intention of forming a settlement was known to Mr. Hudson before his departure in the Princess Royal from Macao; and on his

arrival

arrival before Captain Colnett at Nootka, fuch intention was moft probably communicated to the Spaniards and the native Indians, who appeared to have been long in expectation of the Argonaut's arrival, and had referved the greateft part of their furs for the purpofe of exchanging them with Captain Colnett, for the articles with which, they had learned, his veffel would be freighted.

Under the ideas which Captain Colnett entertained, that this part of the coaft of North Weft America belonged to Great Britain, he had no fear of entering any of its ports, becaufe he was duly authorized by the South Sea company to trade in thofe feas, and had leave to abfent himfelf from his Majefty's fervice, being at that time a lieutenant in the royal navy. As a defence againft hoftile Indians, the Argonaut had twelve carriage guns, befide fwivels and fmall arms; but not apprehending any thing unfriendly from the inhabitants of Nootka, nor having become acquainted before he left China, that any difference exifted between the courts of London and Madrid, when he arrived off Nootka, on the 3d of July, 1790, the guns of the Argonaut were difmounted, and were all in the hold of the veffel.

About nine o'clock that evening, when at the diftance of about three leagues from the entrance into the port, a boat was obferved coming to-

C c 3   wards

wards the Argonaut; but, as the weather was
very hazy, it could not be difcovered to what nation it belonged.   On being hailed, the perfons
in her laid upon their oars, and requefted, in Spanifh, permiffion to come on board, with which
Captain Colnett inftantly complied.   Soon after
another Spanifh boat, and one belonging to an
American veffel, came alongfide his veffel, and
Captain Colnett now underftood that there were
two Spanifh men of war, and an American fhip
and floop, at anchor in Friendly cove.   On receiving this information, Captain Colnett hefitated for fome time, whether he fhould, or not,
go into Friendly cove; as he had fome doubts as
to the propriety of putting himfelf under the
command of Spanifh fhips of war.   This objec-
tion being made known to Don Martinez, who
had arrived in the firft boat, he requefted, through
an interpreter, that Captain Colnett would, neverthelefs, afford him fome affiftance, as the veffels
under his command were in great diftrefs for the
want of provifions and other neceffaries; and as
he had paid fome attention to Mr. Hudfon, the
commander of the Princefs Royal, one of the four
veffels under Captain Colnett's directions (as
would be feen by a letter which he produced to
Captain Colnett from Mr. Hudfon) Martinez
hoped Captain Colnett would not be wanting
in a return of civility, and intreated him, in the
moft

moſt earneſt manner, to enter Friendly cove; pledging his word of honor, not only as com⁻mander in chief of all the ſhips belonging to his Catholic Majeſty, on the northern coaſts of the Pacific Ocean, but alſo as nephew to the viceroy, and in his capacity at Nootka, as the repreſen-tative of the king of Spain; that Captain Colnett ſhould be at liberty to depart whenever he might think proper; Don Martinez ſtating, at the ſame time, that he was then at Nootka for the ſole purpoſe of watching the operations and proceed-ings of the Ruſſians. Theſe aſſurances induced Captain Colnett to conſider Don Martinez as an officer of high rank and character; and as he did not entertain the moſt diſtant idea that any falſehood was attempted to be impoſed upon him, or that he was in the leaſt danger of being treated by Martinez with duplicity, he ſuffered the Spa-niſh launches to tow the Argonaut into port, where ſhe did not arrive until midnight.

The next morning Don Martinez invited Cap-tain Colnett to breakfaſt on board the Princiſſa, and afterwards accompanied him on his return to the Argonaut, where Captain Colnett ordered ſuch proviſions and ſtores as he could ſpare to be got to hand, gave a liſt of them to Don Martinez, and, at the ſame time, requeſted his acceptance of them, with which civility he appeared to be highly pleaſed and thoroughly ſatisfied. Don

Martinez had not been long on board the Argonaut before he felected Captain Colnett's boatfwain from the reft of the crew, who being a native of Gibraltar, fpoke the Spanifh language very
fluently. After fome converfation with this
man, Don Martinez demanded him of Captain
Colnett, as a fubject of his Catholic Majefty, and
as the boatfwain was very defirous of leaving the
Argonaut, Captain Colnett remitted the balance
then due from him on account of his wages, and
difcharged him from his fervice. This circumftance was by no means a pleafant one to Captain
Colnett; but, as Don Martinez feemed to be extremely anxious to obtain the releafe of this man,
Captain Colnett did not think it would have been
prudent to have refifted his application. His
doubts, however, of the profeffed fincerity of
Don Martinez, became increafed, by his foon
difcovering that the Indians declined all fort of
trade with the Argonaut. This induced him to
determine upon leaving Friendly cove with all
poffible difpatch, and he acquainted Don Martinez that he purpofed to depart in the courfe of
the day. Upon this the Spanifh officer offered
his launch to affift the Argonaut out of the cove;
and it was at this time agreed, that the articles
with which Captain Colnett could fupply Don
Martinez, fhould be fent to him by the return of
the Spanifh launch. The promifed affiftance of
this

this boat not arriving fo foon as Captain Colnett had expected, he fent one of his mates to Don Martinez, for the purpofe of reminding him of his engagement, and to procure the launch; but, to his great furprize, inftead of the officer returning with the Spanifh boat, Captain Colnett received a meffage from Don Martinez, defiring that he would inftantly repair on board the Princiffa, and produce his fhip's papers for his examination. With this requeft Captain Colnett immediately complied, and Don Martinez had fcarcely looked at them, before he pofitively afferted that they were all forgeries, although he did not underftand a fingle word of the language in which they were written. With this declaration he threw them on the table, and infifted that the Argonaut fhould not fail from Nootka until he fhould think proper to grant permiffion for her departure. On Captain Colnett complaining of this breach of promife and good faith, Martinez quitted the cabin in an apparent rage, and inftantly difpatched an armed party from the deck, who, after knocking Captain Colnett down, arrefted him, and detained him as a prifoner on board the Princiffa. Don Martinez then fent his launch on board the Argonaut; ftruck the Britifh, and hoifted Spanifh, colours; ordered the Columbia, an American fhip, to fire into the Argonaut if fhe attempted to unmoor; made the

officers

officers prifoners, and put the crew into irons.
After this the veffel was unloaded, and every individual was robbed of fuch parts of his private
property as was chofen by the Spaniards. In
this fituation the Argonaut, officers, and crew,
remained for ten days, when the Princefs Royal
appeared in the offing; and on Mr. Hudfon, her
commander, being perceived by Martinez to be
coming near the fhore in his boat, he fent out his
launch armed, feized the boat, and brought Mr.
Hudfon on board the Princiffa, where a letter
was prepared for him to fign, ordering the officer, whom he had left in charge of his veffel, to
deliver her up without any refiftance. At the
yard-arm was rove a rope, with which Mr. Hudfon was threatened to be hanged, if he declined
figning the letter, or if the floop under his command fhould fire at the launch then ready to
carry the propofed letter, and which, under thefe
circumftances, he was compelled to fign on board
the Princiffa.

From the 5th to the 14th of July, 1790, arrangements were making on board the Argonaut
for the confinement of the officers and crew
during their paffage from Nootka to St. Blas,
whither Captain Colnett was given to underftand
they would be fent as prifoners.

The treatment which Captain Colnett received
whilft on board the Princiffa had nearly proved
fatal

fatal to him; he was feized with a violent fever, attended with a delirium, which did not abate until he was removed on board his own veffel; here he was made a clofe prifoner, and confined to the mate's cabin, a place not fix feet fquare. Such parts of the Argonaut's cargo as Martinez thought proper to reject, were returned into the veffel again, and all the officers, and fixteen of the crew, who were Britifh fubjects, were, on the 14th of July, fent in the Argonaut under confinement from Nootka to St. Blas.

Notwithftanding the great diftinction with which it had been reprefented to Sen' Quadra, and urged by him to me, Captain Colnett had been received on his arrival at this port, and which he does not deny, in point of treatment, was infinitely better than he had experienced during the time he was under the power and directions of Martinez; yet the remainder of his cargo, ftores and provifions, was taken from out of his veffel at St. Blas, and a part only of the former was afterwards reftored, whilft the wages of the Spanifh navy that were paid to him, for himfelf, officers, and crew, were nearly counterbalanced by the heavy expences brought againft his fhip's company during the time of their captivity, for their maintenance, medical and other affiftance.

The hardfhips which were endured, according

to Captain Colnett's reprefentation, by himfelf, his officers, and the fix een Britifh feamen, during a paffage of thirty-two days to St. Blas, are not to be defcribed; but as a detail of thefe circum- ftances would lead me into extraneous matter, unconnected with the object (the ceffion of the territories at Nootka) which made a ftatement of Captain Colnett's tranfactions in Friendly cove neceffary in the former part of my journal, I fhall forbear to mention any thing on that head, and only infert a paffage, tranflated from the Spanifh paffport, granted by the viceroy of Mexico to Captain Colnett, at the time of the reftoration of his veffel, and his liberation from the Spanifh territories in America; by which it will appear, that although Don Eftevan Martinez had no efpe- cial directions to capture either the Argonaut, Princefs Royal, or any other Britifh fhip, yet all veffels not belonging to his Catholic Majefty, might have been retained at Nootka as good and lawful prizes: this will neceffarily leave the reader in fome doubt as to the means that were pur- fued by the American traders then at Nootka, to preferve the privileges which they feem to have enjoyed; and I fhall conclude this relation of the bufinefs from the teftimony of Captain Colnett, by briefly ftating how he conducted himfelf, on receiving a fubfequent paffport from the viceroy of Mexico.

" The.

" The conduct of this officer" (Don Eftevan Jofe Martinez) " was founded on laws and royal orders, which not only do abfolutely prohibit the negociation, eftablifhment, and commerce, of aliens on our coafts of the fouth feas of both Americas; but ordain alfo, that they the faid aliens, fhall be looked upon and treated as declared enemies, without its being underftood to be a breach of the good faith, or contrary to the treaties of peace; for in that concluded in the year 1760, and confirmed in the fecond article of that in 1763, the arrival of all alien veffels, or their introduction, paffage, or commerce on the faid coafts, are completely prohibited.

" Under thefe circumftances, agreed to by the treating parties, and pofitive declarations of the court of Spain, the veffels Argonaut and Princefs Royal might have been retained as good and lawful prizes; but, being defirous to preferve that harmony which at prefents exifts between our court and that of London, and confidering alfo that the fovereigns of both kingdoms will, upon reafonable and juft terms, amicably agree to the reftoration of the faid veffels, I grant a free and fafe paffport to their Captains James Colnett and Thomas Hudfon, that they may proceed to Macao, or fail to any other place they may choofe, with the exprefs prohibition that they fhall not put into any port or bay of our coafts without

fome

some very preffing neceffity, or eftablifh them-felves there, or trade in them with the Indians, becaufe they may do this in other places or iflands not the dominions of his Catholic Majefty."

After Captain Colnett had received this paff-port, he petitioned the viceroy that he might be permitted to difpofe of the remaining part of his cargo on the coaft of North Weft America, but this was pofitively refufed by the viceroy, who ftated that he was bound to give that preference to the fubjects of his Catholic Majefty. Not-withftanding that he did not grant Captain Col-nett this indulgence, he tranfmitted to him another paffport, in which Captain Colnett was directed to proceed to Nootka, with orders to the commanding officer there, to deliver up the Princefs Royal, which veffel had been directed to repair to that port, after having been fome months employed in the Spanifh fervice. On Captain Colnett's return to Nootka he did not find the Princefs Royal there, nor could he learn any tidings of her deftination, and therefore he made the beft of his way from Nootka to Macao, agree-ably to the injunctions contained in the fecond paffport from the viceroy of Mexico.

In the year 1792, the fur trade, between the north-weft coaft of America and China, gave employment to upwards of twenty fail of fhips and veffels, whofe names, and the countries to

which

which they belong, I have thought proper to infert, for the purpofe of fhewing that my opinions, refpecting the value of this trade, were not only founded upon obfervation, but confirmed by the practice of feveral European ftates, and adventurers from the Afiatic, Chinefe, and American fhores.

Ships and veffels.	Commanders.	To what country belonging.
Ship Butterworth, - -	Brown,	London.
Sloop Le Boo, - -	Sharp,	ditto.
Cutter Jackal, - -	Steward,	ditto.
Brig Three Brothers, -	Alder,	ditto.
Schooner Prince William Henry,	Ewen,	ditto.
Ship Jenny, - -	Baker,	Briftol.
Brig Halcyon, - -	Barclay,	Bengal.
Brig Venus, - -	Shepherd,	ditto.
Snow —— - - -	Moor,	Canton.
Brig —— - - -	Coftidge,	ditto.
Brig —— - - -	Barnett,	ditto.
Ship Columbia, - -	Gray,	Bofton, America.
Sloop Adventure, - - } (Built at Clayoquot, tender to the Columbia)	Hafwell,	ditto.
Ship Jefferfon, - -	Roberts,	ditto.
Brig Hope, - -	Ingraham,	ditto.
Brig Hancock, - -	Crowell,	ditto.
Brig Wafhington, - -	Kendrick,	ditto.
Ship Margaret, - -	Magie,	New York.
Ship Ephigenia, - -	Viana,	Portugal.
Brig Fenis and St. Jofeph,	Andrede,	ditto.
Ship —— - - -	Unknown,	France.

Befide thefe, the veffels already mentioned in my journal, belonging to his Catholic Majefty, frequently reforted to the port of Nootka.

When fuch a fpirit for enterprize as this, is thus

thus manifested by the people of so many different nations, and directed from all quarters of the
globe to these shores, there can remain no more
doubt, with respect to the commercial advantages which are likely to be attendant on such
speculations, than that many unjust proceedings
will take place amongst the several persons concerned, who, in the avidity for promoting their
respective interests, become competitors for the
commodity of which each is in pursuit, and de-
stroy the general benefits which, under wise and
good regulations would result to all. A retro-
spective view of these circumstances, and the behaviour of Senr Quadra, in the negociation which,
with him I had the honour to conduct, respecting the cession of the territories at Nootka to the
crown of Great Britain; will serve to shew in
what an important light the court of Spain be-
holds her interests in this valuable country, and
what also are the commercial advantages that
most probably would accrue to the adventurers
on the coast, were their dealings properly re-
strained, and their general conduct wisely regulated.

Although we did not meet with any Russian
vessels at Nootka, yet I am clearly of opinion
the people of that nation are more likely than
those of any other to succeed in procuring furs,
and the other valuable commodities, from these

shores

fhores, with which a moft beneficial trade might
be eftablifhcd between North-Weft America,
Japan, and the northern parts of China. Of this
I was well perfuaded, from the accounts I received from Symloff, and from my own obfervations on the general conduct of the Ruffians
towards the Indians, in the feveral places where
we found them under their controul and direction. Had the natives about the Ruffian eftablifhments in Cook's inlet, and Prince William's
found been oppreffed, dealt hardly by, or treated
by the Ruffians as a conquered people, fome
uneafinefs amongft them would have been perceived, fome defire for emancipation would have
been difcovered; but no fuch difpofition appeared, they feemed to be held in no reftraint,
nor did they feem to wifh, on any occafion whatever, to elude the vigilance of their directors.
For fome of our commodities that were valuable
to them, they would offer their furs in ex-
change; but in no inftance did they propofe any
thing of the kind for fale to the difadvantage of
their employers. The Ruffians, moft likely, unable to reduce the inhabitants of the infular country to the fouth-eaftward from Crofs found, have
preferred to fit down amongft thofe to the weftward; where, from the compactnefs of the coaft,
and the lofty impaffable mountains which ap-

VOL. VI.   D d   proach

proach the fea fhore, the natives are reftrained from indulging in the wandering life to which their more eaftern neighbours are accuftomed, and who being a much more warlike race, may poffibly have been found by the Ruffians to be lefs tractable.

Notwithftanding that our furvey of the coaft of North-Weft America has afforded to our minds the moft fatisfactory proof that no navigable communication whatever exifts between the North Pacific and North Atlantic Oceans, from the 30th to the 56th degree of north latitude, nor between the water of the Pacific, nor any of the lakes or rivers in the interior part of continent of North America ; yet, as it is very difficult to undeceive, and more fo to convince the human mind, when prepoffeffed of long adopted notions, however erroneoufly they may have been founded, and efpecially when circumftances may be reforted to which have the appearance of being capable of furnifhing new matter for ingenious fpeculative opinions, it may not be improper to ftate, that although, from unavoidable circumftances, Mr. Broughton* was compelled, in his examination of Columbia river, to defift from attempting to afcertain the navigable extent of the feveral fmall branches which

* Now a poft captain in the royal navy.

fall

fall into that river, yet that gentleman was thoroughly convinced from the view he had obtained of each, and the circumſtances attendant
on them all, that no one of thoſe branches admitted of any navigable communication whatever with the interior country.

With reſpect to the ancient diſcoveries of De
Fuca, they appear to be upheld by tradition
alone, and ought therefore to be received with
great latitude, and to be credited with ſtill more
caution. A celebrated writer on geography* appears to have been perfectly convinced that this
oral teſtimony was correct, although he candidly
acknowledges that " we have no other than ver-
bal report of De Fuca's diſcovery ; he communicated the information to Mr. Lock at Venice,
and offered to perform a voyage," I preſume, for
the further exploring of thoſe regions, " on condition of having payment of the great loſſes he
had ſuſtained, to the value of ſixty thouſand du-
cats, when captured by Sir Thomas Cavendiſh in
the South Seas. John de Fuca, the Greek pilot,
in 1592, ſailed into a broad inlet, between the
47th and 48th degrees, which led him into a far
broader ſea, wherein he ſailed above twenty days,
there being at the entrance on the north-weſt

---

* See Dalrymple's plan for promoting the fur trade. 1789.

coaſt,

coaft, a great head-land or ifland, with an exceeding high pinnacle or fpired rock, like a pillar, thereupon."

This is the whole that can be collected from the information of this fuppofed navigator; which Mr. Dalrymple fays exactly correfponds with the difcoveries of the Spaniards, who " have recently found an entrance in the latitude of 47° 45' north, which in twenty-feven days' courfe brought them to the vicinity of Hudfon's bay." On making inquiries of the Spanifh officers attached to the commiffion of Senr Melafpina, as alfo of Senr Quadra, and feveral of the officers under his orders, who, for fome time paft, had been employed in fuch refearches refpecting fo important a circumftance, I was given to underftand by them all, that my communication was the firft intelligence they had ever received of fuch difcoveries having been made ; and as to the navigators De Fuca, De Fonte, and others, thefe gentlemen expected to have derived intelligence of them from us, fuppofing, from the Englifh publications, that we were better acquainted with their achievements than any part of the Spanifh nation. A commander of one of the trading veffels met with fuch a pinnacle rock in the latitude of 47° 47', but unluckily there was no opening near it, to identify it being the fame
which

which the Greek pilot had feen; but this circumftance can eafily be difpenfed with, for the
fake of fupporting an hypothefis, only by fuppofing the opening to be further to the northward.
That fuch a rock might have been feen in that
latitude is not to be queftioned, becaufe we faw
numbers of them, and it is well known, that not
only on the coaft of North-Weft America, but
on various other coafts of the earth, fuch pinnacle
rocks are found to exift.

On thefe grounds, and on thefe alone, ftands
the ancient authority for the difcoveries of John
De Fuca; and however erroneous they may be,
feem to have been acknowledged by moft of the
recent vifitors to this coaft, who as well as myfelf,
(as is too frequently and injudicioufly the cafe)
have been led to follow the ftream of the current report. By my having continued the name
of De Fuca in my journal and charts, a tacit ac-
knowledgment of his difcoveries may poffibly,
on my part, be inferred; this however, I muft
pofitively deny, becaufe there has not been feen
one leading feature to fubftantiate his tradition:
on the contrary, the fea coaft under the parallels
between which this opening is faid to have exifted, is compact and impenetrable: the fhores
of the continent have not any opening whatever,
that bears the leaft fimilitude to the defcription

D d 3   of

of De Fuca's entrance; and the opening which I have called the *supposed straits of Juan de Fuca*, instead of being between the 47th and 48th degrees, is between the 48th and 49th degrees of north latitude, and leads not into a far broader sea or mediterranean ocean. The error, however, of a degree in latitude may, by the advocates for De Fuca's merits, be easily reconciled, by the ignorance in those days, or the incorrectness in making such common astronomical observations; yet we do not find that Sir Francis Drake, who sailed before De Fuca, was liable to such mistakes.

The discoveries of the Portuguese or Spanish admiral De Fonte, De Fonta, or De Fuentes, appear to be equally liable to objections, as those said to have been made by De Fuca. Little reliance, I trust, will hereafter be placed on that publication of De Fonta's account,* wherein it is stated that " He sailed 260 leagues in crooked channels, amongst islands, named the Archipelago of St. Lazarus, and on the 14th of June 1640, he came to a river which he named Rio de los Reyes, in 53° of north latitude; he went up it to the north-eastward 60 leagues; it was fresh 20 leagues from the mouth, the tide rising

* See Dalrymple's plan for promoting the fur trade. 1789.

24 feet,

24 feet, the depth not lefs than four or five fathoms at low water all the way into lake Belle,
which he entered the 22d of June; in this lake
there was generally fix or feven fathoms; and at
a particular time of tide there is a fall in the lake;
that from a good port fheltered by an ifland on
the fouth fide of lake Belle, De Fonta on the 1ft
of July failed in his boats to a river which he
named Parmentiers; that he paffed eight falls, in
all thirty-two feet perpendicular, from its fource
in lake Belle, into a large lake which he reached
the 6th of July. This lake he named De Fonte;
it is 160 leagues long, and 60 broad, lying E. N. E.
and W. S. W. in length, having in fome places
60 fathoms depth, abounding with cod and ling."

It is here neceffary to interrupt the thread of
De Fonta's curious narrative for a moment, in
order, if poffible, to reconcile the nature of his
voyage with his ftatement of facts. After his arrival in Rio de los Reyes, he failed in his fhip 60
leagues to lake Belle; 40 leagues of this diftance
were frefh water; and then in his boats, through
that lake and the river Parmentiers; where, after
paffing eight falls he arrived in lake de Fonte,
which he finds abounding with cod and ling; but
the extent of lake Belle is not mentioned, nor
whether the water in lake de Fonte was frefh or
falt, though from common reafoning, it is natu-

ral

ral to conclude, that fince the water in Rio de los Reyes was frefh at the diftance of 40 leagues from the lake whence the river derives its origin, that the water in lake De Fonte, where cod and ling are faid to abound, muft be frefh alfo. But to return to the narrative. Lake de Fonte contained " feveral very large iflands, and ten fmall ones: from the E. N. E. extremity of this lake, which he left the 14th of July, he paffed in ten hours with a frefh wind and whole ebb a lake, which he named Strait Ronquillo, 34 leagues long, and two or three broad, with 20, to 26 and 28 fathoms depth. On the 17th he came to an Indian town, where he learnt there was a fhip in the neighbourhood; to this fhip he failed, and found on board only one man advanced in years and a youth; the man was the greateft in the mechanical part of mathematicks he had ever feen: he learnt they were from Bofton in New England, the owner named Gibbons, who was major general of Maltachufett's, and the whole fhip's company came on the 30th of July. On the 6th of Auguft De Fonta made the owner fome valuable prefents, and took fome provifions from them, and gave Captain Shapely, the commander of the veffel, one thoufand pieces of eight for his fine charts and journals. On the 11th of Auguft De Fonta arrived at the firft fall in the

river

river Parmentiers, and on the 16th on board his ship in lake Belle.

The extensive archipelago, in which De Fonta had sailed through crooked channels 260 leagues; the river navigable for shipping that flowed into it, up which he had sailed in his ship 60 leagues; the water becoming fresh after he had entered and passed in it 20 leagues; its communicating by other lakes and rivers with a passage, in which a ship had arrived from Boston in New England; are all so circumstantially particularized, as to give the account, at first sight, an air of probability, and on examination, had it been found reasonably connected together, which is by no means the case; a trifling difference in point of description or situation would have been pardoned.

The Rio de los Reyes Mr. Dalrymple states (according to the Spanish geographers, under the authority of which nation De Fonta is said to have sailed) to be in the 43d; according to the English in the 53d; and according to the French, in the 63d degree of north latitude, on the western coast of North America. If it be necessary to make allowance for the ignorance of De Fonta, or the errors in his observations, any other parallel along the coast may be assigned with equal correctness.

Under

Under the 43d parallel of north latitude on this coaft, no fuch archipelago nor river does exift; but between the 47th and 57th degrees of north latitude, there is an archipelago compofed of innumerable iflands, and crooked channels; yet the evidence of a navigable river flowing into it, is ftill wanting to prove its identity; and as the fcrupulous exactnefs with which our furvey of the continental fhore has been made within thefe limits, precludes the poffibility of fuch a river having been paffed unnoticed by us, as that defcribed to be of Rio de los Reyes, I remain in full confidence, that fome credit will hereafter be given to the teftimony refulting from our re-fearches, and that the plain truth undifguifed, with which our labours have been reprefented, will be juftlyappreciated, in refutation of ancient unfupported traditions.

I do not, however, mean pofitively to deny the difcoveries of De Fonta, I only wifh to invefti-gate the fact, and to afcertain the truth; and I am content with having ufed my endeavours to prove their improbability as publifhed to the world. The broken region which fo long occu-pied our attention, cannot poffibly be the archi-pelago of St. Lazarus, fince the principal feature by which the identity of that archipelago could be proved is that of a navigable river for fhipping

flowing

flowing into it, and this certainly does not exift in that archipelago which has taken us fo much time to explore; hence the fituation cannot be the fame, and for that reafon I have not affixed the name of De Fonta, De Fonte, or Fuentes to any part of thofe regions. It is however to be remembered, that our geography of the whole coaft of North Weft America is not yet complete, and that the French navigators, who have ftated the archipelago of St. Lazarus to be in the 63d degree of north latitude, may not yet be in an error.

The ftupendous barrier mountains certainly do not feem to extend in fo lofty and connected a range to the northward of the head of Cook's inlet, as to the fouth-eaftward of that ftation; and it is poffible that in this part, the chain of mountains may admit of a communication with the eaftern country, which feems to be almoft impracticable further to the fouthward. In this conjecture we are fomewhat warranted by the fimilarity obferved in the race of people inhabit-ing the fhores of Hudfon's bay and thofe to the northward of North Weft America.

In all the parts of the continent on which we landed, we nowhere found any roads or paths through the woods, indicating the Indians on the coaft having any intercourfe with the natives of

the

the interior part of the country, nor were there any articles of the Canadian or Hudſon's bay traders found amongſt the people with whom we met on any part of the continent or external ſea ſhores of this extenſive country.

FINIS.

BOOKS

PRINTED FOR

JOHN STOCKDALE, PICCADILLY.

A GENERAL MAP of GERMANY, ITALY, &c. on Thirty large Sheets. By Captain CHAUCHARD, with a defcriptive Volume, in royal quarto, containing 500 pages of clofe letter-prefs, on fine paper, and twenty-four plans of cities, price 8l. 8s, or fubfcribers' unclaimed copies, 12l. 12s. half bound. Dedicated by permiffion to His Majefty, and patronized by the whole of the Royal Family.

The HISTORY, Civil and Commercial, of the BRITISH COLONIES in the WEST INDIES. By BRIAN EDWARDS, Efq. F. R. S. S. A. To which is prefixed the Life of the Author, written by himfelf, and a Preface, by Sir William Young, Bart. In three large volumes octavo, with twenty-two maps and plates, price 2l. 2s, or on royal paper 2l. 12s. 6d. Dedicated by permiffion to His Majefty.

TRAVELS through the STATES of NORTH AMERICA, and Provinces of UPPER and LOWER CANADA, during the Years 1795, 1796, and 1797. By ISAAC WELD, Junior, Efq. In one volume, quarto, with fixteen plates, 1l. 10s. in two volumes, octavo, with all the plates, 1l. 1s. or in one volume with eight plates, 10s. 6d.

HISTORY of CATHERINE II. Emprefs of Ruffia. Tranflated from the French of J. Caftera. By HENRY HUNTER, D. D. In one large volume octavo, with thirteen portraits, and a view, price 10s. 6d. or on fine paper 13s. 6d.

The VOYAGE of LA PEROUSE round the WORLD, in the Years 1785, 6, 7, and 8. To which are annexed, Travels over the Continent, with the Difpatches of La Peroufe, by M. DE LESSEPS. In two large volumes octavo, with fifty-one plates, 1l. 11s. 6d.

The VOYAGE in fearch of LA PEROUSE, during the Years 1791, 2, 3, and 4. Tranflated from the French of M. LABILLARDIERE. In one large volume quarto, with forty-fix plates 2l. 2s., or in two volumes octavo, 1l. 7s.

HISTORY of the HELVETIC CONFEDERACY, from its Origin to its late Diffolution. By JOSEPH PLANTA, Efq. Sec. R. S. In two volumes quarto, elegantly printed and hot-preffed. Price 2l. 2s. Dedicated by permiffion to His Majefty.

OBSERVATIONS on the MANNERS and CUSTOMS of the EGYPTIANS; the Overflowing of the Nile; and its Effects. With Remarks on the Plague, and other fubjects. Written during a refidence of twelve years in Cairo and its vicinity. By JOHN ANTES, Efq. In one volume quarto, price 10s. 6d.

TRAVELS in UPPER and LOWER EGYPT. From the French of C. S. Sonnini. By HENRY HUNTER, D. D. In three volumes octavo, with 40 plates, price 1l. 7s.

The

The VOYAGE of GOVERNOR PHILIP to BOTANY BAY, with an Account of the Eſtabliſhment of the Colonies of Port Jackſon and Norfolk Iſland. To which are added, the Journals of Lieutenants Short-land, Watts, Ball, and Captain Marſhall, with their new Diſcoveries. In one volume royal quarto, with fifty-five plates, price 1l. 11s. 6d.

An HISTORICAL JOURNAL of the Tranſactions at Port Jackſon and Norfolk Iſland, with the Diſcoveries which have been made in New South Wales, and the Southern Ocean, ſince the publication of Philip's Voyage; compiled from the official papers, including the Journals of Governors Philip and King, and Lieutenant Ball, and the voyages from the firſt ſailing of the Sirius in 1787 to the return of that ſhip's company to England in 1792. By JOHN HUNTER, Eſq. Poſt Captain in the Royal Navy. In one volume royal quarto, with ſeventeen charts and views, price 1l. 11s. 6d. or on fine paper 2l. 12s. 6d.

DISCOVERIES of the FRENCH in 1768 and 9, to the South Eaſt of New Guinea, with the ſubſequent Viſits to the ſame Lands by Engliſh Navigators. To which is prefixed, an Hiſtorical Account of the Voyages and Diſcoveries of the Spaniards in the ſame Seas. By M. FLEURIEU. In one volume royal quarto, with twelve plates, price 1l. 1s.

JOURNAL of a VOYAGE in the LION extra Indiaman, from Madras to Columbo and Da Lagoa Bay, on the Eaſtern Coaſt of Africa, where the Ship was condemned, in the Years 1798 and 9. With ſome account of the manners and cuſtoms of the inhabitants of Da Lagoa Bay, and a vocabulary of their language. By WILLIAM WHITE, Eſq. Cap-tain in 73d Highland Regiment of Foot. In quarto, with two fine plates, price 7s.

A VOYAGE round the WORLD, but more particularly to the North Weſt Coaſt of America, in the Years 1785, 6, 7, and 8, in the King George and Queen Charlotte. By Captains PORTLOCK and DIXON. Dedicated by permiſſion to His Majeſty. In two volumes, with forty-two charts, views, &c. price 2l. 6s. or on royal paper, with the Natural Hiſtory coloured, 3l. 7s. 6d.

T. Gillet, Printer, Salisbury-square.

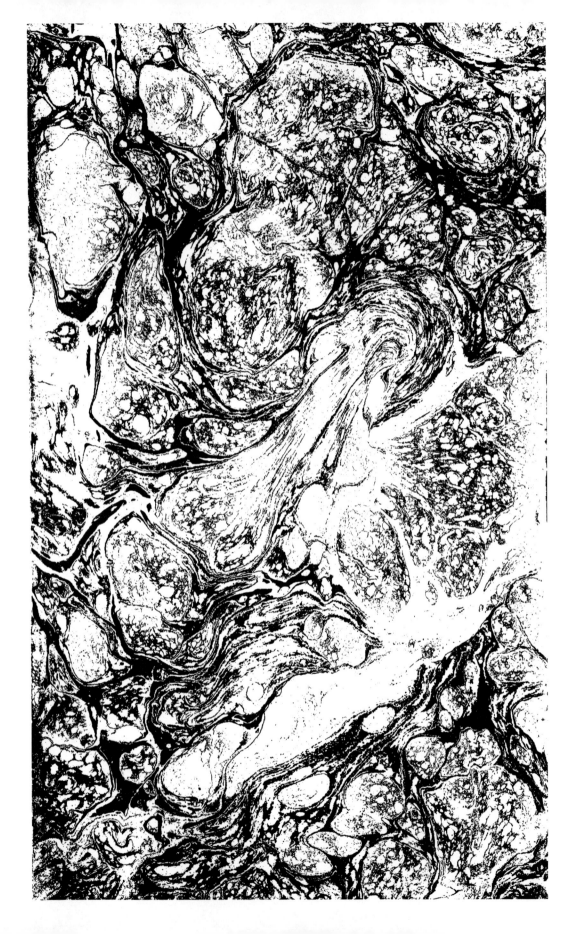

CPSIA information can be obtained at www.ICGtesting.com
Printed in the USA
LVOW030043010512

279737LV00014B/187/P